P9-CEM-386

Management Theories for Educational Change

Keith Morrison worked in primary and secondary education for many years before moving into teacher education. Much of his work has been in the field of continuing professional development, management and curriculum development. His books include: *Curriculum Planning and the Primary School* (with K. Ridley, published by Paul Chapman Publishing); *The Curriculum Handbook* (with T. Brown); *Planning and Accomplishing School-Centred Evaluation*; *Implementing Cross-Curricular Themes*; *A Guide to Teaching Practice* (4th edition, with L. Cohen and L. Manion). He is currently Director of the EdD course at the University of Durham and Editor of *Evaluation and Research in Education*.

Management Theories for Educational Change

Keith Morrison

P·C·P

Paul Chapman
Publishing Ltd

Copyright © Keith Morrison 1998
First published 1998

All rights reserved. No part of this publication may be
reproduced, stored in a retrieval system, transmitted or
utilised in any form or by any means, electronic,
mechanical, photocopying, recording or otherwise, without
permission in writing from the Publishers, except in
accordance with the provisions of the Copyright, Designs
and Patents Act 1988 or under the terms of a licence issued
by the Copyright Licensing Agency Ltd, 5 Dryden Street,
Covent Garden, London, England WC2E 9NW.

 Paul Chapman Publishing Ltd
A SAGE Publications Company
6 Bonhill Street
London EC2A 4PU

SAGE Publications Inc
2455 Teller Road
Thousand Oaks, California 91320

SAGE Publications India Pvt Ltd
32, M-Block Market
Greater Kailash-I
New Delhi 110 048

British Cataloguing in Publication Data

A catalogue record for this book is available from the British
Library

ISBN 1 85396 414 X
ISBN 1 85396 404 2 (pbk)

Library of Congress catalog card number

Typeset by PDQ Typesetting, Staffordshire
Printed and bound in Great Britain by Athenaeum Press,
Gateshead

A B C D E F   3 2 1 0 9 8

For Fun Hei, my Happiness.

Contents

Introduction

The management of change in education has become a topic of perennial interest in the last two decades. Both management and change command huge attention in education in their own right. Put them together and it is hardly surprising that they occupy centre stage in the professional development of educationists at all levels. That the world of education is underpinned by business matters is not new; that education has been put on a business footing certainly is. The *realpolitk* of education is that it has to be costed and cost-effective and that it has to prepare students to contribute to the economic growth of the nation.

However, the reach of this new business mentality extends beyond simply financial concerns. One of the significant developments in the field of education has been the view that the worlds of business and education are not mutually exclusive. A productive, partnership relationship and dialogue can exist between these two worlds. One common focus is their concern to manage change effectively, to identify the pressures for change, to plan the direction of change, its contents and processes and to implement it to everybody's collective advantage.

It is striking how much of the stuff of educational management derives from the world of business. Indeed one intention of this book is to identify the business sources that inform educational management. However, the purposes of the book go beyond this. Not only does this book intend to identify the business pedigree of many change management issues in education but, in so doing, it also intends to indicate the complexity of the change process and how this complexity can be addressed manageably. One purpose of the book is to raise an agenda for the management of educational change that stems from the agenda of managing change in the worlds of business, manufacturing industries and commerce, from product-focused businesses to service-orientated businesses.

Hence many examples are presented that are drawn from specific business organizations and practices, and they are addressed in a way that makes them amenable to being translated into educational matters. Clearly the selection from the field of business is just that – selective. Specific matters of financial concern and calculation are not addressed in this book because they are not relevant to the discussions of the management of change. However, care has been taken to ensure that justice is done to the discussions of the business literature on change.

The book falls into two parts. Part I sets a range of macrocontexts of change and Part II sets a range of microfactors (institutional and personal) involved in change. Part I provides an overview of the range of issues involved in planning change. Change in education is located in the contexts of social, cultural and economic changes. An explanation for change is provided in terms of social and economic theories and an account of society and business that sees them moving from modernism to postmodernism. Such a move is mirrored in industry where businesses are changing from large, monolithic organizations to flexible, consumer and employer-conscious organizations with niche marketing and customer satisfaction.

Part I then, addresses key macrocontexts in approaching the management of change. Part II is premised on the notion that, in practice, the success and effectiveness of change are premised on the participants involved. Hence, whilst Part I focuses on macrofeatures of change, Part II shifts from outside the organization and into the organization itself – the microcontexts of change. The business literature has a wealth of contributions to make to understanding and developing individuals and organizations for effective change.

In reading this book one can isolate chapters but, like the synergy for the effective management of change that is advocated throughout the book, one strength of the book is the coherence of its several elements and their contribution to a cumulative, developing argument. Hence readers will maximize the contents and arguments contained in the book by seeing it as a whole as well as reading its several sections.

The management of change is a messy, untidy, complex and, importantly, human enterprise that potentiates individuals and organizations. One of the principles of the effective management of change is its power to empower, its power to create and operate win/win situations. That can only be done by addressing the human side of the organization. The strength of the business literature is that, far from advocating the austere, dehumanized and objective pursuit of profit at all costs, it suggests that the effective management of change is an affirmation of the humanity of businesses. That clearly is a message of great significance for education.

Acknowledgements

This book owes a lot to the groups of higher degree students with whom I have been working for several years, and to teachers and other educationists with whom I have had contact. Acknowledgements are given to the following for permission to reproduce material in this volume: Lung, C. L., for material from 'School improvement: effective management of personal and social education in an era of change', paper submitted towards the award of Doctorate of Education, School of Education, University of Durham; Burridge, E., Ginnis, P., Hammond, L., Smith, A. and Birmingham City Council Education Department for material from *Quality Development Resource Pack*; Cassell Publishing for material from Bottery, M. *Lessons for Schools*; Gower Publishing Company Limited for material from Hastings, C., Bixby, P. and Chaudhry-Lawton, R. *The Superteam Solution*; FT Management for material from Bowring-Carr, C. and West-Burnham, J. *Managing Quality in Schools*.

Part I
Macrocontexts of Change

1

The context of change

Introduction

The industrialist Senge wrote that yesterday's solutions become today's problems (Senge, 1990: 57). This 'soundbite' indicates that change is inescapable, it is inbuilt into developing societies. Uncertainty and change are ubiquitous and the case for having to cope with change does not need to be made. The need to be able to live with change is one of the great truisms of the present day. Change is accelerating and the paradigms that are being used to analyse society are themselves changing (Dalin and Rust, 1996: 31). Hammer (1996: 105) suggests that new technologies are being used not to render existing practices more efficient – 'paving the cow paths' – but to revolutionize the way we think about things. There are no longer absolutes; values are debatable and indeed are debated. The aims, objectives, content, pedagogy, evaluation and direction of education are not fixed but fluid.

The wholesale scale of change is being experienced in all walks of life, in society, in science, in political, economic and educational practices. Education is part of these broader currents of society and change is a fact of life; it is irresistible and unstoppable. At the forefront of many developments are changes in the economy and the bringing of a business mentality in many spheres of life; hence this chapter provides a justification for the underlying premise of the book, viz. that, though there are fundamental differences between the worlds of business and education, nevertheless practices for the management of change in business and industry have a vast amount to offer the world of education in its management of change.

Changes in society

We are moving from a modernist world and a modernist conception of the world and industry to a postmodern world and a postmodernist conception of the world and industry (Clegg, 1992). A modernistic, closed view of the world separates the family and work, brings mass production and the industrialization of the workforce, with international monopoly capitalism and socialism striving for profit and survival. The modernistic institution is the large, hierarchical, bureaucratic, departmentalized, demarcated, specialized, mechanistic, standardized, ordered, Fordist, technocratic, impersonal, inflexible organization with clearly defined strata of power, control and decision-making. Conception and execution are sundered. It is the great manifestation of the success of science and technology elevated to scientism.

We are moving from a modernist society towards a postmodern society, with the decline of the large-scale factory system, the increasingly rapid production of smaller, niche-targeted goods, the rise of the service sector (Handy, 1991), the growth of international capitalism, the move from 'organized capitalism' to 'disorganized capitalism' (Lash and Urry, 1987), the expansion of the information revolution, the cult of immediacy and post-Fordist forms of organization and production. Flexibility, responsiveness, consumerism and client satisfaction are the order of the day, with flatter management organization and organic rather than mechanistic views of an organization (discussed in subsequent chapters), multi-functional and fluid teams, multiskilling, and an emphasis on team rewards, personal fulfilment and empowerment, and trust in senior managers. The typical organization here adopts the Japanese model (discussed in Chapter 3).

Whilst it is perhaps invidious, in the definition of postmodernism, to prescribe the nature of postmodernism, nevertheless Jameson (1991) argues that there are several elements that characterize postmodernism and its partner – late capitalism:

1) the 'tendential web of bureaucratic control' (*ibid*.: xviii);
2) the absence of grand metanarratives or overall coherence;
3) the valorization of discontinuity, difference and individuality;
4) the rise of consumerism and commodification in all walks of life – the economic, cultural and aesthetic;
5) the supremacy of a market mentality and market forces;
6) an 'utter forgetfulness of the past' (*ibid*.: xii) and the autoreferentiality of the present (*ibid*.: 42);
7) the celebration of heterogeneity, depthlessness and multiple super-ficialities together with a concomitant emphasis on the irresponsible, the complacent, the decadent;
8) the appeal to populism and populist culture.

Further, Jameson argues that the logic of late capitalism is dispersive, atomistic and individualistic, 'an antisociety rather than a society' (*ibid*.: 343).

However, postmodernism itself brings difficulties, for example the rise in experiences of fragmentation, anomie, alienation, uncertainty and a search for meaning and authenticity, the thrust towards opportunism and impression management, the need for flexibility and problem-solving capability, the problem of coping with unpredictability, volatility and impermanence, the elevation of the individual over the social, the compression of time and space that can lead to stress and premature burnout, the uncertain, tentative and provisional nature and status of knowledge. All is in flux! Jameson (*ibid.*: 376) suggests, too, that much of postmodernism is an indulgence of the affluent and is too time-bound (see also O'Neill, 1995: 199; Morrison, 1996).

What one can see in a postmodern reading of society is that change inheres in society because society is fragmenting, partly in response to the ever-changing and metamorphosing requirements of capital, partly in response to the cultures of difference and personal freedoms of expression, and partly in response to rampant bureaucratization.

Change and reform in education are inescapable. Regardless of how one views society, education, as a significant component in sociocultural and economic renewal and development, is caught up in change. These changes are wide-ranging and question the aims, structure, contents, organization of schools, schooling and other educational institutions. Hargreaves (1994), for example, argues that most large educational institutions typify modernistic conceptions of education as mass schooling on the factory model, whilst Toffler (1990) reinforces the message so far that schools will need to change to become 'moving mosaics' of small and often independent units, i.e. to become postmodern institutions.

The impact of theories of chaos and complexity

One feature of postmodernism is its celebration of disparateness and chaos. Not only in social theory but also in the scientific community change and uncertainty are ubiquitous. As metaphors for change, emergence, uncertainty, unpredictability and instability, the need for self-organization and adaptability, recent theories of chaos and complexity are potent reminders of the need for a paradigm shift in the way we view the world, from a stable world-order to an ever-changing, unfixed scenario.

In the physical sciences Laplacian and Newtonian theories of a deterministic universe have collapsed and have been replaced by theories of chaos and complexity in explaining natural processes and phenomena, the impact of which is being felt in the social sciences (e.g. McPherson, 1995). For Laplace and Newton, the universe was a rationalistic, deterministic and clockwork order; effects were functions of causes, small causes (minimal initial conditions) produced small effects (minimal and predictable) and large causes (multiple initial conditions) produced large (multiple) effects. Predictability, causality, patterning, universality and 'grand' overarching theories, linearity, continuity, stability, objectivity, all contributed to the view of the universe as an ordered and internally harmonistic mechanism in an albeit complex equilibrium, a rational, closed and deterministic system susceptible to comparatively straightforward scientific discovery and laws. The link between this view of the universe and the project of modernity is not difficult to discern; both are premised on the same principles for progress.

From the 1960s this view has been increasingly challenged with the rise of theories of chaos and complexity, themselves capturing the spirit of change, uncertainty, openness and unpredictability of earlier in the century (with Heisenberg's uncertainty principle, quantum physics and theories of relativity). Central to chaos theory are several principles (e.g. Gleick, 1987):

- small-scale changes in initial conditions can produce massive and unpredictable changes in outcome (for example the movement of a butterfly's wing in the Caribbean can produce a hurricane in America);
- very similar initial conditions can produce very dissimilar outcomes (for example using simple mathematical equations – Stewart, I., 1990);
- regularity and uniformity break down to irregularity and diversity;
- even if differential equations are very simple, the behaviour of the system that they are modelling may not be simple;
- effects are not straightforward continuous functions of causes;
- the universe is largely unpredictable;
- if something works once then there is no guarantee that it will work in the same way a second time;
- determinism is replaced by indeterminism; deterministic, linear and stable systems are replaced by 'dynamical', changing, evolving systems and non-linear explanations of phenomena;
- continuity is replaced by discontinuity, turbulence and irreversible transformation;
- grand, universal, all-encompassing theories and large-scale explanations provide inadequate accounts of localized and specific phenomena;
- long-term prediction is impossible (in matters as diverse as the weather and the economy).

More recently theories of chaos have been extended to complexity theory – the 'edge of chaos' (Waldrop, 1992; Lewin, 1993), itself applied to the realm of economics (Waldrop, 1992; Kauffman, 1995) as a 'complex adaptive system' with components at one level acting as the building blocks for components at another. A complex system comprises independent elements (which themselves might be made up of complex systems) which interact and which give rise to patterned behaviour in the system as a whole (e.g. Åm, 1994). Order is not totally predetermined and fixed, but the universe (however defined) is creative, emergent (through iteration, learning and recursion), evolutionary and changing, transformative and turbulent.[1] Order emerges in complex systems that are founded on simple rules for interacting organisms (Kauffman, 1995: 24); life is holistic, if complex.

Through feedback, recursion, perturbance, autocatalysis, connectedness and self-organization, higher and greater levels of complexity and differentiated, new forms arise from lower levels of complexity and existing forms. These complex forms derive from often comparatively simple sets of rules – local rules and behaviours generating complex global order and diversity (Waldrop, 1992: 16–17; Lewin, 1993: 38; Åm,

1994). Dynamical systems (Peak and Frame, 1994: 122) are a product of initial conditions and often simple rules for change – the dynamics of change. General laws can govern adaptive, dynamical processes (Kauffman, 1995: 27). There are laws of emergent order. The basic rules and components are simple but give rise to emergent complexity through their interaction (Waldrop, 1992: 86). Complex behaviours and systems do not need to have complex roots (*ibid.*: 270).

Systems, however defined, are complex, unstable, emergent, adaptive, dynamical and – significantly for our purposes – changing. In human terms disequilibrium can be accounted for by intentionality, competition (e.g. Åm, 1994), intelligence, creativity, the independent behaviours of acting individuals, etc. It is a requirement that a system be perpetually out of balance (*ibid.*); order emerges as the system (however defined – from ant colonies to economic practices) strives for unachievable equilibrium. Complex adaptive systems are constantly modifying and rearranging their building blocks in the light of prediction, experience and learning (Waldrop, 1992: 146, 177). They display 'perpetual novelty' (*ibid.*: 147). Importantly (as discussed in Chapter 2), in complexity theory organisms demonstrate a propensity for problem-solving approaches (*ibid.*: 168). Self-organization is the order of the day.[2]

Whether one wishes to adopt the notions of chaos and complexity at the level of metaphor (e.g. Doll's (1993) work on the curriculum) or as practice the message confirms that of the preceding sociological analysis – that change, uncertainty, openness are the order of the day and that a premium is placed on organizations (and self-organizations!) that can respond to, live with, cope with and lead change. Postmodernism, chaos theory and complexity theory are blood brothers.

The impact of market forces in education

Policy-making for education in the 1980s and 1990s changed schools, bringing them much more on to a business footing than previously, principally through the devolution of budgetary control to school and the impact of marketization on schools. The advocacy of the market view was initially premised on the neoliberalism of Hayek (1960; 1973; 1979; 1986) and was endorsed by the then prime minister's (Margaret Thatcher's) mentor, Keith Joseph (1976: 57). Thatcherite politics moved towards a strongly interventionist role of government in promulgating a market mentality. This was premised on competition, consumerism, choice, diversity, freedom from constraint, privatization, quality control, information and efficiency (Morrison, 1994; 1994b). Competition, it can be noted, is a prime mover in theories of complexity in business.

In educational terms market forces were evidenced in a series of Education Acts and papers (DES, 1986; 1988; DFE, 1992; 1993a) designed to touch and change every aspect of education – the total jigsaw: open enrolment into schools (no restriction on choice of school); the introduction of local management of schools, i.e. devolution of budgets from local authorities to schools; the reduction of the power of local education authorities; privatization of services in schools, to be bid for in competitive tendering; the assisted places scheme to enable students from economically disadvantaged backgrounds to attend private schools; the rise of city technology colleges (specialist schools whose funding comes directly from government and industry); the rise of grant-maintained schools (those that opted out of local authority control); the orchestration of a moral panic about putative falling standards in schools, giving rise to accountability systems, inspections, appraisal and publication of schools' results of national tests; the espousal of the notion of 'magnet' and 'sink' schools; the rise of parental choice and parent power on governing bodies; the reduction of the power of the unions through the imposition of Pay and Conditions of Service for teachers; the rise of the statutory National Curriculum and assessment; the reform of the General Certificate of Secondary Education and vocational qualifications; the rise of marketing of schools through the publication of prospectuses. The picture is as familiar as it is totalizing.

There was an advocacy of the value of introducing the competitive edge of commercialism into education, for example the Adam Smith Institute (1984) argued that a commercial firm which failed to satisfy its customers would quickly lose them to its competitors, but that this competitive pressure did not exist in the state sector. The Adam Smith Institute suggested that without this source of consumer pressure it was impossible for a service to be run in the interests of customers (*ibid.*: 1). 'Producer capture' had to be replaced with consumerism.

More recently, Tooley (1996) argues that the evidence from the literature on school effectiveness is enough to show unacceptable disparities between similar schools (p. 57). 'Free marketeers' have advocated the furtherance of commercialism and consumerism into education and the reduction of state intervention in education. Tooley (1996: 23), for example, makes the case that markets enable schools to become entrepreneurial, to act on their vision. Whether one consider his advocacy of 'authentic' market forces in education to be merely seductive or indeed to be the way forward does not concern us here; the issue is that there is a case for market forces in education that draws the links between education and business ever more tightly. Freeing up the 'supply' side of the education market to meet the demand side of the market was a powerful message of the Conservative government of the 1980s and 1990s.

The claims for market forces from business thinking to operate in education cannot be dismissed easily, including, for example, the claims that market forces will

- increase efficiency;
- increase choice and diversity;
- promote equity and equality;
- further democracy;
- increase liberty;
- meet consumer demands;
- enhance standards and quality;
- increase motivation;
- develop entrepreneurialism;

- reduce 'producer capture';
- revitalize education to meet the demands of a changing society and economy;
- increase accountability and responsiveness.

On the other hand, the adoption of market principles in education is the subject of trenchant criticism. Ball (1990: 2–3), for example, attacks markets because in them inequality is both necessary and inevitable in order to stimulate competition through incentives. Levitas (1986: 84) argues that markets cannot but increase inequality of opportunity. Ranson (1990) and Ball (1994) argue that, whilst masquerading as a neutral device for driving up standards, the market reinforces and perpetuates existing social and economic inequality and privilege for some at the expense of the many – it is a class strategy (Ranson, 1990: 15; Ball, 1994), a view echoed by Jonathan (1989: 323) in her comment that students commence the educational race from different starting points – to which the market is blind. Tomlinson (1993: 4) argues that to cast the parents merely as consumers is to foster suspicion rather than partnership in education; parents become the 'vigilantes' of education rather than its supporters. Blackstone *et al.* (1992) argue that markets create winners and losers (and that this is ethically and morally questionable – Bridges and McLaughlin, 1994). It is unclear whether, in practice, markets do guarantee efficiency and raised standards (Bowe *et al.*, 1992), whether consumers are equipped and realistically able to choose, whether enlightened self-interest (Dale, 1989; Ball, 1994) and 'possessive self-interest' (Ball, 1990) ought to be encouraged, whether citizenship and the debate on ethics and morality are compromised when market forces are put before community interests (Grace, 1994; Morrison, 1994).

Whether or not education should become aligned with market forces and principles in a sense is a non-question, because: 1) market forces are already operating because of funding arrangements; 2) public perception of several aspects of a market mentality (e.g. consumerism, information, accountability, efficiency, 'standards') is here to stay – it is embedded in the broader current of social and economic change (e.g. Ball, 1994).[3] Bottery (1994: 130) takes further the debate concerning whether schools can or should be educationally free from or involved in a market enterprise. He teases out six important differences between commercial and non-profit organizations:

- commercial organizations tend to rely on material *incentives* to maintain impetus; non-profit organizations tend to rely on non-material rewards such as prestige, or job satisfaction, to maintain impetus;
- commercial organizations are dominated by the motive of *profit*; profit serves little or no part in the determination of a non-profit organization's goals in its definition of success;
- commercial organizations exist in a *competitive* market; non-profit organizations are bounded by an ethos of co-operation;
- commercial organizations vary their *mission*, depending on the climate and market; non-profit organizations have clearly defined missions from which they wander at their peril;
- commercial organizations are characterized by *hierarchy* and degrees of

delegation; non-profit organizations are characterized by (or at least pay lip-service to the ideals of) equality, egalitarianism and participation;
- commercial organizations have a limited number of *goals and constituencies* to which they must answer; non-profit organizations have numerous and conflicting goals and constituencies.

Weller and Hartley (1996) add to this their view that

- schools have very limited control over the 'materials' (the students) who come to the school;
- schools have no control over the outside forces and influences which impinge on education (e.g. decisions about funding and resourcing);
- there is disagreement on the aims, objectives, contents and pedagogy of education;
- whereas business is agreed on how best and how frequently to evaluate a product the same is not true for education (evaluating schools, students, curricula, pedagogy);
- whereas businesses' products yield returns/resources which can be channelled back into the company (e.g. for research and development), schools have limited resources and little control over funding;
- some businesses pay greater salaries than those in education, thereby maintaining higher-quality staff.

Despite these differences, it is dangerous to adopt an 'either/or' mentality in discussing the links between education and business, industry and commerce – either business or education, either markets or non-markets, either consumerism or non-consumerism. This is the failure of bivalent thinking (Kosko, 1994) and it is more fruitful to think in multivalent terms. The management of educational change can benefit from certain aspects of a business mentality.

Why use business models in the management of educational change?

Folklore has it that there has been some traditional antipathy between education and business/industry. The business community makes accusations against education of falling standards, of failure to prepare students for the demands of work, producing illiterate, innumerate and work-shy employees. In turn the educational community has accused the world of work as being the graveyard of the aspirations, creativity, flexibility, adaptability, breadth and problem-solving capabilities that schools have taken painstaking care to develop in their students (Entwistle, 1981). Education is not a commodity to be bought, sold and haggled over as one would a car or an item of furniture, and schools do not turn out a single, sole product. Competition is not an attribute that schools wish to encourage, and so on. Moreover the educational community has been suspicious of introducing industrial models of management into education, seeing them as furthering the narrow, line-management, coercive mentality that sits uncomfortably with schools as person-centred institutions, arguing that schools are not production lines and that students are not passive objects to be moulded. Wilby (1997: 18) suggests that education should not introduce business practices because business is amoral (silent on values and morals), undemocratic, self-serving, rapacious, acquisitive, obsessed with image rather than substance, distrustful of partners and driven by profit.

There is truth in all these concerns. Of course schools are not production lines; of course students are not passive objects; of course we should all be concerned with standards; of course schools should prepare future citizens and workers; of course some employers and employment might not be perfect. Simple polarities – bivalent thinking – do not catch the complexities of the industrial or the educational spheres and institutions. So let us leave aside prejudices, suspicions and distrust that one community has of the other. Partnerships and synergies are much more positive and productive, turning the vicious win/lose circle into the virtuous win/win circle; everyone can benefit from lengthening and embracing their own and each others' perspectives respectively.

One of the main messages of this book is that not only are very many business practices compatible with practices in education but, indeed that they are also highly desirable. Indeed it could be argued that education would benefit enormously from the resource input that graces the business and industrial community!

The view that business and educational practice are, in very many areas, compatible entails a shift of perception and, perhaps, an abandonment of prejudice on the part of educators who might hold a negative view of business as being essentially exploitative, driven by the thirst for naked profit, dehumanized and dehumanizing, impersonal, alienating, auto-cratic, steely cold and cut-throat in its internal relations, boring, repetitive and dispassionate. That is an outmoded view of business that was characterized by Taylorism.

Many commercial companies are far more person-centred than many schools. Business has realized that it behoves the company to invest in its employees in a multiplicity of ways that will be addressed in this book, because to do so enhances productivity. Business organizations are becoming human organizations. To the argument that they are often only producing a standardized product one can suggest that this only serves to suggest that humanizing practices is even more applicable to education, which is producing a non-uniform, human 'product'. It is to make the human services yet more human. Further, with the rise of the service industries – of which education is one (a human service) – more human practices are entering industry (even if they are providing material services, e.g. British Airways). Therefore one could argue that it is even more necessary to have to change education as a human service. It is a sobering exercise to read the recent business literature because it is replete with example after example of just how effective management and organizations have been in becoming person centred, in many cases massively more so than in the world of education.

In a sense this might be because it is too great a problem for industry to ignore. For example, O'Leary (1993) and Cartwright and Cooper (1994) indicate that some 90 million working days each year are lost because of employees having some form of mental illness, that between 30 and 40 per cent of absence from work involves some form of stress or mental illness; that alcohol abuse costs industry some £1 billion per year, and that at any one time up to 20 per cent of any workforce will be experiencing personal problems that impact on their performance at work. These frightening statistics not only point to the 'intensification thesis' (the thesis that work is increasingly pressured through greater and overloaded demands being made upon employees with less time to fulfil them and with multiple innovations having to be addressed in conditions of poorer working conditions) but also that companies are having to place a premium on the 'people' aspect of their organization. Whether or not work itself is the main contributor to these problems is, of course, a moot point.

Education could be informed usefully from business perspectives on the management of people and organizations.[4] Further, the business community is at the forefront of change because not to be so would be to court failure, closure and demise. The logic of survival leads to the logic of managing change. What does the business world do to keep up with, advance and manage change? In many ways the business community could be considered to be the experts at managing change because that is their stock-in-trade. Hence, in true business benchmarking style (where one organization looks at other successful organizations to see how they develop and sustain their successes), there is nothing to be lost and everything to be gained in the world of education by educationists adopting a less insular and more eclectic view of effective practices in the management of change, moving beyond the parochialism of 'this is the way we do it in education' to a much more open view of 'how might we do it better'? Why not look at the best practice in business and industry to see if there are messages for managing change in education?

Of course, the educational community, quite properly, will say that theirs is not a problem of managing change because that, too, is their everyday experience. Indeed innovation overload and its concomitant fatigue are the order of the day, an order that is not of the making of the educational community but which has been thrust upon it, often against professional advice. However, that does not negate the potential benefits that can be gained from looking at how other organizations manage change; indeed it could be argued that it makes the case for this to be done. Being involved in practice should not blind one to the need to improve practice. Indeed, as will be demonstrated in this book, one of the great lessons from Japanese industry is its commitment to continuous improvement through people.

If one looks to the source of several innovations in education in recent years then their pedigree and parentage in business and industry are clear. For example:

1) the topical issue of quality and quality development derives in large part from industry;
2) the move towards flatter management styles and team practices has its counterpart in industrial management;
3) organizational theory that is being used in planning and managing educational change has much of its basis in the literature of industrial practices;

4) the debates on leadership and management styles are informed hugely by practices in industry;
5) the need to develop empowering organizational cultures has its roots in industry;
6) much of the educational discussion of resistance to change and ways of overcoming it owes several of its key concepts to industry;
7) much of the discussion of motivation in organizations has its seminal work in industry;
8) much of the management of planning change and strategy development has its roots in industry;
9) many of the concepts and practices of change agents and facilitators derive from the world of industry and business;
10) there is a wealth of literature from business and industry that addresses the personal and emotional aspects of management of change, from workplace counselling to functional and dysfunctional emotions in the management of change;
11) much of the discussion of teamwork and leadership has its roots in industry.

Indeed a visit round most business schools will reveal a startling array of up-to-date journals and literature about effective person-centred management that can be applied straightforwardly to, and inform, a vast range of issues in the management of change in education.

Hence not only does the business world spawn a broad and in-depth literature on the management of change but, to do justice to the educational literature on the management of change it is also useful to trace its roots back into the literatures from the business and industrial communities. Such an enterprise is one purpose of this book. This volume takes as its chapter headings key features of the management of successful and effective change in business, and then teases out from these key features and the literatures from business and industry their implications for education. This book provides a straightforward introduction to the relevant business and industrial literature and, from it, derives several implications for the successful management of change in education. The book deliberately goes to the business rather than to the educational literature. The insights, concepts and examples that are available from the business and industrial literature are fascinating and transfer directly into the world of education.

Notes

1.   Prigogine and Stengers (1985), Toffler (1985; 1990), Waldrop (1992), Lewin (1993) and Kauffman (1995).

2.   Prigogine and Stengers (1985: 156–9) provide a fascinating example of self-organization in the lowly slime-mould where, responding to pressure from external factors (lack of nutrients in the environment), the slime-mould cells aggregate, metamorphose, migrate, fruit and disperse. What a lesson in adaptability, responsiveness and change this is for higher forms of life!

3.   It has been argued that education is a quasi-market rather than a fully fledged market. Le Grand (1990), Bowe, *et al.* (1992) and Bridges and Husbands (1996) argue that education is a quasi-market rather than a market because: 1) most schools neither strive to be, nor cannot be, profit-making organizations; 2) the consumers/customers do not spend their money directly in the education market – it is largely 'spent'/allocated for them; 3) most schools are not privately owned; (4) ownership structure is not clear and it is unclear exactly what they are striving to maximize in the market.

4.   Indeed there is a move in professionally qualifying teachers for compulsory study of business practices (Whitehead, 1997: 9).

2

Elements of change

Defining change

Change can be regarded as a dynamic and continuous process of development and growth that involves a reorganization in response to 'felt needs'. It is a process of transformation, a flow from one state to another, either initiated by internal factors or external forces, involving individuals, groups or institutions, leading to a realignment of existing values, practices and outcomes.

Needs assessment/analysis is an important feature in commencing the planning of change. Here the question of a definition of need (e.g. as discrepancy, as preference, as want, as deficit, as desired, as necessary) leads planners to assess the size of the need, the priorities for the needs, the numbers of people who are likely to be affected, the consequences if the needs are not met, how the needs can and should be met, the resources required to meet the needs and how to operationalize needs.

Whether the process of change is highly planned or less planned in detail is a matter of conjecture. For example Mintzberg (1987) argues that one can accept a definition of change that emphasizes its preplanned, predictable nature or, alternatively, an emergent approach that begins with the assumption that change is continuous, open ended and a largely unpredictable process to align and realign an organization because of the changing environment of that organization. This is precisely the case in education, where the environments of education – most recently the political, economic and technological – have changed dramatically, and where schools have had to cope with changes both to their external and internal environments. The rise of school development planning can be seen as an attempt to insert a rational model of school planning and change into a frequently disordered and fluctuating system whose overall direction is mutable.

The rational model of change is very powerful and appealing, suggesting that change can be planned and sequenced. This is evidenced in the staged and sequenced approaches to change discussed later in this chapter. However, it will be argued that this belies the complexity of change in education because, as a human service and human enterprise, different conceptions of rationality and rational action can often clash.

Echoing the discussion of Chapter 1 on theories of chaos and complexity, Mintzberg argues that strategies are emergent, that successful companies do not necessarily set out with detailed strategic plans but, rather, their strategies emerge over time and stem from the pattern of decisions they take about the key features of their activities. He argues that detailed visions and carefully laid plans might be counterproductive in trying to manage more open-ended change, producing counterproductive strategies. Mintzberg's suggestion is that companies that are successful in a chaotic environment are those which develop dynamic agendas, focusing on change at several levels so that their organization develops organically. Again, this has direct parallels in education, where development planning proceeds on several levels – for example management, curriculum, resources, carefully selected focuses for change – and where school development plans are updated on a yearly basis to take account of new pressures for change and emergent focuses, derived from both internal and external sources.

From the mid-1970s onwards[1] there is a clear literature to suggest that change possesses certain characteristics:

- it is structural, systemic and system-disturbing rather than superficial (Cuban, 1990, regards superficial changes as 'first-order change' and structural change as 'second-order' change). Regarding change as structural recognizes that change in one part of an organization will have a knock-on effect on other parts of an organization;
- it is a dynamic process – over time – rather than an event (see the discussion below of the stages of change);
- it is non-linear (Carnall, 1995), echoing theories of chaos and complexity;
- it is a multidimensional phenomenon (embracing objectives and functions, organization and administration, structures, knowledge, skills, behaviours, beliefs, values, roles and relationships, curricular aims, content, organization, pedagogy, resources, assessment, evaluation);
- it embraces multiple perspectives (Hopkins *et al.*, 1994) and, therefore, assumes resistance and conflict (though conflict is to be regarded as an opportunity rather than an insuperable difficulty – Dalin *et al.*, 1993);
- it requires investment in structures, institutions, people, technological and psychological support;
- it requires involvement of people, bringing anxiety and uncertainty together with the need to develop new skills;
- it is a personal as well as an organizational matter;
- organizational conditions exert a strong effect on the likelihood of success;
- practices often change before beliefs (Fullan, 1991; Hargreaves, 1994) – the adage 'drag them by the hair and their hearts and minds will follow' is perhaps pertinent here; conflict and negotiation are inescapable;
- it is better to think big but start small (i.e. to identify 'levers of change'), though the areas of highest leverage are often the least obvious (Senge, 1990: 63; Hargreaves, 1994: 10);

- effective change is in response to real needs and felt needs (Dalin *et al.*, 1993: 134);
- innovation and information are very closely linked with each other (Carnall, 1995);
- evolutionary planning works better than linear planning (Hargreaves, 1994: 10), echoing the discussions of 'emergence' in complexity theory;
- policy cannot mandate what actually happens in schools and classrooms; the critical site of change is the classroom and the teacher (Dalin *et al.*, 1993; Hargreaves, 1994);
- innovation is creative and requires the ability to identify and solve problems;
- change is learning, with schools as learning organizations (Dalin *et al.*, 1993);
- effective change integrates top-down strategies with bottom-up strategies.

The principal feature that run through these characteristics is that change concerns people more than content. This is a critical factor, particularly in the human services like education. Change changes people but people change change! The best laid plans stand or fall on the people involved (e.g. Hoyle, 1975; 1976; Dalin *et al.*, 1993). Macrodecisions about change are mediated (accepted, subverted, altered, diverted, rejected) by micropolitics of institutions. The changes in education of the last two decades bear witness to this very clearly.

Change, therefore, concerns human resource development and human resource management. Indeed Hargreaves and Hopkins (1991) argue that managing change may involve changing management. Though many staff might welcome this as legitimating the replacement of management, in fact it need not be so drastic! Successful change is about successful management; successful management is about managing successful change. It is no accident, perhaps, that management training has featured amongst the highest resource priorities for in-service education at a time when there is wholesale change in education.

Whilst one can plan for change in a careful way, in practice the plan seldom unfolds in the ways anticipated. People change things! People respond to change in a variety of ways. Some will resist, some will adapt, some will adopt an innovation. People will respond to the way in which they perceive the change, echoing Thomas's (1928) view that if people define their situations as real, they are real in their consequences. If I think there is a mouse under the table I will behave as though there is a mouse under the table, whether there is or not! Part of the successful management of change is to identify participants' perceptions, attitudes, values, beliefs and opinions and to ensure that these are fully informed.

Hall *et al.* (1986) suggest that people have different concerns during the process and unfolding of an innovation in education. They may commence with requiring further *information* about it; they may have anxieties and concerns about how the changes will affect them *personally*, how the changes will take place and be *managed*, what the *consequences* of the changes will be, how *collaboration* will occur, what will *proceed from* the change. One task of the management of change, then, is to identify and address the concerns that people have at different stages of the innovation. Micropolitics mediates macropolitical will. Planned change might be too rationalistic if it neglects the perceptions and values of participants.

People mediate change plans. Several *sequiturs* flow from this. For example:

- the research, development and diffusion (R, D & D) model of change is too simplistically unidirectional, even if it builds in extensive dissemination strategies; change is recursive as well as linear; the traditional R, D & D sequence is replaced, through teamwork, by synchrony, with people working together from across departments;
- the R, D & D model of change is too clean and 'antiseptic' to be used as a fair model of the change process – it is product focused rather than people and process focused. Change in education is a messy business simply because it involves people and is focused on people;
- strategies of change must build in 'ownership' (Dalin *et al.*, 1993: Chap. 7) and involvement of participants;
- the strategy of change to be used must be careful to identify, and work within, the locus of power within or outside the organization. Typically in education this involves not only ensuring the support of the senior management/governors of the educational institutions but also the influential staff in an institution (the issue of micropolitics – discussed in Chapter 6.

The problem-solving model offers an alternative to the R and D approach, as it assumes the ability of participants to identify, operationalize and solve problems – a 'bottom-up' strategy rather than a 'top-down' model. Moreover, a problem-solving model is an attempt to build in ownership, engagement and involvement of all participants actively rather than as passive recipients of prefigured decisions.

The nature of change

The success of the change will depend not only its successful management but also on the specific contents and characteristics of the change itself,[2] for example:

- its *centrality* (how far the change is perceived to alter the core patterns and norms of the institutions);
- its *complexity* (how many groups within the institutional setting will be affected by the change and the difficulty or ease of its implementation);
- the *nature* and *amount* of the change (the level of difficulty which the innovation has for an individual);
- the *consonance/compatibility/congruence* of the change (the degree of fit between the innovation and the existing institutional practices and values);
- the *visibility* of the change (how far the change is public);
- the *communicability* of the change (how straightforward the change is to communicate);

- the *divisibility* of the change (the possibility of trialling the change on a partial and limited basis);
- the *clarity* of the proposed change;
- the *relative advantage* of the change over existing practice;
- the *reversibility* of the change;
- the *ease of solution* that the change presents to a problem;
- the *scale of the benefit* that the change brings;
- the *contribution to the overall vision of the organization* that the change will bring;
- the *specificity* and *concreteness* of the change proposals.

Change is likely to be successful if it is: congruent with existing practices in the school; understood and communicated effectively; triallable and trialled; seen to be an improvement on existing practice by the participants; seen to further the direction in which the institution is moving. On the other hand, change is likely to be unsuccessful if it is: overcomplex, not understood; poorly communicated; overdemanding on the individuals and existing resources; unclear; untested (particularly if it will affect large numbers of people); of questionable benefit over existing practice; unclear on its benefit in meeting the institution's general direction; too incompatible with the existing practices, values and beliefs of the organization and the people in it; brought in without real consultation.

This latter describes the introduction of the National Curriculum where significant hostility was encountered from professionals in the system, leading ultimately to an expensive review of the National Curriculum, a boycott of testing and assessment, the replacement of successive Secretaries of State for Education, a moratorium on subsequent change and declining morale amongst the teaching profession. Indeed, under such circumstances, it is hardly surprising that the National Curriculum had to be brought in by the force of statute in order to over-ride hostility. As Coffield (1989: 46) suggests, it was doomed to succeed.

More positively, what is being suggested here is that there will be occasions when decisions will have to be taken which might upset several staff. If that is the case then it might be the case that a power-coercive strategy is necessary. A new headteacher might be brought into a school in order to bring in radical changes with a staff who are marked by inertia and where practice has stagnated. In these cases it might be necessary to initiate change in the face of staff opposition, simply because not to do so would be to perpetuate the problem. Of course, the effective headteacher will ensure that the appropriate combination of pressure and support is applied.

Effective change occurs in response to felt need. This is the essence of many formula-driven approaches to understanding change that one finds in business. For example Clarke (1994) suggests that there is an equation for effective change which can be written as $C = (ABD) > X$, wherein C = change, A = dissatisfaction with the status quo, B = the desirability of the proposed change, D = the practicability of the proposed change, and X = the cost of the change. This is echoed by Carnall (1995) who discusses a formula for effective change in which $EC > Z$, with EC (the energy for the change) having to exceed Z (the perceived cost of making the change). Carnall breaks down this formula into a multiple of constituent elements, rewriting it as $EC = ABD$, where EC = the energy for change, A = the perceived or felt dissatisfaction with the present circumstances and situation, B = the level of knowledge of the practical steps forward, and D = the shared vision. Buchanan and Boddy (1992) adopt Gleicher's formula for effective change ($KDV > C$) arguing that change will occur where K (knowledge of the first practical steps to be taken), D (dissatisfaction with the status quo), and V (the desired vision of the future state) exceed the cost C (e.g. psychological, financial, material) of the movement. They also cite Pettigrew's (1985) formula, in which change occurs if $CVL > I$, where pressures and arguments for change are present in the *context* of the organization, there is the presence of *visionary* leadership, the proposals for change are seen to be *legitimate*, and these three factors exceed the organizational *inertia* that is being sustained by existing practice and ideology.

Though one can argue that these formulae strive for a perhaps spurious, quasi-scientific respectability, nevertheless they are useful in identifying key features for successful change. For example, they focus on the value of considering force-field analysis, where the locus, nature and strength of inhibiting factors are weighed against the locus, nature and strength of facilitating factors (discussed in Chapter 4). Formula-driven approaches suggest that managers of change need to consider:

- dissatisfaction with the status quo;
- the desirability of the proposed change;
- the practicability of the proposed change;
- the cost of the change (e.g. psychological, financial, material);
- the energy for the change;
- the level of knowledge of the practical steps forward;
- the shared vision of the future;
- knowledge of the first practical steps to be taken;
- pressures and arguments for change are present in the context of the organization;
- there is visionary leadership;
- the proposals for change are seen to be legitimate;
- the organizational inertia that is being sustained by existing practice and ideology.

An example of how these factors might be addressed is presented in Figure 2.1.

Stages of change

One can identify several stages to a change, for example: invention, development, diffusion/dissemination, adoption, implementation, institutionalization, recommendation. Fullan (1991: 47–8) identifies the phases of

1) *initiation* (mobilization, adoption);

The results of a school's National Curriculum assessments for mathematics at Key Stage 3 are disappointing. The staff review the possible causes of this and decide that one major reason is that the mathematics scheme is too based on students working from textbooks and worksheets to the neglect of instructional activities; in effect that students are 'teaching themselves'.

Reducing the amount of worksheet/textbook work will free time to provide more whole-class interactive instruction. Most of the mathematics staff, including the Head of the Department, agree on this but a significant and influential minority of respected staff argue against this, suggesting that the problem is: 1) that the scheme already in existence is under-resourced in terms of time, materials and staff expertise; 2) that, given the school's adherence to the philosophy of mixed-ability teaching, to teach in a whole-class style would be to neglect different abilities and minimize differentiation and effective matching; 3) that they would feel unhappy in adopting a new teaching style without appropriate in-service education; 4) that students at Key Stage 3 should be taught that they must be able to take greater responsibility for their own learning rather than relying on the teacher to shoulder that responsibility; 5) that the new scheme has only been running for three years and its longer-term effects have not had time to surface; 6) that whole-class teaching will increase discipline problems as disruptive students will be able to gain the attention of the whole class.

The whole mathematics team agree that the issue of mixed-ability teaching and student-centred learning – central features of the school's mission statement – should not cloud the fact that students are not responding to the existing mathematics teaching. It is recognized that support for the proposed change must include considerable staff development for a more whole-class instructional style, that it should be run on a trial basis for two years with all the mathematics staff participating and then a review should be conducted, and that facilities will be increased for the withdrawal of seriously disruptive students. Further, it is agreed that there should be frequent and regular meetings of the mathematics team – in school time – in order to discuss developments and provide feedback.

The proposed change was discussed openly, was responsive to felt need and external pressure in the form of published results; decisions were taken democratically, and a combination of pressure and support was present; the change was in line with the overall mission of the school, the Head of Department was supportive of the change and was pressing for its introduction but was also prepared to take account of evidence rather than simply listening to preference.

In terms of the formula-driven view of change, the pressure for change, the dissatisfaction with the status quo, the energy and supporting developments for change, the support of the leadership, the democratic nature of the decision-making and the perceived legitimacy of the change (for improving students' performance), combine to outweigh dissenting voices, the increased workload and the inertia of particular staff – however respected they are.

Figure 2.1 Changing the school mathematics curriculum

2) *implementation* (initial use);
3) *continuation* (incorporation, routinization, institutionalization).

He adds a fourth stage of *outcome* to complete the overview of the change process.

One can expand on this by suggesting a seven-stage model of change: invention → development → diffusion/dissemination → adoption (awareness ⇨ interest ⇨ evaluation ⇨ trial ⇨ adoption/rejection) → implementation → institutionalization → recommendation. Though this sequence is typical of the research, development and diffusion (R, D & D) model it can apply, with modifications (e.g. to the stage of diffusion/dissemination) to a 'bottom-up', problem-solving, action research model of change. The management of an innovation has to plan for each stage of the innovation. This might entail identifying 1) the tasks to be accomplished at each stage (i.e. what actually has to change); 2) the roles and tasks of participants; 3) facilitating factors at each stage; 4) inhibiting factors at each stage; 5) the strategies to be used to address the inhibiting factors; 6) the leadership tasks at each stage; 7) the nature of the support needed at each stage; 8) the criteria for evaluating the success of each stage. This is shown in Figure 2.2.

In the business literature there are several references to a staged approach to planning and managing change. What characterizes the business literature is the rationalistic approach that it adopts, regarding change as able to be closely and carefully planned. The question to be asked, perhaps, is the extent to which such a rationalistic approach is either desirable or matches up to the reality of change in education. The issue is immense, for much of the business literature adopts an objectives-driven approach to the management of change that belies the complexity of the issues when one encounters people in a person-orientated service. This is not to deny that such an approach is not useful, nor that it builds out people; it is rather to suggest that it might oversimplify a complex phenomenon of change.

Problem-solving approaches

The essence of many problem-solving approaches is that one 1) identifies a real problem – a process of careful focusing and information gathering; 2) moves to a divergent phase of generating solutions; 3) thence to a convergent phases of deciding on the approach or solution; 4) thence to implementation; 5) finally to evaluation of the extent to which the problem has been solved. Much of the business literature constitutes variations on this theme. For example Buchanan and Boddy (1992) suggest a nine-stage approach:

1) identifying the problem;
2) gathering relevant data;
3) analysing the data gathered;
4) generating possible solutions;
5) selecting a solution;
6) planning the implementation of the solution;
7) implementing the solution;
8) evaluating the implementation and outcomes;
9) continuing to improve.

Bank (1992: 174) echoes such an approach, identifying six steps to problem-solving:

	INITIATION	IMPLEMENTATION	CONTINUATION
1) Tasks to be accomplished			
2) Roles/tasks of participants			
3) Facilitating factors			
4) Inhibiting factors			
5) Change strategies			
6) Support required			
7) Leadership roles/tasks			
8) Evaluation criteria			

Figure 2.2 Planning each stage of an innovation

Stage One: Identifying the exact problem (prioritizing problems if there are more than one).

Stage Two: Identifying the causes of the problem, using, for example cause-and-effect diagrams (fishbone/*Ishikawa* diagrams discussed in Chapter 4), brainstorming possible causes of the problem and prioritizing causes.

Stage Three: Generating possible solutions to the problem, brainstorming possible solutions to the problems and prioritizing possible solutions.

Stage Four: Choosing the most appropriate solution and translating it into action plans, prioritizing solutions, costing possible solutions and resources needed, clarifying tasks to be undertaken and action planning; presenting clear and firm proposals.

Stage Five: Implementing the chosen solution, ensuring that the project is controlled, that commitment is high and that any contingencies are anticipated and planned for.

Stage Six: Evaluating the outcomes to see how effective the solution has been, involving monitoring procedures and measuring results.

Bank suggests that it is worth while devoting considerable time to the early stages, first to ensure that the problem is correctly perceived (e.g. avoiding the confusion between symptoms and causes and correcting faulty perceptions), and secondly to explore fully the possible causes before reaching conclusions in Stage Two, thereby enabling solutions to be more carefully matched to correctly identified problems. One can see the clear link here between problem-solving approaches and action research programmes; both commence with problem identification, both are strongly rooted in reality, both involve the move from analysis to practice, both build in ownership and involvement.[3]

Carnall (1995) suggests some principles to guide the process of problem-solving whilst encouraging creativity, for example: 1) keeping thinking loose and fluid until rigour is needed and suspending disbelief; 2) ruling out initial criticism of new ideas and celebrating new ideas, focusing on the positive aspects of ideas and avoiding evaluating ideas too soon; 3) ruling out status or position in a hierarchy; 4) supporting confusion; 5) being positive and optimistic; 6) valuing the opportunity to learn from mistakes and sharing risks; 7) building on ideas. One can see here the emphasis being placed on adopting a non-judgemental and divergent approach to the early stages of problem-solving.

In this process the value of brainstorming has been emphasized. Effective brainstorming has several conventions (e.g. Adair, 1987; Bank, 1992: 175–6). For example:

- separate the process of suggesting from evaluation and rule out initial evaluation/judgement/criticism, i.e. suspend judgement as criticism might inhibit creativity;
- any suggestion is acceptable, however fanciful it might appear at first sight;
- the aim is for quantity – as many ideas as possible, regardless of their quality;
- write everything down so that everyone can see what has been suggested, choosing a fast writer who can record the suggestions on a

flip-chart/overhead slide at great speed;
- encourage 'wild' ideas;
- build on other people's suggestions;
- leave evaluation until after the brainstorming session.

Following the brainstorming the group can decide on evaluation criteria for evaluating ideas, can review obvious 'winners' and eliminate unusable suggestions, can sort and assemble the types of suggestions that have been made in order to select the best of each type. Brainstorming, then, is a skill that can be learnt and practised; it is not merely a matter of inspiration. It should encourage openness and as many ideas as possible, therefore anything that might block the free flow of ideas is to be minimized. Brainstorming is a valuable tool as a technique for generating ideas in the problem solution stages.

There will, of course, frequently be blocks to problem-solving, just as there are to change. Carnall (1995: 44) argues that people will have

- blocks in perception (e.g. stereotyping, inability to isolate and identify problems or to see others' points of view; saturation with data – an inability to see the wood for the trees!);
- blocks in emotion (e.g. fearfulness of risk-taking, inability to tolerate uncertainty and ambiguity);
- blocks in the culture (e.g. humourlessness, tradition that is hostile to change, taboos, a focus on rationality at the expense of creativity and intuition);
- blocks in the environment (e.g. inability to accept criticism, lack of support, overdominating senior managers);
- blocks in cognition (e.g. inability to think flexibly; incorrect data, using incorrect language and concepts).

Burnes (1996) argues for a planned approach to organizational change using an action research model; action as well as research is advocated in order to overcome what Peters and Waterman (1982) term 'paralysis through analysis' – the inability to progress beyond analysis (research) into action, itself a function of having too many dominant personalities in a group (Belbin, 1981). The action research model is a powerful way of planning change because it is rooted in a problem-solving approach, itself the essence of effective learning for the learning organization. The action research and problem-solving models are exemplified in Figure 2.3.

The three-step model – unfreezing, moving, refreezing

The 'three-step' model derives from the seminal work of Lewin (1958), which is an attempt to ensure a degree of permanence in a new change and to overcome regression to the initial state after the impetus for change has receded. The three stages are:

Stage One: Unfreeze the present situation;
Stage Two: Move to the new situation;
Stage Three: Refreeze the new situation.

Clarke (1994) and Burnes (1996: 182–3) argue that unfreezing usually

A secondary school is concerned to reduce the incidence of bullying amongst students. It examines the extent of the problem, its incidence, nature and particular groups of bullies and victims. It consults widely with all involved parties in order to identify the most and least important causes of the problem. Interviews are conducted with bullies and victims in order to gather further data about bullying in the school and its causes. A short, anonymous questionnaire is given to all students to ascertain the frequency, location, perpetrators, timing, types and severity of the bullying; the same questionnaire is given to teachers to gather their perceptions, so that they can be matched with the students'.

These data about the issue and its multiple causes are then sorted into major causes, frequency, location, perpetrators, timing, types and severity of the bullying. One cause is defined as the opportunity for bullying, another is the lack of action when bullying is reported, another is the presence of bullies in the school, another is the gradation of bullying incidents in the school. For each factor a brainstorming exercise is conducted to generate possible solutions to the problem – the exercise being conducted both with student groups and teachers. Once these have been generated, evaluation is undertaken of each possible solution using the criteria of practicability, cost, extent of positive benefit (amount and type of benefit), extent of subsequent trouble (amount and type), importance in tackling the range, amount and severity of bullying. From a shortlist of ten actions six are selected and their implications for action and practice are worked out in detail, time frames for introduction and implementation are agreed, and success criteria established. The actions are implemented over the course of a school year, their effects evaluated and the project is shown to have had partial but significant success.

Here a problem-solving approach builds in wide consultation and involvement, moves to the identification of actual causes, has a divergent phase in which possible lines of action are generated, has an evaluation phase in which possible actions are evaluated, decides which actions will be implemented – a convergent phase – and then implements and evaluates these.

Figure 2.3   An action research/problem-solving model of change

requires a recognition that existing practices are no longer effective, the reduction of the forces that are maintaining the organization's present behaviour, and some form of confrontation or re-education for participants and organizations (through team-building). To 'unfreeze' – to destabilize – the status quo Clarke suggests several activities that organizations can undertake, for example:

- increasing the rate of the unfreezing process;
- identifying major forces for resistance, perhaps using attitude surveys;
- enabling dissatisfactions in the organization to surface, perhaps through the construction of a forum for this to happen;
- engineering a crisis situation or feeling;
- being self-critical;
- recruiting mavericks (see the discussion of plants in Chapter 7);
- using external consultants and change agents.

Moving involves taking action after having identified the need to move from the existing situation. Here a range of alternatives for action is considered and the most appropriate is selected. Clarke (1994) suggests that careful support and the creation of 'safe circumstances' for change are necessary here. Refreezing strives to restabilize the organization in its new state, i.e. to avoid reverting to the previous state. This involves careful attention to support strategies and mechanisms, rewards and incentives, and the development of the organizational culture and the practices that constitute the new culture.

An example of Lewin's model in education is presented in Figure 2.4.

A secondary school is trying to improve its careers education programme. The school has a high academic profile and a stable staff who are committed to the school preserving its academic route into higher education. Many teachers do not regard careers education either as their 'domain' or as a high priority because most of the students go on to higher education. Any move to destabilizing the existing, traditionalist teaching is being resisted by a narrow majority of the staff. The school has two large and well resourced careers rooms that are underused.

To 'unfreeze' the existing situation the senior management team (SMT) presents data to show that a significant minority of students are leaving school without going into further or higher education and with no immediate employment prospects. However that fails to impress many of the staff, who argue that some of these students have not made the most of opportunities presented to them and that to try to cater for this group of students cannot be done without extra resources of staffing and time. The SMT then states that this situation cannot continue as several parents have expressed concern that their children are not being catered for satisfactorily – by being inadequately prepared for employment/further education, and by insufficient advice being given for higher education. Further, the development of careers education is seen as a major way of meeting the school's mission statement of preparing all students for adult employment. The SMT places this issues as a high priority on its development planning, securing the agreement of the governors for this, and the school devotes three curriculum development days for this in the school year.

A four-pronged development is planned. First, a careers officer is appointed on a promoted post. Secondly, the SMT requires curriculum teams to plan how to ensure that their area of the curriculum addresses careers education with continuity and progression. Thirdly, timetabled time is released from personal and social education, so that classes use the careers rooms during class time, and the rooms are staffed continuously throughout the day. Fourthly, careers interviews and student self-assessment are conducted as a result of the careers education programme and work placement periods, together with facilitated action planning and target-setting between students and teachers. A time frame of one year is set for the development to be in place, with the new programme being implemented immediately afterwards.

To unfreeze the present situation data are provided to show that the existing situation is unsatisfactory, that existing teaching practices cannot solve the problem and that the customers are complaining. The SMT provides normative arguments to show how careers education furthers the school's expressed mission. This is coupled with a more coercive, perhaps confrontational management style to insist that developments to address the problem are planned (the headteacher is prepared to be unpopular in the interests of the students). What is being described here is a cultural change that affects everybody, reaching into the heart of the culture of the organization – the new initiative is everyone's responsibility. This is necessary as the initiative has to address the demonstrated inherent propensity of the organization to inertia.

Figure 2.4 An example of unfreezing, moving and refreezing

Staged and phased models of change

Staged approaches to change are premised on the view that innovations and changes can be planned in a more or less rational, linear view. This demonstrates high optimism, for it assumes that planners will have been able to anticipate fully the views, values, attitudes and behaviour of participants. Staged and phased models have the attraction of a degree of putative precision. Bullock and Batten (1985) adopt a four-phase model of change:

Stage One is an exploration phase, in which participants become aware of the need for change which, in turn, might involve seeking outside assistance.

Stage Two is a planning phase, in which participants collect information to ensure a correct diagnosis of the problem that has to be faced. This moves forward to setting goals and taking decisions on the appropriate actions to achieve them, together with securing from key decision-makers their support for the proposed changes.

Stage Three is an action phase, in which the necessary arrangements are made in order to manage the change process effectively and efficiently, together with gaining support for the actions.

Stage Four is an integration phase, in which the new practices and behaviours are reinforced (for example through support structures, feedback and reward systems).

The key elements of these approaches are the identification and diagnosis of problems and needs, the planning and evaluation of action, the implementation of the plans and the subsequent evaluation of their success in practice. However, Burnes (1996: 185–6) cautions against relying too greatly on detailed planning, arguing that it might be more advisable to adopt a more open-ended view of change that is responsive to emerging factors, internal politics and possible conflicts that could not have been anticipated. Predictable, preplanned steps give way to a much more pragmatic view of planning for change. Such a view clearly resonates with the notion of emergence in complexity theory outlined in Chapter 1 and contingency theory.

Contingency theory rejects the view that there is only 'one best way' to effective change and management that can be used as a blueprint for all organizations (Carnall, 1995; Burnes, 1996). Organizations differ in the situations and circumstances – the contingencies – that they face, hence their structures and content and management of change will be situationally specific.

ICI in the 1980s was very aware of contextual variables, regarding change, in Pettigrew's (1985) terminology, as 'the management of meaning'. Pettigrew advocates a 'processual' approach to change, to take account of traditions, cultures, structures and environments. A processual agenda includes the specification of goals, the specification of roles and tasks, effective communication and negotiation of the change, and the ability to 'manage up' in the organization.[4]

The significant contingencies that most organizations face are technology, size, resources and environment, including the 'human factor' (Child, 1984; Carnall, 1995; Burnes, 1996). Burnes (1996) comments on the rise of 'human relations' approaches which suggest the need for organizations to take very seriously the fact that: 1) people are emotional, sentient rather than rational-economic beings; 2) organizations are social and dynamical systems rather than mechanistic; 3) formal structures in organizations are complemented strongly by informal networks, practices, procedures and norms. In the human relations model emphasis is laid on communication, effective leadership, the significance of motivation (discussed in subsequent chapters of this book), and the creation and utilization of organizational structures and practices that support and promote involvement and flexibility (*ibid.*: 56)

To say that organizations approximate more closely to contingency theory than to a mechanistic view of structure and process is to face the reality of the complexity of organizations and their essentially social nature.[5] An example of staged approaches within a context of contingency theory and 'the management of meaning' is set out in Figure 2.5.

Change, then, is to be regarded less in a rational, linear, objectives-driven way, and more in a human, processual and contextually sensitive way. This view distinguishes two types of business literature. On the one hand there is the business literature that regards the management of change as comparatively 'uncontaminated' by people. On the other hand there is the view that it is precisely the presence of humans – that people are the key components and motors of change – that renders change so tricky to manage.

An example of the former can be seen in the work of Egan (1993), who sets out a three-stage model of change that moves from analysis to action.

Stage 1: the current scenario assesses the current state of affairs

What is going on? What are our current problems and challenges? What opportunities need developing?

Step One: Telling the story.
Step Two: Identifying blind spots and developing new perspectives.
Step Three: Establishing priorities and searching for points of leverage.

Stage 2: the preferred scenario creates a picture or map of the desired package of outcomes

Step One: Developing preferred scenario possibilities.
Step Two: Crafting an agenda.

- cast in outcome language – what should be in place;
- specific enough to drive action;
- challenging – capable of capturing the imagination of those who are to carry it out;
- realistic, even though people might have to stretch;
- substantial – it should have a real impact in the business;
- sustainable – the agenda should have staying power;

A primary school wishes to improve its science curriculum at Key Stage 2. The newly appointed science co-ordinator in the school has identified the need to integrate investigational work within the context of content-specific fields, e.g. electricity, forces and motion. The Key Stage 2 staff are unsure of their abilities here; they feel they have insufficient subject knowledge and require further guidance on how to plan for progression in investigational work and how to integrate this within a cognate scientific field.

The science co-ordinator plans a curriculum development day. In the morning she sets out the elements of investigational work, how progression in investigations can be planned, and how assessment and recording can be undertaken, focusing on electricity experiments and knowledge. In the afternoon teachers set a timetable for the change: 1) planning out a term's timetable for developments, with year-team meetings, tasks to be undertaken (with staff identified) and feedback and review sessions, so that at the end of the development time a range of science activities to address the issue will have been developed; 2) planning the implementation and ongoing review in the second term, with two end-of-term meetings to undertake a more formal evaluation and to set further development priorities.

However, during the first term – the planning phase – it becomes clear that there are very marked differences in class teachers' subject knowledge and confidence to handle the work. Some are unclear on the meanings of investigational work and its links to pedagogic strategies and classroom organization. The science co-ordinator responds by bringing to meetings examples of published materials and schemes, only to find that this appears overwhelming to some colleagues. One teacher asks to go on a short course to improve his subject knowledge, but is turned down.

Then it becomes clear that there are insufficient material resources in the school to undertake some of the planned changes, so the science co-ordinator has to submit equipment lists and costings. Some of the teachers trial some of the materials and identify a range of problems with them in assessing and recording children's progress. Then the teachers subdivide into development working groups but it becomes clear that there are different views of the purposes of the groups. The science co-ordinator does not join with these subgroups. The outcomes of their activities, even though an initial remit was provided, are very discrepant.

There is confusion on responsibilities, tasks, definitions of investigational work and where the whole development process is going. This generates antipathy, complaints and dissension within and between the subgroups; staff lose heart and motivation slips. Some staff place the responsibility back on the science co-ordinator, complaining of poor leadership, ineffective communication and lack of direction, culminating in a general view that it is the science co-ordinator's task to develop programmes and that she should 'get on and do it'.

What began as a positive, needs-driven activity has rapidly descended into difficulties. Initially the leader took insufficient account of the factors concerning the staff, resources, development needs – the 'contingencies'. A blanket response was provided (bringing in published materials) that compounded the problem by failing to address real needs (those that the staff expressed), working only on those needs that the co-ordinator perceived. Insufficient account was taken of the genuine concerns and perceptions of staff, and the management of the innovation was neglected. Staff were 'cut adrift' from each other and from sources of expertise and support when they fragmented into subgroups, and communication was broken. Further, the science co-ordinator did not intervene when human concerns and relations were a problem.

What we have here commenced by being a clean plan of action, following a very rational – predetermined – sequence. However, this plan was untouched by the people involved, it had no room for them and therefore it was unsuccessful. The lesson here is to take very seriously the human factor in the planning of change. The science co-ordinator had seen the development of the science as an essentially content-driven matter, whereas it turned out to be a person-driven problem.

Figure 2.5   A staged approach to planning within contingency theory

- flexible – it should be able to be adapted to a changing environment;
- compatible with the resources and culture of the business;
- cast in a reasonable time frame.

Step Three: Securing commitment.

Stage 3: action strategies are designed to move the system from the current to the preferred scenario

Step One: Brainstorming strategies.
Step Two: Choosing the best strategies.
Step Three: Formulating a plan.

The model of change here is silent on the human and processual factors. It builds out people and, thereby, is simplistic. Whilst it might have a certain attraction for clear planning, it belies the complexity of the phenomenon it is trying to model.[6]

An attempt to inject a human dimension is undertaken by Doz and Prahalad (1988) in their four-stage model of change:

Stage One: Incubation (e.g. of ideas, needs, vision, mission).
Stage Two: Variety generation (the identification of possible ways of meeting needs).
Stage Three: Power shifts (the destabilization of the status quo).
Stage Four: Refocusing (renewal and refreezing).

Clarke (1994) argues that making change human and manageable is premised on a culture of sharing, collaboration and communication. He argues that a staged approach to change could proceed in six stages:

Stage One: Research the internal and external markets to identify the need for and direction of change.
Stage Two: Anticipate resistance and obstacles to change.
Stage Three: Develop a shared vision in the organization.
Stage Four: Mobilize commitment to the proposed change.
Stage Five: Plan and communicate the plan for change.
Stage Six: Constantly reinforce the change.

A more complex model of the change process builds in the human dimension and the significance of processual factors and, thereby, not only becomes more realistic but, significantly, also more detailed – there are very many stages in Clarke's (*ibid.*) twelve-stage model!:

Stage One: Identify and become sensitized to external pressures for change – the external environment.
Stage Two: Examine the organization's capability for change and diagnose what needs to change and what the 'levers' of change might be.
Stage Three: Examine your own values, attitudes, assumptions and leadership styles.
Stage Four: Examine the process of change – how to spread the experience of what is happening in the change (e.g. communicate extensively).
Stage Five: Create and develop a culture for change (maybe through the

creation of an internal market for change).

Stage Six: Anticipate resistance, identify how this can be managed and how commitment can be mobilized.

Stage Seven: Practise visionary leadership (see Chapter 8).

Stage Eight: Unfreeze the existing situation, destabilizing the status quo and the comfort of inertia.

Stage Nine: Communicate continuously and ensure involvement.

Stage Ten: Manage incremental change through careful attention to timing, time frame and the management of transitions (see the comments above on moving).

Stage Eleven: Implement it.

Stage Twelve: Support, sustain and reinforce the change to ensure institutionalization in the longer term (see the comments above on *refreezing*).

An example of Clarke's twelve-stage process can be seen in Figure 2.6.

Clarke's model is much more sophisticated than others because it succeeds in catching the dynamic quality of change and in incorporating this within a planned approach to change that looks at the human dimension, the processual dimension, the management dimension, the organizational dimension – the culture of the organization – as well as the substance of the change itself. One can see that the process of a staged approach is a move from understanding the environment to planning strategy and thence to planning the implementation of the change (see also Grundy, 1994; Carnall, 1995: 166).[7] A useful activity for understanding the planning of a staged approach to educational change is presented in Figure 2.7.

Managing change, then, involves: 1) the identification of pressures for change (internal and external); 2) the setting and clarification of aims and plans; 3) the careful integration of the new with the existing situation; 4) the ability to operate in existing and changing organizational cultures; 5) the ability to manage transitions effectively; 6) the ability to mange the micropolitics of the organization; 7) the provision of appropriate support (e.g. for risk-taking and learning) and training; 8) ensuring the involvement and ownership of participants; 9) the ability to catch and develop the motivation and self-esteem of participants; 10) the provision of feedback, and the management of stress; 11) the ability to change the organization and move towards a learning organization (Carnall, 1995). This, surely, is a set of criteria that the educational world could embrace readily, as many recent reforms in education have violated nearly every one of these!

Incremental and radical change

The approaches outlined above emphasize the incremental view of change, as opposed to the radical, transformative nature of change. An incremental view of change is one in which small steps together build into strategic decisions; change is a continuous process which evolves from and demonstrates continuity with the past and present situations (Johnson,

A comprehensive school was formed from the merger between a grammar school and a smaller secondary school. Though there is only a small number of former grammar school teachers still on the staff, the school is known as the 'academic' secondary school in the locality and its academic achievements are high. The school has recently been informed that it will be inspected by OFSTED within nine months.

The new headteacher was appointed deliberately to initiate changes in the internal organization and management of the school. She sees as a priority the need to develop collegiality in the school in order for a climate of change and innovation to be promoted. As part of this she is actively developing team approaches to planning and management. She has set into place a system of faculties in the school and the senior management team (SMT) comprises the headteacher, deputy headteachers and the four faculty heads – humanities, communication, sciences, arts. Most of the former grammar school teachers are heads of departments in the school but the faculty heads are deliberately not drawn from the heads of departments.

The move towards creating faculties was strongly resisted by many of the former grammar school staff, all of whom are in long-standing promoted posts. For example, the head of history, a former grammar school teacher, has been at the school for many years and clings to the academic tradition of history teaching. He is very certain that he should have control over the academic planning of 'his' department and that the faculty organization is an unnecessary tier in the management structure of the school. He believes that promoted posts should be given for subject and departmental responsibility in the school and that creating a new management structure is little more than costly bureaucracy that takes experienced teachers out of classrooms, putting unacceptable burdens of teaching on to less experienced staff. This, he believes, will ultimately contribute to falling standards, reducing the academic excellence for which the school is known. The costs of further promoted posts in the school, he believes, are at the expense of resources and additional classroom teachers, and he believes that, in a climate of budgetary stringency, this will lead to unhealthy competition between faculties for money and resources. He is quite happy to work collegially within 'his' department but regards more extended forms of collegiality as unworkable.

The SMT recommends a modular structure devolved on to student-centred learning for the school's curricular organization at sixth-form level. When this was first mooted there was immediate and vocal resistance from the department heads who saw this as yet another encroachment on the academic standards of the school and further undermining of their own professional expertise.

Setting this into Clarke's (1994) 12 stages one can re-present the planning thus:

Stage One: Identify and become sensitized to external pressures for change – the external environment: a) the pressure from the proposed OFSTED inspection; b) the need to respond to the changing demands on schools – beyond the academic; c) the need to respond to extended forms of assessment and examination.

Stage Two: Examine the organization's capability for change and diagnose what needs to change and what the 'levers' of change might be: a) limited capability for change because of the power of tradition in the school (particularly the academic); b) limited capability for change because of the autonomy of departments and teachers and the absence of crossdepartmental collegiality and a tradition of team approaches; c) resistance to change from senior and long-established teachers.

Levers of change are: a) the push for change from the headteacher; b) the development of faculties in the school; c) the generation of a new SMT that over-rides traditionalism in the school; d) the introduction of a modular structure of organization; e) the development of crossdepartmental team approaches to planning and management.

Stage Three: Examine your own values, attitudes, assumptions and leadership styles: a) the headteacher regards a collegial approach and the creation of a new structure for the SMT as essential for school development; b) the headteacher identifies the need to cater for the broad spectrum of abilities and qualifications in the school – beyond the narrowly academic; c) an extended view of leadership is desirable, with faculty and departmental heads.

Stage Four: Examine the process of change – how to spread the experience of what is happening in the change (e.g. communicate extensively): a) a series of ongoing staff meetings and meetings with heads of faculties and departments; b) the development of several different types of team, e.g. curriculum teams, cross-curricular teams (e.g. to work on the proposed modular structure), whole-school issues teams (e.g. for assessment, for discipline and pastoral work, for work experience), with each teacher having multiple team membership to facilitate communication and; c) regular feedback sessions in face-to-face meetings and written reports (where necessary).

Stage Five: Create and develop a culture for change: a) introduce multiple innovations with clearly defined purposes, devolved tasks and responsibilities, and within specified time frames; b) ensure that team approaches are adopted, where appropriate, for planning, implementation and monitoring of the changes; c) ensure devolved leadership on to faculty and departmental heads within the strategy and direction of the school; d) curtail the power of the traditionalist departmental heads; e) ensure equitable distribution of funding for changes within the school's development plan; f) adopt a problem-solving, consultative and bottom-up approach to planning and implementing developments.

Stage Six: Anticipate resistance, identify how this can be managed and how commitment can be mobilized: resistance from: a) departmental heads who have had others promoted over them (addressed by ensuring early involvement and much consultation); b) former grammar school staff who see the changes as threatening academic standards (addressed by making clear that the change concerns maintaining academic standards whilst broadening the work of the school, talking it out and the presentation of logical and compelling benefits, wearing out and waiting out resisters); c) heads of department who see that their power base is being undermined (addressed by communicating how autonomy and control will operate in the realigned organization and reducing the potential for loss of status); d) those who see the furtherance of unproductive bureaucracy (addressed by indicating how the 'system' will work to everyone's advantage); e) those who see the changes as a poor use of funds (addressed by democratic decision-making on funding and/or consultation to identify the micropolitics of the organization); f) those who see the changes as essentially divisive (addressed by the provision of extensive information to indicate how new alliances, groups and teams will break down the existing divides; g) those who see the changes as an encroachment on their professional expertise (addressed by discussion of how the changes extend professionalism and professional autonomy within an aligned organization).

Stage Seven: Practise visionary leadership (see the discussion of leadership in

Chapter 8): a) effectively assessing the environment, needs and micropolitics of the situation; b) setting the context and direction of change; c) creating the critical mass in the SMT for change; d) communicating the need for change extensively; e) generating a shared vision of where the organization is heading; f) appointing effective managers of the changes; g) setting challenging targets and negotiating/ discussing ways of achieving them; h) making key strategic promotions; i) communicating clearly the key features of the change; j) asking demanding questions; k) utilizing high organizational skills; l) bringing together key people in teams with identified responsibilities.

Stage Eight: Unfreeze the existing situation, destabilizing the status quo and the comfort of inertia: a) making new appointments, new management structures and new lines of decision-making, all coupled with *actual* new decisions to be taken; b) reducing the power of former locuses of decision-making; c) creating multiple teams and multiple team membership; d) rechannelling funds; e) making it clear that the existing emphasis purely on academic standards is insufficient for the range of the student population, identifying the range of qualifications that students will be expected to gain.

Stage Nine: Communicate continuously and ensure involvement: ensure that a) ongoing briefings, consultations, communications take place throughout the period of discussion, development and implementation; b) members of the SMT are present for other team meetings; c) each member of staff is a member of several teams; d) the tasks, responsibilities and time frames for teams are clear; e) departments produce development plans that are aligned to the overall school development plan; f) staff development days and crossdepartmental modular programmes are timetabled.

Stage Ten: Manage incremental change through careful attention to timing, time frames and the management of transitions: a) require outline delineation from teams of proposed developments on a half-termly basis in advance, to include initial tasks, follow-up tasks and criteria for ensuring that the tasks have been successful; b) identify the overall stages of the developments in the crosscurricular modular programme development, so that the school moves, as far as possible, in tandem, one team with another, to maintain momentum and mutual support; c) ensure that the SMT is on hand during development and implementation times to engage in discussions and communication; d) ensure that there is careful differentiation of small and large tasks.

Stage Eleven: Implement it: a) ensure that the plans for implementation are sufficiently 'tight' to provide direction and momentum and yet sufficiently loose to be able to accommodate to unforeseen issues, the human dimension, the processual factors; b) be prepared to make modifications to plans as circumstances dictate.

Stage Twelve: Support, sustain and reinforce the change to ensure institutionalization in the longer term (see the comments above on refreezing): a) the proposed change will be irreversible in terms of developing the organizational culture for change, a subsequent evaluation and review might lead to further management changes; b) ensure that planning and development are undertaken for all major innovations through the team structures; c) establish the success criteria for the change and evaluate both formatively and summatively.

Figure 2.6 Implementing a staged approach to change

---

1) Identify a series of stages or steps – in sequence – that planners can follow and address in planning a change. Identify the main issues to be faced for each stage of the planned change. For example, a simplified model might be:

   Needs assessment → Selection of focus → Development of programme to meet focused need → Preparation of organizational culture to introduce the change → Implementation → Evaluation.

   Construct a fuller flow chart with appropriate laterals and arrows.

2) Be prepared to justify the sequence and series of issues.

3) Then devise a very different series of stages or steps – in sequence that planners can follow and address in planning a change, again, providing prescriptions for practice. Identify the main issues to be faced for each stage of the planned change.

   It may be that you simply resequence the previous model, or it may be that you generate a completely different set of considerations. Construct a flow chart with appropriate laterals and arrows.

4) Be prepared to justify the new sequence and series of issues.

5) Prepare an overhead transparency to illustrate *one* of your models, and please prepare a presentation of no more than five minutes to introduce your model.

You may find it helpful to take an actual example in order to focus your discussions.

Time allowed: 1¹/₂ hours.

Figure 2.7   A task to address the staged planning of educational change

1993: 58–64). Planning for incremental change enables the contingencies, the human dimension and the processual factors of change to be addressed, as managing incrementalism involves: being sensitive to needs; enlarging and communicating understanding and awareness of the existing situation and needs; developing credibility and legitimizing perspectives and opinions; suggesting partial solutions to problems and tentative trial concepts; developing support for the change; identifying and managing areas of indifference, resistance, opposition, commitment, support, possible coalitions; altering the risks that people will take; restructuring for required flexibility; excising undesired options; sharpening and making concrete the focus and the development of consensus; formalizing agreed undertakings, tasks and roles.

Quinn (1993: 65–6) argues that an incremental style enables managers to plan consciously and proactively in

• improving the quality of information that organizations use in corporate decision-making;

- managing time frames, with subroutines and contributory elements built into programming and decision-making;
- identifying and coping with possible resistances and micropolitical difficulties;
- developing organizational awareness and the commitment of those affected by and implementing the change;
- increasing the certainty of decisions and directions through effective communication and involvement of participants;
- improving the quality of decision-making by involving participants and avoiding premature closure of discussions.

For Quinn (1980; 1993), strategic planning on an incremental model is more akin to fermentation in biochemistry than an industrial assembly line, itself echoing the significance of the organism acting with and reacting to its environment. The model is one of inclusion, participation, collaboration and involvement rather than exclusion, passivity, coercion and disengagement.[8] This is a point of major importance, for likening the process of change to a process of fermentation breaks with the narrow and simplistic linearity of most of the staged approaches outlined earlier. The 'fermentation' approach builds in people rather than regards them as potential contaminants in the antiseptic process of change; it is a very powerful metaphor. It recognizes that change is messy and often piecemeal. An example of incremental change is given in Figure 2.8.

Strategy development

A significant message that is emerging from the material presented so far is the need for strategy development. Whilst everyday parlance would hold that a strategy is simply an operational plan, in the business literature it can have several meanings. For example Mintzberg *et al.* (1988) suggest five definitions of strategy that are inter-related, in which strategy can be conceived as: 1) a plan (a deliberate course of action planned in advance); 2) a ploy (a manoeuvre designed to outsmart enemies or opponents); 3) a pattern (where an organization operates in an identifiably consistent way, e.g. 'our marketing strategy'); 4) a position (where an organization deliberately positions itself in order to maintain or develop its competitive superiority); 5) a perspective (an idea or concept that people keep in their minds, e.g. to guide their thinking) (see also Normann and Ramirez, 1996).

Whichever of these interpretations is adopted does not diminish the significance of strategy as an essential ingredient of the planning process. Whether one discusses it in terms of vision, aims, objectives, mission statements, policies or operationalized practices the message is clear that strategy development and strategizing is a significant, if not critical, component of managing successful change. Central to effective strategic planning is the drawing up of objectives, aims, goals, targets – whichever terminology one uses the message is clear, an effective organization knows where it wants to go, it is future orientated (Pettigrew, 1988). Burnes (1996: 323) argues that successful organizations focus their objectives on four phases in the change process: the trigger (how to commence the change, the impulse

A secondary school is introducing teacher-facilitated student self-referenced assessments. Teachers realize that this demands a different style of teaching and learning and that the 'social distance' between teachers and students has to alter. In-service development is undertaken to implement new teaching styles to incorporate the change. Many staff feel that valuable teaching time will be lost as time will be spent on self-assessment, target-setting and action planning. New timetabling arrangements are made, and staff have to develop the abilities and practices of incorporating greater self-assessment in the teaching and learning process.

To facilitate self-assessment, teachers need to develop sensitive 'counselling' skills, including active listening and providing support, the abilities to prompt, probe, summarize, empathize, tolerate, persevere, initiate, facilitate, clarify, focus on the positive, etc. Hence a series of workshops is run, with the involvement of a trained external counsellor. Money to support this is taken out of other development areas.

As student self-referenced assessment unfolds, it becomes clear that significant crosscurricular issues are involved, e.g. the use of language and mathematics across the curriculum, and the relationship between work in one curriculum area and another. Hence there is a need for much greater co-ordination of the curriculum than heretofore, so that students' learning is facilitated through co-ordinated effort. The difficulties students might be facing in one aspect of their learning impact on other aspects of their learning, for example their motivation, confidence and self-esteem. The need for communication about these aspects of a student to all teachers involved becomes significant.

This high-profile innovation is the responsibility of one of the senior management team, appointed to give greater legitimacy and administrative efficiency to the innovation. Once the move to self-referenced assessment has been implemented, its use, together with action planning, is seen to link very closely with the school's record of achievement, involving 1) accreditation by outside agencies; 2) sponsoring by a local business partnership; 3) significant clerical time, computer access, stationery and storage issues; 4) using self-referenced assessment and action planning in a programme of careers education and preparation for employment.

The project has snowballed quickly from being a bounded, singular innovation to spawning a multiplicity of initiatives in a wide range of aspects of the school, for example: curricular, pedagogic, pastoral, in-service, budgeting, management, accreditation, community relations, sponsorship, careers and employment, time-tabling, administration, resourcing, assessment, reporting. In this respect the innovation has brought about a ferment of other issues, people and practices through a series of comparatively small-scale, incremental changes.

Figure 2.8   An example of incremental change

for change), the remit (the tasks and purposes of the change), the assessment team (their purposes, roles and tasks in feeding into the process of change), and the assessment of the impact and effectiveness of the change itself.

Owen (1993) suggests that strategies tend not to materialize if their implementation cuts across existing organizational practices or structures, if data for monitoring the implementation of the strategies are inadequate, if the organization is resistant to change and if payments reward retrospectively (i.e. for achievements) rather than provide incentives for the achievement of future goals. He argues that successful strategy implementation flows from several factors:

- the allocation of clear accountability and responsibility for the success of the project;
- placing limits on the number of strategies that are operating at any particular moment;
- the identification of actions that need to be taken in order to achieve strategic objectives;
- the allocation and agreement of specific responsibilities for the actions to be taken;
- the identification of clear 'milestones' or progress points and criteria that can be evaluated during the project;
- the identification of the key performance measures that will be used for monitoring throughout the life of the project, together with an appropriate recording system.

The language here is very close to the language of school development planning (e.g. Hargreaves and Hopkins, 1991) with its references to targets, routes, initial tasks and success criteria. Additionally here there is an injection of accountability and responsibilities, attempting to ensure that strategies can become translated into action. Strategy development is akin to development planning, particularly in its twin concerns for development through collective staff involvement, empowerment and open consultation. It is concerned with the process and management of change.

Mintzberg (1994) suggests that there are several fallacies in strategic planning, including fallacies of prediction (when the future is unpredictable), detachment (from the whole picture) and formalization (and its dehumanization). He argues that adhocracies might be the most advisable order of the day, echoing the comments earlier on the importance of emergence and evolutionary planning.

Strategy development concerns products – product manufacture, placement, marketing etc. – seeking to maximize efficiency and effectiveness through rational planning. Whether this is possible, or indeed desirable, in education is contestable, for it suggests a certain instrumentalism, controlled predictability and manipulation that might be undesirable in education. Moreover, it is an open question whether strategic planning interpreted as mission statements, vision statements, policy formation, etc., actually improves practices and standards of achievement, whether and how they impact on practice. The senior management team and governing body of a school might be better advised to concentrate on specific practices and concrete innovations than to spend time on developing strategies, because the context of education is changing so rapidly. This is not to deny the importance of an organization knowing clearly where it is going; it is to recognize that this is only a starting point – none the less critical – for more closely planned change. An example of strategy development is given in Figure 2.9.

The example indicates an attempt by the school not only to maintain its existing tasks but also to seek development roles and directions. Hargreaves and Hopkins (1991) are explicit that school development plans should seek to balance maintenance with development.

An urban secondary school is seeking to establish a clear identity in the area. It decides to specialize in languages, as it draws on a very mixed ethnic and multicultural community and because no other secondary schools in the area offer this. A three-pronged development is planned, first to increase the focus on English for second-language users, secondly to increase the amount of non-English mother-tongue community language use, and thirdly to increase the range and emphasis of international languages used. To this end meetings are held to identify a development team for this initiative, whose task it is to

- set targets for the uptake of these three features within a specified time frame in terms of actual numbers on designated courses, together with targets for achieving publicly recognized qualifications in languages;
- audit current practices in the school so that needs, gaps and areas for development can be identified;
- identify resource needs (e.g. staffing – full time and part time; materials, administrative, financial, space);
- develop publicity materials and to disseminate this widely in the community;
- to prepare bids and budgets, attracting funding into the school and networking with a range of external agencies to ensure that the project can be funded adequately;
- devise a staged development plan that identifies targets, routes, initial tasks, responsibilities and success criteria (performance measures) for each stage of the process, together with staffing and timetabling implications;
- prepare formative evaluations of the development and implementation of the initiative.

What can be seen in this example is that the overall direction of the school (its strategy-as-position) is complemented by: 1) a statement of the main features of this strategy (strategy-as-pattern and strategy-as-perspective); 2) proposals for action (strategy-as-plan); 3) identification of niche targeting (strategy as invention of value or maybe strategy-as-ploy).

Figure 2.9 An example of strategy development

Change as organizational development

The implicit message, it has been argued here, is that effective change, from a business perspective, engages the whole question of organizational development. Whilst this is a topic that will be addressed in subsequent chapters, it is important to signal that message here – effective change requires organizational learning. Dunphy (1981) argues that successful change possesses 15 important features in the field of organizational development in the business community:

1) clear and unambiguous objectives;
2) a realistic scope which is planned and simple;
3) informed awareness of the change right around the organization;
4) the identification and selection of appropriate strategies for intervention;
5) effective timing;
6) real and genuine participation;

7) the support from the key power groups in the organization;
8) the use of existing power structure and experiences in the organization;
9) the adoption of open evaluation and assessment before implementation;
10) the establishment of majority support for the perceived benefits of the change;
11) the provision of competent staff in order to offer temporary resource support;
12) the ability to integrate new methods into routine operations;
13) the ability to transfer, disseminate and diffuse successful innovations;
14) the presence of continuing monitoring, review and modifications;
15) the provision of adequate rewards and incentives for participants and those affected by the change.

Nadler (1993: 87) breaks down the elements of an organization into four components, each of which is susceptible to change, viz. the organization's tasks; the individuals in the organization; the formal organizational structures, procedures and arrangements; the informal organizational procedures, norms and arrangements. This reinforces the message that effective organizations take seriously the 'people' dimension and echoes the comments earlier about the significance of adopting the human relations theory of organizations (see also Pugh, 1993: 109–10). Pugh (*ibid.*: 111–12) sets out six rules for managing organizational change successfully:

1) work strenuously to establish the need for change;
2) think out the change and think through it, anticipating issues and problems;
3) initiate the process and contents of change through informal discussion in order to receive feedback and to encourage and develop participation;
4) welcome and encourage those affected to voice their objections;
5) be open and prepared to have to change yourself;
6) monitor, support and reinforce the change.

Beer *et al.* (1990) suggest six steps to effective organizational change:

Step One: The mobilization of commitment to change through joint diagnosis of problems.
Step Two: The development of a shared vision of how to organize and reorganize in order to manage effectively for competitiveness.
Step Three: The fostering and development of consensus for the new shared vision, the development of competence to put it into practice, and the establishment of cohesion amongst staff to progress the change.
Step Four: Spreading the message and practice of revitalization across all departments without pushing it unnecessarily from senior management.
Step Five: The institutionalization of the revitalization through the development and implementation of formal policies, systems, networks, structures and infrastructures.
Step Six: The development and implementation of monitoring and adjustment strategies and practices in response to problems encountered in the processes of revitalization.

An example of organizational development is provided in Figure 2.10.

An all-age school for 80 students with moderate learning difficulties is experiencing considerable staff turnover and, indeed, the long-standing and highly autocratic and unpopular headteacher has recently retired. A new headteacher has been in post for one term. Many staff have berated the former headteacher for her absence of consultation, her inability to handle disagreement, her hostility and over-reaction to genuine criticisms and suggestions made, her disparagement of longer-serving and senior members of staff and her overt support for newer staff to the school whom she could manipulate. These have led to an atmosphere of suspicion, distrust, factions and cliques, the disempowering of the senior staff, the low morale in the school and an unwillingness to do more than the basic minimum for students. Most of the teachers have 'given up' because there is no incentive to do otherwise.

The new headteacher has decided that the poor personal, interpersonal and cultural aspects of the school should be the target of immediate development. Upon taking up the post he conducts individual interviews with all the staff in which they are each asked to identify the main strengths, weaknesses, problematic areas and areas for improvement. This is complemented by whole-staff meetings where, through the use of devices such as nominal group technique, focus groups and general staff discussions, the problems in the school are aired and discussed in a spirit that tries to avoid blame and recrimination and to move forwards, recognizing that genuine grievances and problems will need to be 'talked out'. The intentions of the meetings are to set and address agendas for development. The headteacher gives a high priority (through staff meetings and development days) to whole-school identification of, and agreement on, the ways forward, to further the achievement of an agreed, collectively devised mission statement and set of aims. Immediate steps to be taken are

1) an audit by curriculum co-ordinators of the curricular practices, assessment and achievements in the school;
2) team planning of the curriculum, resources, teaching arrangements, assessment and reporting;
3) the introduction of weekly senior management team (SMT) meetings to monitor activities, developments and to plan consultatively and collegially;
4) the addressing of whole-school matters by cross-school development teams, for assessment, record-keeping, documentation for planning, behaviour, links to mainstream education, progression and continuity in the curriculum.

The headteacher recognizes that the early steps will need to be premised on team approaches (e.g. cross-school, cross-age phase, crosscurricular and crossdepartmental teams), on genuine, frequent and open consultation, on democratic agreement and decision-making, on participatory styles of development and decision-making, and that the early stages of organizational development will be the raising of morale through the revaluing of the staff in the school. This needs a concrete focus, and so the SMT identify specific concrete practices and activities for development.

Figure 2.10 An example of organizational development

This example shows that the four elements of the organization – tasks, individuals, formal structures and informal arrangements – set out above by Nadler are all addressed in moving forward the institution collegially, democratically and collaboratively. This is sensitive to the history and micropolitics of the organization and to the need for trust and morale to be re-established. It recognizes that people matter in organizations and that their motivation is essential for effectiveness.

Nadler (1993) reinforces the need to plan carefully for people-focused organizational change as the context for other substantive changes in businesses (e.g. products and manufacture). He identifies three basic problems in changing organizations and suggests how they might be addressed:

1) *overcoming resistance* (i.e. the need to motivate change). Action is required to motivate the change, identifying and exposing current dissatisfactions, building in involvement and ownership, providing real incentives and rewards for adopting the changes, ensuring adequate and appropriate resource support for the change (e.g. in terms of time and opportunity to 'let go' of emotional attachment and investment in existing practices and beliefs, to have appropriate materials and training);
2) *ensuring control* (i.e. managing the transition effectively). Action is required to develop and communicate a vision and picture of the desired future state, identifying and utilizing several points of leverage into the new practices and support systems to enable the transition to proceed as smoothly as possible, and developing monitoring and feedback systems and practices;
3) *managing power* (i.e. shaping the political aspects and dynamics of change). Action is required to ensure and develop the support of key power groups in the organization, identifying leadership and the nature of leadership support, and using an array of practices that will create energy for the change and sustain motivation and commitment for the change.

A key leitmotiv that runs through this literature is the centrality of working with, and on, the motivation of individuals involved in or affected by the change. The business literature is redolent with references to agreement, involvement, need, assistance, consultation, reward, support, motivation, incentives, reinforcement, celebration of success – terms that reinforce the need to view change not through the mechanistic lenses of Taylorism but as focused on people.

The work of Kanter *et al.* (1992) draws together the key organizational, personal, interpersonal and managerial features introduced in the preceding sections. For Kanter and her associates there are 'ten commandments' for the successful implementation of change:

1) the need for analysis of the organization and the identification of the need for change;
2) the creation of a genuinely shared vision that provides direction;
3) the need to separate past activities from current and future activities, to break with the past;
4) the need to create a sense of urgency for change:
5) the need for a strong and supportive leader of change and senior management:
6) the need to attract, develop and employ political sponsorship:

7) the careful development of the plan for implementation:
8) the creation of structures in the organization that will support the change:
9) the need for widespread communication, honesty with people and the building up of their involvement:
10) the need to reinforce change in order that it will become sustained and institutionalized.

If one did not know that this emanated from the business community it would be difficult to detect this. The message can apply equally well to education as it can to the business world.

Notes

1.   Dalin, 1978; Cuban, 1990; Senge; 1990; Fullan, 1991; Dalin *et al.*, 1993; Hargreaves, 1994; Dalin and Rust, 1983; 1996; Miyashiro, 1996a.

2.   Rogers and Shoemaker, 1971; Berman and McLaughlin, 1979; Kanter, 1983; Kanji and Asher, 1993.

3.   Bank (1992: 138) provides an example of the problem-solving strategy adopted by the Xerox company in the context of quality development. In this a six-stage process is involved. Buchanan and Boddy (1992) cite the five-stage approach to managing change that was adopted by British Telecom: Stage One was the proposal for quality improvement. Stage Two was the statement of the problem and its causes. Stage Three was the education and communication of the action plan. Stage Four was the detail of the implementation, the concrete actions to be taken. Stage Five was the implementation.

4.   Buchanan and Boddy (1992) suggest some problems with Petti-grew's analysis. Nevertheless Pettigrew's work is useful in signalling not only that change is a process rather than an event but also that it requires sensitivity to many levels of planning, operation and interpretation.

5.   For a critique of contingency theory see Carnall (1995) and Burnes (1996: 68–70).

6.   Kanter (1983) identified three waves of change: 1) identifying the problem and the collation of information about it; 2) identifying and mobilizing a supportive coalition of participants; 3) completion of the task.

7.   Wickens (1995: 335), echoing the work of Deming (see Chapter 4) describing the conditions for the 'ascendant organization' in business, makes several acute observations about the management of successful change: senior managers need to establish a shared understanding of the present and desired future situation; appointing the best people is critical, ensuring, meanwhile, that they do not have the monopoly of wisdom; support for change from the senior managers is essential; remove insecurity and fear and develop trust; encourage experimentation and support it with training; identify the critical factors and criteria for success; use outsiders if appropriate; stage the changes so that people are not overwhelmed; elements of the old and the new can coexist.

8.   Carnall (1995) argues that there are three fundamental conditions if change is to be effective: awareness, capability and inclusion. He cites an example from IBF Ltd (a design company). Incrementalism is not without its critics (see Champy and Nohria, 1996a; 1996b; Goss, *et al.* 1996: 121–2).

3

Managing change: the Japanese model

Introduction

The dazzling rise of Japanese companies has brought a transformation into business practices such that industries across the world are emulating them. It is difficult to underestimate the impact that Japanese practices have had not only on other automobile producers (e.g. the Rover group) but also on other non-automobile companies (e.g. British Telecom, British Airways). The material introduced in this chapter signals major implications that are covered in subsequent chapters of the book, for example, human resource development, teamwork, quality development, organizational development and leadership.

In some respects it is perhaps a misnomer to call the practices described in this chapter distinctly Japanese for, as will be seen in the subsequent chapter on quality development, several of the practices in Japan were inspired from the first wave of 'quality gurus' from America, for example Deming, Juran, Crosby and Feigenbaum. Nevertheless, for the sake of shorthand convenience these practices will be termed 'the Japanese model'. Further, for the sake of clarity, this chapter will use a worked example from the Japanese automobile industry – the Nissan Motor Manufacturing Company (UK) Limited (hereafter referred to as Nissan) – as a vehicle for studying Japanese practices. The UK plant is a vast complex employing some 4,000 workers and is highly successful, producing its millionth car within ten years of first arriving at a greenfield site in 1984. It provides an interesting example of a Japanese company operating in the cultural context of the UK; hence it enables us to examine the transferability of Japanese practices out of Japan, to examine the strengths and weaknesses of some of the Japanese practices in a non-Japanese cultural context.[1]

Principles of Japanese organizations

There are several principles of Japanese organizations, in the field of personnel and business practices,[2] for example:

1) the emphasis on co-operation and obligation;

2) the value of self-discipline and patience;
3) the employees' expectation of lifetime employment in the company (*sushin koyo seido*) and the security this brings;
4) the practice of making promotions from within the company (the internal market);
5) the practice of promotion based on seniority (*nenko garrets*);
6) the strong emphasis on teamwork, strong informal group relations, the ethos of the group and the comparative intolerance of 'deviants';
7) an emphasis on group co-operation rather than individual creativity;
8) an emphasis on long-term planning and the persistent pursuit of objectives and goals;
9) a single-union policy;
10) an emphasis on continuous training and education;
11) the practice of extended company concern for employee's welfare;
12) the expectation of loyalty to and praise for the company together with a strong commitment to its aims and practices;
13) an expectation of hard work and continuous improvement at work, together with personal development and improvement;
14) the ethos of co-operation rather than conflict;
15) the emphasis on total quality management;
16) a highly homogeneous internal culture within the organization;
17) workers' commitment to the organization rather than to their particular occupation.

These points can be applied to, and reinterpreted in, an educational context. With reference to point 1, one can suggest that schools should be predicated on collegiality and mutual responsibility, regardless of seniority or position in the school; they have an essentially human nature. Decision-making should be based on the force of the argument rather than the positional power of the protagonist. Point 2 can be interpreted as the need to be self-reliant and to be reliable, both important aspects of professionalism.

With reference to point 3, the expectation that employees will remain in a company/school for life is unrealistic nowadays; indeed, as will be shown later in this chapter, this is also the case in Japanese business. It is perhaps much more realistic to expect a higher degree of insecurity in employment, with the rise in fixed-term and part-time contracts brought about by funding formulae for schools. Indeed, the current recruitment and retention difficulties in teaching suggest that teachers themselves are becoming consumers, and that they are not prepared to enter or remain in teaching posts they find unsatisfactory. They are prepared to develop their own portfolios and profiles (Handy, 1989).

With regard to internal promotion and promotion based on seniority (points 4 and 5), in Japanese companies this is predicated on the fact that workers will have been 'multiskilled' rather than specialized, and will have demonstrated a commitment to the organization over time. In educational terms this sits very comfortably with the view that teachers acquire experience in a variety of aspects of school life, not simply teaching their own subject(s), for example: middle and senior management positions, curriculum development, mentoring of new colleagues, pastoral and community involvement, whole-school issues (e.g. assessment and reporting, behaviour), planning and strategy development groups, age-phase responsibility. That this is a *de facto* practice in most schools, where teachers have membership of several groups, attests to the power of this view of promotion.

On the other hand there are five concerns about applying this practice in education. First, it might well be the case that, even though there is staff development for internal promotion, there might not be, in fact, the 'right person for the right job' in the school, and therefore it might be more appropriate to look outside. Related to this is the issue of equity, viz. that applicants from within and outside the organization must be able to apply on an equal footing so that the best possible person for the post is appointed. Secondly, there is a danger that the institution might stagnate for want of 'new blood' in important positions, i.e. recruitment from outside the organization of people who have not been socialized into the school's existing culture and accepted practices. Thirdly, one has to question in educational contexts the notion of the 'internal market' in the Japanese model, for one person's internal promotion might bring an undesirable competitiveness and the unpleasant, factional, side of the micropolitics of the organization into sharp focus; it might cause significant interpersonal problems. Fourthly, internal promotion might be used by the institution as a way of saving money, simply heaping on to individuals extra work with a salary increase which is less costly than paying for an additional member of staff. Fifthly, if promotion is based on seniority, this might be a real disincentive for those staff who seek a fast track to promotion; indeed it might be seen to lead to a situation where older, more conservative staff might be in senior positions in the school, impeding change.

One very powerful educational implication of the Japanese model is the development and practice of teamwork and collegiality (points 6 and 7 above), and this book devotes a complete chapter (7) to this feature, its strengths, weaknesses and implications. The notion that institutions should be 'people centred' resonates entirely with educational contexts, where the means has to be found to address the 'idiographic', person-centred dimension of the organization *through* the 'nomothetic' structures, systems and practices of the organization (Hoyle, 1976).

In Japanese companies loyalty to the group is very pronounced, with employees belonging to a very limited number of groups. Quite how far this is straightforwardly applicable to education is not so clear, for typically teachers are members of multiple groups with different remits, purposes and tasks. Further, in Japanese companies group loyalty is seen as a mechanism, or organization, to reinforce or serve the company's singular mission, i.e. it is located within an accepted company philosophy. Hence dissension from the company view is not tolerated. This might not translate so comfortably into education – which is an 'essentially contested concept' (Hartnett and Naish, 1976) – and schools, which are flexible and strive to encourage a much more open-ended view of development, personal contributions and personal fulfilment. This is not to deny the significance of staff all 'pulling in the same direction' in education, nor for the need for a school to know where it is going; indeed one of the central features of an effective school is that it is 'aligned' – it knows where it wants to go and staff all contribute to moving in the same direction.

However, the role of dissension is important in education, for it fosters debate and, importantly, education through creative conflict. Schools perhaps should be suspicious of the negative construction of 'deviance' (ref. point 7 above). Human institutions thrive by dint of individual creativity rather than by 'group-think' or a single 'management line'. In this respect, then, one has be cautious in applying the Japanese model too completely to education, lest the benefits of teamwork and corporate commitment stifle individual creativity and constructive criticism.

Teams, then, are not simply devices for controlling workers within a given corporate identity; they are powerful engines for developing the organization in ways that genuinely empower their members in open, uncertain and perhaps contestable ways. In this respect teamwork in education connotes a different mind-set than in the Japanese model. Teamwork, thus construed, is an important developmental mechanism in schools. Further, because teams cut across bureaucratic hierarchies, they can be seen as the embodiment of 'flat' management organizations, 'delayered' companies and non-hierarchical organizations, themselves strongly advocated in business organizations (discussed in subsequent chapters).

With regard to point 8, the persistent pursuit of objectives in education has a twofold outcome. First, this underpins the notion of target-setting as a means for development planning and school development plans in an objectives model (DES, 1989; Hopkins *et al.*, 1994), setting targets, then routes, then initial tasks (Hargreaves and Hopkins, 1991). The 'objectives' model has never been far away from education this century, finding its voice in curriculum terms in the 'Tyler' rationale for curriculum planning (essentially a managerialist model), in development terms in the school improvement movement, and in assessment and action planning terms through the notion of target-setting and formative assessment.

Secondly, the notion of persistence is important in point 8, for the Japanese model is scrupulous – or relentless – in achieving goals. In Japanese companies this is evidenced in terms of production targets, quality assurance targets and comparatively easily operationalized goals (themselves often limited and mutually reinforcing). How straightforwardly this can be translated into education is, perhaps, a moot point, for educational goals are multiple, non-uniform and sometimes tension-ridden (Pollard, 1982) and cannot be operationalized straightforwardly, e.g. simple figures-based views do not address the unmeasurable, but equally valuable, aspects of education.

Nevertheless, the single-mindedness of the exhortation to 'persistence' is, perhaps, a salutary reminder for schools to 'stick to their knitting' (Peters and Waterman, 1982) – to identify what they are there to do and to ensure that they are not deflected from this. Reynolds and Farrell (1996: 55) suggest that effective schools concentrate on a limited number of goals that are attainable, often of an academic nature.

With regard to point 9, this is not a practice that is defensible in education, for it breaches the right of workers to belong to any appropriate union of their choice, without prejudice.

Point 10 is a significant factor for education, for not only does it give impetus to the notion of lifelong learning (Coffield, 1997) in which schools have a significant part to play but it also lays emphasis on the fact that such developments require sustained resource support. It recognizes that initial teacher education is no more than a strategy for preparing beginning teachers, and that continuing professional development (CPD) is essential.

Point 10 links significantly with discussions of quality assurance (see Chapter 4), where it is recognized that quality can only be assured if everyone in the organization not only has responsibility for quality but also that everyone is suitable equipped (through education and training) to develop and recognize quality. This requires investment in training and education, developing reflective practice.

Points 11 and 12 are mutually reinforcing for, in return for company loyalty, Japanese company workers are provided with many extra benefits, for example health insurance, reduced-cost purchase of the company's products, sports facilities. Indeed Wickens (1987) indicates that it is not uncommon for employees to have present at their wedding representatives of the company. The corollary of this is that it is expected that the employee will be entirely committed to the company and will not speak badly of it or of the conditions inside it. Whether one sees these twin concerns as seeking the welfare of the individual or gagging criticism is a moot point. Certainly it has the effect of reinforcing adherence to the company's philosophy and, therefore, of keeping the company's philosophy intact, unchallenged. Criticism of the company from within is not tolerated; by a process of selection and self-selection, those employees who do not agree with the system do not work in it.

In educational terms, points 11 and 12 are perhaps not as widespread as in industry, except perhaps in the independent sector of education, where market forces and responsiveness to wealthy consumers are felt sharply. Certainly, in the state sector the notion of financial or additional inducements to stay in the 'company', other than the inherent motivation for teaching and the possibilities of promotion, is largely chimerical. Indeed education trails significantly behind business in the concern that it shows for the motivation and welfare of employees – they do not become issues until they become problems (e.g. the difficulty in teacher recruitment, retention and stability of staff in a school).

It is important to note that in point 13 the expectation of hard work and continuous improvement is coupled with personal development and improvement, suggesting that the two have to be addressed together. In educational terms the expectation of hard work does not need to be mentioned; it is a commonplace (e.g. Pollard *et al.*, 1994). The problem comes in the interpretation of point 13, for Japanese companies expect absolute and undistracted work during working hours – the expropriation of the labour force, in which the company, in effect, buys the worker's complete compliance during working hours. Here the personal development is confined to that which is necessary for the more efficient working practices. Whether that is a model one would wish to impose in education is questionable, for it is perhaps too exploitative and instrumental, dehumanizing what should be a humanistic profession and rendering education narrowly behaviourist. If, on the other hand, one is to interpret point 13 as the need for hard work – which teaching is – to be matched by appropriate support and development coupled with the recognition that improvements are always possible, then this might be more palatable and certainly less instrumental. It is not a recipe for slackness, rather for humanity.

Point 14 is a valuable lesson from Japanese industry. Decisions are reached after extensive consultation and consensus, requiring much discussion time before they are taken. This is an important model for education, for it suggests not only that genuine consultation within a collegial organization is necessary but that decisions are also made on the basis of the best evidence and widest data available – the force of the argument – rather than on the positional power of the proponents in a hierarchy. This is not to suggest that co-operation can only operate in a collegial structure; indeed one of the characteristics of the Japanese model – through the notion of *nenko garrets* discussed above – is of a hierarchy based on very clear differentials of power, such that disagreement can lead to termination of employment. It is arguing for widespread consultation where the consultation can actually affect the outcome. Point 14 emphasizes working with people rather than against them, with the grain rather than against it.

Point 15 will be discussed fully in Chapter 4. Here one should note, perhaps, that total quality management, as its title suggests, involves attention to the people in the organization as well as to structures and systems in the school. People, personalities, values and emotions are a management issue rather than a management problem. Total quality management has commanded a high profile in educational circles for a decade, and Chapter 4 addresses this as one main impetus for and substance of change.

Point 16 is significant for education, and is itself problematic. On the one hand the Japanese model suggests that the company should comprise like-minded individuals who contribute to an agreed philosophy and set of practices and that this ethos should permeate the culture and the organization. On the other hand one has to be aware that this is a product-focused environment where this might be possible. The extent to which one might wish to emulate this in schools is contentious. Schools, perhaps, should be developing, respecting and celebrating diversity in staff and students rather than homogeneity, and certainly they are not simply assembly lines whose task it is to deliver 'products', however customized these might be. As mentioned in point 7 above, in the Japanese model the individual is certainly less important than the team; how far one would wish to have a parallel with this in education is contentious. This argues for an extended view of homogeneity – the view of 'loose-tight' or 'loosely coupled' organizations – where general principles and a set of agreed practices and protocols do not obstruct individuals from exercising their individuality to promote learning.

Point 17 returns to the notions of multiskilling from point 4 and commitment from points 11 and 12. One of the claimed attractions of multiskilling is that it makes for flexibility. However, one of the claimed disadvantages is that it renders the employee less employable outside the organization – it only equips employees to work in a variety of (frequently low-skilled) jobs within the company and, thereby, fetters them from leaving the company. It argues against narrow specialization.

This point has interesting ramifications for education. In one sense it is patently not the case the teachers will be more committed to their organization than to their everyday tasks with specific students; to suggest this is to misrepresent seriously the realities of everyday teaching. Further, it misrepresents the value of the specialist teacher who has the subject and pedagogical expertise in a certain curriculum field, and to argue for extending that role to other curriculum fields might have questionable educational benefits. On the other hand point 17 recognizes that effectiveness is multifaceted and teachers have very many differing responsibilities and tasks. They are not simply teachers of X to Y, but are involved in an ongoing dialogue with students to promote learning.

Pucick and Hatvany (1991) suggest that Japanese management systems are based on the paradigm of effective human resource management in which intensive socialization of workers takes place into the company philosophy, which is accompanied by open communication, consultation, teamworking and a genuine concern for employees.[3] To facilitate internal promotion senior management ensures that there are always some unfilled management positions. Kenney and Florida (1988: 135) suggest that internal promotion and the retention of staff combine to ensure that the collective memory of shared knowledge in the organization stays in the organization. This latter point is an important feature for education where premature retirements, staff turnover and the funding formula which render older teachers 'expensive' can diminish the 'collective memory' and experience of schools. Combine this with those senior staff who are disaffected because of demotivating external forces from outside in the last decade, and the prospect for building on the collective expertise is diminished. It tends not to be the case that staff members receive salary or additional incentives to remain in the institution; indeed the opposite is much more typically the case. The implications of the Japanese model are to suggest that addressing real, meaningful and substantial incentives not only to stay in a school but also in education generally are long overdue.

Herbig and Palumbo (1996), in echoing the comments in Chapter 2 about the value of incremental rather radical change in the Japanese system, stress a significant difference between the Japanese and western cultures and companies. They argue that process, 'downstream' innovation is the Japanese speciality, perfecting existing products, rather than the 'upstream', radical, basic, blue-skies research being undertaken, for example, in the USA. The Japanese, they suggest, are strong on perfecting rather than inventing the wheel. In terms of Cuban's typology of change from Chapter 2, the Japanese are more concerned with first order rather than second-order change (see also Wickens, 1995: 316).

In educational terms the picture is not as clear cut as this. In one sense the message in education *is* very similar to the Japanese model: teachers receive a prescribed National Curriculum and strive to 'deliver' it most effectively, efficiently and with the maximum level of assessed outcomes and achievements. This is clearly the 'downstream' model. On the other hand, in a very real sense each situation in teaching is a new situation because it concerns inducting new students into new areas of knowledge, value systems, skills and attitudes. Further, the impact of constructivism on notions of learning, arguing for the need to view situations and concept formation through learners' eyes – or brains! – suggests a view of learning that is diverse. Students and teachers do create ideas and knowledge as well as re-create and receive them.

Education, then, has some affinity to the Japanese model but transcends it in many respects. Many of the features of Japanese companies noted above are rooted strongly in Japanese culture and contrast with the working practices in the west (a feature that might make it difficult to apply elsewhere – Harvey-Jones, 1988: 17). Clarke (1994: 179–80) notes the Japanese celebration of small-scale, incremental growth through considerable lead-time in consultation and the achievement of consensus, with rapid implementation following this. He contrasts this with the American style of deciding on a change and then ensuring – over years – that it is implemented. The model of change recently in the UK has certainly been American rather than Japanese; indeed what has characterized many of the changes in the UK has been the telescoping of consultation, the absence of consensus and trialling, and the stress placed on schools in attempting to cope with the fallout from rapid, multistranded change. Indeed, in this respect, perhaps the education service should have taken closer note of Japanese advocacy – and practice – of slower but more carefully thought-through and agreed change. Wickens (1995: 314–15) highlights several contrasts between Japan and the west. These can be presented in terms of education in Table 3.1, with examples given below (see also Reynolds and Farrell, 1996: 54–9).

We should be careful not to assume that the Japanese model of education applies in Japan (for example the notion of 'product variety' in the Japanese model fares very poorly in a climate of intense examination pressure and 'crammer' schools in Japan), or to assume that the model of the west applies so generally (*ibid.*). For example, one could suggest that schools in the UK simply do not have the luxury of 'waste', that flexibility and diversity in the UK are seriously attenuated by the National Curriculum and its assessment, and that whole-school planning is intended to prevent problems from arising.

It can be seen that the relative merits or demerits of Japanese (and western) practices are inextricably woven into the values and cultural fabric of the societies from which they originated. That is not to say that the practices of one culture will not translate into those of another; indeed the whole premise of this chapter is to suggest the opposite. Rather, it is to suggest that one cannot straightforwardly accept or dismiss practices without attention to the principles that underlie them.

Consensus, consultation and involvement

If a decision has to be made then the people affected by that decision are consulted. The Japanese *ringi* system emphasizes the need to circulate new

Table 3.1 The Japanese and western industrial practices in educational terms

Japan	The west
Waste elimination – efficient resource management (e.g. time, space, materials, people, support)	*Decision to live with waste – inefficient resource use (e.g. time, space, materials, people, support)*
Focused whole-class interactive teaching and extended use of information technology. Ensuring understanding first time round. Avoidance of duplication of effort or materials. Expectation that all students will achieve highly. Intensive monitoring. Sets of textbooks. Limited movement around the school	Multiple group work with repetitious teaching and students thrown on to their own learning resources. Failure to check students' understanding. Poor use of teachers, e.g. as highly paid secretaries/ photocopier operators. Acceptance of a 'trailing edge' of underachievement. Limited monitoring. Multiple and non-uniform textbooks. Time wasted in moving from room to room
Product variety – multiple educational outcomes to suit consumer needs	*Single products – standardized educational outcomes to suit consumer needs*
Curriculum diversity to meet specialist requirements and individual needs. Extended view of the 'basics'	Standardized National Curriculum reinforced through standardized assessments of achievement of levels of performance. Emphasis on a narrow view of the 'basics'.
The standard operation – heavily prescribed and uniform practices	*Flexible operations – autonomously decided and non-uniform practices*
Rote learning and traditional pedagogic practices	Pedagogical diversity decided through autonomous professional decision-making and leading to diverse outcomes
Continuous small improvements to existing practices	*Major wholesale, radical change and development*
Improvements to the teaching of reading and mathematical computation	Introduction of local management of schools and the National Curriculum and its assessment
Long-term planning	*Short-term planning*
The introduction of new categories of school, restructuring of post-16 education	School development planning on an annual basis
Problem prevention	*Problem-solving and post-hoc rectification*
Training in effective curriculum planning, pedagogy and diagnostic, interventionist, demanding teaching. Strategies to improve student motivation for learning. Ensuring that students have understood first time round. Use of specialist teachers for consultation in planning. Recruiting highly capable staff	Rescue and recovery programmes to lift the 'trailing edge' of underachievement brought about by low expectations. Repeating work and teaching. Use of specialist teachers to work with 'failing' students. Providing support for staff when problems have been identified

Group motivation/group rewards/ teamwork	*Individual motivation/rewards/ individualism and initiative*
Collaborative teaching where appropriate. Funding for group development projects. Group planning	Individual promotion and incentive allowances. Unrewarded, interest-based motivation and additional work
Consensus and co-operation, team meetings called to share ideas	*Competition, meetings called to make decisions*
Team planning during programmed school time. Consultation on policy issues. Partnerships with all stakeholders. Community schools	League tables of schools' performance in published assessments/examinations. Selective schools and streamed classes. Specialist colleges
Respect for authority and seniority	*Challenges to authority and seniority*
High status of teachers. Respect for experience, expertise in decision-making. Respect for senior management in school. Acceptance of the legitimacy of senior managers to make decisions	Disregard for positional power of staff. Emphasis on the micropolitics, interest groups and factions in a school. Questioning of the legitimacy/credibility of senior staff in a school. Recognition of seniority by dint of expertise rather than position in a bureaucracy
Involvement and welfare of all aspects of the worker	*Concern for the individual solely as worker*
Matching of needs of school with needs and interests of teachers. Concern for each teacher's welfare. Extended consultation	Extracting the maximum from staff regardless of cost to personal stressor preferences. Pigeon-holing staff without attention to their needs, abilities, expertise, interests, choices. No consultation
Non-specialist career development	*Specialist career development.*
Deliberately moving staff around school, age phase, subjects, ability groups, responsibilities, types of task	Fast-tracking to promotion through specialization. Restricted job specification. Opportunities for specialization.
Leadership as facilitating the evolution of decisions with an eye to details (with careful listening and harmonization with the whole group)	*Leadership as decision-making with an eye to the 'big picture' (with speaking and leading from the front)*
Consultative decision-making. Prolonged discussion of the implications of decisions to evaluate possibilities, strategies and their ramifications	Leadership to make decisions, if necessary autocratically. Decisions made on the basis of principle and general direction, with managers to ensure that it takes place

proposals or ideas for policy or procedural changes throughout the circle of those affected, in order for full consultation, understanding and consensus to take place before implementation is attempted (*nemawashi*). Though this might be time-consuming it does ensure that, as far as possible, matters are 'right first time' (an essential feature of quality development discussed in Chapter 4). There is considerable emphasis on co-operative and collaborative approaches, consensus-forming rather than conflictual decision-making. At Honda, for example, any employee, from the most junior to the most senior can call for an open discussion session – a *waigaya* session (Goss *et al.*, 1996: 136–7). The principles of procedure here are that people speak openly and frankly about problems and that nothing is excluded from the discussions. Goss *et al.* (*ibid.*) suggest that the *waigaya* session regards disagreement and problem-airing as the starting point of learning, harnessing conflict for everybody's good – disagreeing without being disagreeable.

Drucker (1993: 404) comments that the strength of the Japanese derives in part from their acceptance that living together effectively cannot be premised on adversarial relations but, rather, that there is a shared common interest and mutuality of trust. Wickens (1987: 23), too, suggests that group harmony is more highly valued than individuality. Of course, consensus and harmony do not appear overnight, so it is characteristic of Japanese companies that there will be a long lead-time in the preparation of new products as widespread consensus is sought, followed by rapid production. Indeed Nissan started employing and training employees for up to nine months before production commenced in the UK. An example of these principles applied to education can be seen in Figure 3.1.

Kaizen and its significance

Perhaps the most widely known Japanese business term is *kaizen*, which is frequently translated as 'continuous improvement', though it also connotes the notion of improvement through the accretion of multiple, continuous, small-scale improvements (Wickens, 1995, mentions the hundreds of 0.01 per cent improvements that together make for significant overall improvements, echoing the comments in Chapter 2 on incrementalism), and the notion of improvement through teamwork.

Kai can be translated as 'modify' and *zen* as 'goodness'. Nissan includes in its company philosophy statement the commitment to seek continuously to improve in all its actions, for example in terms of saving money, time, materials, staffing or in improving quality, safety and productivity. *Kaizen* applies anywhere and everywhere in the organization and can arise from an individual, team or other group,[4] i.e. it is universally used, no improvement is too small to be considered and, because continuous improvements are built into the system, they become institutionalized and, therefore, sustained, automatically. The practice of *kaizen*, then, builds in involvement, participation and engagement, echoing Wickens's (*ibid.*: 35) comment that for the Japanese the process of involvement is as important as the product. The principle of *kaizen* is of fundamental importance as it indicates a distinct management and organizational philosophy that

A primary school staff has been involved in a series of development sessions to improve the assessment and reporting throughout the school, investing considerable money in time, materials and purchase of samples of reporting, with a group of staff from across the school to develop this. The school now wants to evaluate the progress to date, i.e. a formative evaluation. A member of staff is appointed to conduct the formative evaluation and she gathers data using nominal group technique (NGT) (Morrison, 1993: 94–6) at a staff meeting.

She provides the staff with a series of open-ended and closed questions and statements that are designed to elicit responses about the development sessions, the samples provided, the development sequence, the focus and contents of the sessions and the assessment pro-formas, the reporting documents, the balance of standardization and open-endedness, etc. She decides to conduct a four-stage process of data collection during the staff meeting:

Stage 1: A short time is provided for individuals to write down without interruption or discussion with anybody else their own answers, views, reflections and opinions in response to the questions and statements provided.

Stage 2: Their responses are entered on to a sheet of paper which is then displayed for others to view. The evaluator invites individual comments on the displayed responses to the questions and statements, but no group discussion, i.e. the data collection is still at an individual level, and then writes these comments on the display board. The process of inviting individual comments which are then displayed for everyone to see is repeated until no more comments are received.

Stage 3: At this point she asks the respondents to identify clusters of displayed comments and responses, i.e. to put some structure, order and priority into the displayed items. It is here that control of proceedings moves from the evaluator to the respondents. A staff discussion takes place since a process of clarification of meaning and organizing issues and responses into coherent and cohesive bundles is required which then moves to the identification of priorities.

Stage 4: Finally she invites any further group discussion about the material and its organization.

At stages 3 and 4 the process involves discussion, clarification, agreement (or an agreement to disagree) and the identification of a set of issues or responses, i.e. there is a clearly identifiable outcome to the sequence of activities and discussions.

NGT enables individual responses to be included within a group response. This technique is useful for gathering data from individuals and to assemble them into an order which is shared by the group, e.g. of priority, of similarity and difference, of generality and specificity. It allows individual disagreements to be registered and to be built into the group's responses and identification of significant issues. It gives equal status to all respondents in the situation. NGT can also be used to further group interaction and collegiality (*ibid.*). It is designed to identify issues about which there is consensus, and to involve everybody who will be affected by the decision.

Figure 3.1   Consensus, consultation and involvement

respects the professionalism and autonomy of workers. Wickens (*ibid.*: 34) argues that it is the person who is doing the job who know more about it than anybody else – clearly a message for educational policy-makers! – and that people have minds and brains as well as bodies and hands (*ibid.*: 132). The Japanese extol the virtue of *sunao* (the untrapped mind) in bringing improvements to the company.[5] It is a salutary exercise in *kaizen* for teachers to ask themselves on a daily basis two questions:

1) What have I done today to improve teaching, learning, achievement, other aspects of the school?
2) What steps have I taken to ensure that these actions have been discussed and disseminated to teams with whom I am concerned?

The closest systematic educational equivalent of *kaizen*, apart from the improvements that teachers routinely make to their own practice as part of their development as reflective practitioners, is in the notion of action research. Here a need or problem is identified, an intervention to meet the need is identified and planned, the intervention is implemented and its impact and effects are evaluated. An example of this can be seen in Figure 3.2.

The Key Stage 2 teachers in a primary school are concerned about the students' mathematics standards of achievement:

Stage 1: Needs/problem analysis. The teachers concerned identify possible causes of the problem and decide that a major feature could be that students work largely individually and at their own levels and rates through the commercially produced mathematics scheme. This means that the teacher has very limited contact time with each child, and indeed those children who can 'get on' unsupervised are largely teaching themselves; the teachers spend much of their time marking and keeping track on where students are going – i.e. procedural and managerial tasks rather than instructional tasks. The problems, then, are: lack of teacher contact; lack of teacher instruction – 'teaching'; inefficient use of the teacher.

Stage 2: Planning the intervention. The teachers suggest that more whole-class interactive teaching and more group activity, rather than individualized work, would address the three problems. Taking the suggestion from Pacific Rim countries (Reynolds and Farrell, 1996: 57), the teachers decide to increase the amount of whole-class interactive teaching to 50 per cent,[6] to reduce the amount of group work to 10 per cent, and to reduce the amount of completely individualized work to 40 per cent. Targets and success criteria are set to evaluate the programme.

Stage 3: Implementing the innovation. The new programme takes one term to plan; it is implemented for nearly two terms, and its effects are evaluated.

Stage 4: Evaluation. The students' achievements are assessed just before the commencement of the intervention and at the end of it. At the end of the programme the teachers review the extent to which the targets have been met and the reasons for this, the effectiveness of the programme in meeting the problems identified and identify other strengths and weaknesses of the programme and its outcomes.

Figure 3.2   An action research programme

What is being advocated in *kaizen* is a much more routine, programmed and perhaps systematic view of continuous improvement than the often *ad hoc* developments in schools. For example, at Nissan, there is work time deliberately and routinely devoted to this. Continuous improvement, in education as in Japanese industry, concerns improving people and improving systems and processes. In educational terms, then, this implies ongoing continuing professional development which, as was argued earlier, is a central pillar of sustaining and meeting the demands of change. This is more than the 'suggestion box' mentality (Wickens, 1987); in educational terms *kaizen* is arguing for all colleagues to be alert to possible improvements that can be made (first and second-order changes) and to make these public.

It is the task of management to create the conditions so that *kaizen* can be utilized to its maximum, both to the benefit of the individual and the company. Herein lies a key feature both for business and for education – that of the win/win situation – wherein both the company can benefit from having the worker's contribution and the individual can benefit from being valued and being able to contribute positively to the organization, thereby enhancing motivation, involvement and self-esteem. Indeed this is echoed by the industrialist Senge (1990: 95) in his comment that one should not push growth, rather one should remove the factors that limit growth.

This emphasis on empowering individuals marks the difference between a coercive and enabling management style. This is not a new feature in business management. For example McGregor's (1960) Theory X suggests that

1) people dislike work and will avoid it if they can;
2) people must be forced or induced to make the effort;
3) people would rather be directed than accept responsibility;
4) people will seek to avoid accepting responsibility;
5) most people are not very creative except in avoiding work.

This negative view of people can account for the need for line-management, hierarchical, bureaucratic models of management. On the other hand in his Theory Y McGregor adopts a much more generous, positive and dynamic view of human behaviour (Galbraith and Lawler, 1993) in which

1) work is necessary for a person's psychological well-being and development;
2) people want to be interested in their work;
3) given the right conditions, people will enjoy work. Most humans do not dislike work;
4) people will direct themselves towards a target to which they feel committed;
5) commitment to goals is a function of the rewards that attach to their achievement;
6) people will seek and accept responsibility under the right conditions;
7) self-discipline is more effective than imposed discipline; it can also be more severe and self-demanding than imposed discipline;

8) given the right conditions, people are motivated to realize their own potential;
9) creativity, imagination and ingenuity are widely, not narrowly, distributed in the population and are largely underused;
10) the expenditure of mental effort is as natural as play.

Theory Y represents a more optimistic view of human motivation; it asserts that people will direct and control themselves in the service of objectives to which they are committed. From such a view it is up to management to create the conditions so that members of the organization can achieve their own goals most effectively by directing their activities towards the corporate success of the organization (McGregor, 1960: 49). This embraces the potential creativity of participants, avoiding Hargreaves' (1994: 14) interesting comment on education that many teachers are treated as though they are recovering alcoholics who need step-by-step training).[7]

The Japanese industrialist Ouchi (1981) adds on to McGregor's Theory X and Theory Y his own Theory Z. Theory Z places employees as the key to the success and productivity of the company and recommends the practices of lifetime employment, progression within the company, collective and participatory approaches to decision-making. Ouchi (*ibid*.: 81–3) argues that people can use their discretion and can be trusted to work without close supervision in a culture of consent, co-operation and commitment. Indeed, anticipating the flexibility of Nissan and the commentary on it by Wickens (1987), Ouchi argues for flexibility rather than high degrees of specialization. *Kaizen*, then, links into McGregor's Theory Y and Ouchi's Theory Z. It is the motor of many developments at Nissan.

Efficiency in Japanese companies and the just-in-time system

Japanese companies place a premium on the elimination of waste (*muda*), the key Japanese writers here being Ohno (1988) and Shingo (1988), who argue that waste can occur anywhere in production. What is being advocated here is 'lean production' – doing only what is necessary to ensure quality and add value, using the minimum number of people, and efficient use of resources. Shoji (1988) identifies the elimination of three factors as being important: *muda* (waste), *muri* (unreasonableness) and *mura* (unevenness – see the discussions of high-reliability organizations in Chapter 4).

To cope with the increased efficiency arising from eliminating wasteful practices, Japanese companies practise 'five Ss' (Wickens, 1995: 171; Ho and Gimil, 1996: 45–9). Though these typically refer to low-level physical factors in industry, nevertheless they can apply to the world of education:

- *seiri* (organization and consolidation): identifying those aspects of the organization and production that are necessary and those that are not; eliminating those that are not and keeping to a minimum those that are and keeping them in a convenient location. In educational terms this is arguing for teachers to identify their prime purposes and to adhere to these stringently ('sticking to their knitting' (Peters and Waterman,

1982)). This often has implications for time management where they need to prioritize what must be done, what should be done, and what can be done, and to ensure that these priorities are matched to the time and importance devoted to them;

- *seiton* (orderliness and neatness): ensuring that materials and objects are stored in a safe place and that they are easy and quick to store and access. In educational terms this not only refers to classroom materials and layout but also to the burgeoning field of documentation;
- *seiso* (cleaning): cleaning is done by everyone (at Nissan all the production workers are responsible for keeping their work areas clean); keeping everything clean and ensuring – through checking – that materials and equipment are in a safe condition, replacing where necessary. In educational terms this is not necessarily to suggest that teachers must become cleaners; however it is to suggest that maybe the students and teachers themselves are required to ensure that all materials are returned to the place from, and in the condition in which, they were found;
- *seiketsu* (standardization): keeping premises and working areas clean and organized, e.g. transparency of the storage. In educational terms this is arguing for the provision of appropriate and sufficient resource storage facilities within classrooms, in libraries, in central resource areas, etc. (not simply to embrace physical resources but, for example, to include data storage in standardized form on computers), and to ensure that students' work and property is effectively and securely stored;
- *shitsuke* (discipline): doing the five Ss every day and ensuring that everyone is trained in the rules and procedures of the organization and is expected to adhere to them. In educational terms this is arguing for whole-school policies to be devised and implemented.

This is a salutary lesson for schools; for example it would be easy to recall even over a single day the time and energy that are wasted on finding and copying materials, sorting out textbooks, photocopying and duplicating, attendance at meetings, rescheduling meetings, unproductive INSET, repeating and explaining tasks and instructions, checking and confirming matters, seeking clarification, leaving matters incomplete, returning to work from previous days, telephoning and waiting, repairing and servicing equipment, covering for others (Greenwood and Gaunt, 1994; West-Burnham, 1997).

However, efficiency does not end with the elimination of waste in the day-to-day servicing and operating of Japanese companies. Concomitant with this is the rise of 'just-in-time' (JIT) practices and even synchronous delivery. Here stockpiling (tying up space, money and time for inventory) and large production runs are often replaced by rapid supply and small numbers per batch of supplies. As Wickens (1995: 166) comments, in Japan the emphasis is on the *just* – the minimum required. Just-in-time replaces the 'just-in-case' mentality of stockpiling.

At Nissan the JIT system has meant the highly co-ordinated, synchronized and frequent supply of parts from external sources (e.g. seats that are put into cars will only have been ordered and made within

A secondary school is aware that a considerable amount of teaching time is being lost (up to an hour per day) as a result of much movement of students and teachers around the school between sessions. Students are arriving late for sessions: this wastes the teachers' time in repeating the introduction and instructions, it makes teachers irritable so that they spend time in telling off tardy students, it makes for a poor start to sessions, reducing their impact. Those students who arrive on time become bored and frustrated with waiting for everyone to arrive. Further, because most sessions are only of 40 minutes duration and up to 10 minutes could be lost per session, some teachers feel it not worth their while setting up interesting resources or activities, so teaching became arid and expectations and demands are low.

The school takes steps to address this problem, in several ways. First it condenses the school day into fewer but longer lessons. Secondly, lessons are timetabled so that students only need to move at break times and lunchtimes. Thirdly, it staggers the lunch break to relieve congestion at changeover times. Fourthly, teaching rooms and their usage are reviewed to reduce distances for students to travel. Fifthly, sanctions are applied against those students who are unacceptably late in arriving for session. Sixthly, wherever possible (within the constraints of having to move resources around the school), it is teaching staff who move rather than the students.

Figure 3.3 An example of the just-in-time system in schools

the preceding two hours). In turn this has meant extensive and efficient communication. At Nissan large batch supply was seen to lead to limited flexibility, hence unresponsiveness to customer demand, money being tied up in unsold products, whilst small batch supply led to high-flexibility, high-quality, lower inventory levels – 'zero inventory' (Beale, 1994) – low cost, high ability to change, release of money into the organization, rapidity of production and responsiveness to customer demand.[8] One educational implication of the JIT system is to ensure that resources in schools and outside are well co-ordinated. This is a familiar picture for those teachers who are involving students in work placement programmes.

The JIT philosophy makes for high efficiency, increased throughput, high quality ('right first time' because there is no back-up), effective communication, careful scheduling, attention to the details of co-ordination, the surfacing and exposure of any problems and responsiveness to customers (*ibid.*) – all essential messages for schools. The application of the JIT system argues that everything and everyone must be in the right place at the right time. This requires careful and realistic timetabling and co-ordination. An example of the JIT system for education is presented in Figure 3.3.

Though the JIT system makes for efficiency, nevertheless it can create problems. For example just-in-time systems are fragile and very vulnerable to absenteeism and problems with suppliers, putting suppliers under tremendous pressure and leading to the 'just-in-case' mentality; small delays and faults can exert a disproportionately high effect on the whole operation and can result in work overload for employees in the assembly plant (Beale, 1994: 41; Wickens, 1995: 68). It is management by stress and can lead to substantial staff turnover. Wickens suggests that in this philosophy there is no place to hide! In schools, too, the chain of resources (however defined) and its organization in the JIT system would be only as strong as the weakest link. At one level this argues for the need for the high reliability of resources to be ensured (see the discussion in Chapter 4 of high-reliability organizations) so that human frailty does not become a problem! At another level a human organization should, perhaps, adopt a less ruthless and stressful view of management.

Further, one has to note that the several practices outlined above are all designed to render the 'standard operation' more efficient, to reduce unevenness in different stages of the production (*muri*). One should not lose sight of the essential importance of the assembly line and assembly-line mentality in the production processes set out above. Wickens (1987; 1995) argues for the centrality of rendering the standard operation – each element of the assembly-line process – more efficient.

It is important here to note that there are some non-negotiable factors, for example the materials used are preordained – one produces the best car for the price rather than the best car regardless of cost (the Rolls-Royce model!). This model cannot apply to education, for teachers have almost no control over their intake (though the revival of some degree of selection might attenuate this). It also translates into the definition of quality as 'fitness for purpose' (discussed in Chapter 4) rather than as 'excellence'.

Further, the standard operation is another non-negotiable factor. The Nissan plant assembly line has broken down all the tasks of assembly into the tiniest component elements (bringing about the longest assembly line in Europe), so that each task can be performed with maximum efficiency in a matter of seconds. Workers have their tasks preordained; the agenda is given. Whether this is a model that one would wish to install in education is perhaps questionable, though it has been argued that the effects of the National Curriculum has been to do just that – to regard teachers as semi-automatons or technicians, deliverers of a preordained curriculum (a standard operation) that is designed to produce the same standard outcome.

Poka yoke and its significance

Prevention is more effective and efficient than cure. It is common to see in company literature such phrases as 'we don't inspect in quality, we build in quality'. *Poka yoke* – the prevention and avoidance of mistakes, or rendering the system foolproof – is another fundamental premise of Japanese practice that features very highly in discussions of quality (see the work of Shingo and Chapter 4). The model is one of quality assurance – building in quality – rather than quality control – detecting errors and faults some time after they have been made (e.g. at the end of the assembly line).

To leave a fault until it has been created and subsequently discovered at inspection is to build in failure and waste, it allows failure and error to exist, for however short a time. Rather, the model of *poka yoke* is to prevent the error or fault from arising in the first place. Hence continuous checking is the order of the day, with each worker responsible and accountable for ensuring that her/his task is perfect before it is passed on to the next worker in the assembly line. Immediate detection of fault and immediate remediation, coupled with immediate responsibility, avoidance of failure and the repetition of error, ensure that this principle contributes to increased efficiency and the reduction of waste.

In order to ensure that the product has zero defects requires careful scrutiny and awareness of all participants in the process of production. For example, in Nissan where an assembly line is operating at several thousand pounds per minute, any stoppage – even for a matter of seconds – is hugely costly. With one car being produced every one and a half minutes, and each car taking less than eleven hours to build from scratch (raw materials coming into the factory) it is essential that mistakes and stoppages are eliminated entirely. Therefore staff are trained to spot faults and there are support mechanisms that can be called up immediately to deal with problems.[9] At Nissan there are no additional online quality inspectors, responsibility for quality resides with each worker.

In educational terms *poka yoke* is a slippery concept to address fully, because the exactness and control over the inputs (the materials), the process and the product that one might legitimately expect in industry are not so in education. Teachers do not have such a degree of control or precision; neither, perhaps, would such a degree be desirable. Nevertheless there are other aspects of error prevention or 'passing on faulty products' that can be addressed. One implication might be that students do not progress on to the next stage of the work until the teacher is convinced – with evidence – that the student has understood everything that is required, and that any problems in the students' learning are fully addressed and remediated (see Reynolds and Farrell's (1996) comments on the significance of this aspect of whole-class interactive teaching). What is being argued here moves towards the need to have resources in place to support and remedy problems as efficiently and effectively as possible, even if this means that a student's progress might not be as rapid as others'.

The attraction of *poka yoke* is that it focuses on causes rather than symptoms of difficulty, it tries to explain them fully so that effective action can be taken to eradicate rather than simple to postpone or bury the problem. Whilst this might be a relatively simple matter in the manufacture of cars, in the management of change and schools it might be less straightforward. An example of *poka yoke* is provided in Figure 3.4.

In management practices the educational implications of *poka yoke* might be to ensure that if people disagree with proposals by the senior management team or other leaders in the school, or that if decisions are causing problems, then these are addressed fully rather than being allowed to fester and cause rancour. An example of this can be seen in Figure 3.5.

Both examples of the success of *poka yoke* hinged on the expertise of the leaders of the innovation. In the first the teacher had to have subject and pedagogical expertise, in the second the senior management team had to have expertise in the management of change and the management of people. Neither of these sets of expertise are developed overnight. In

A student at Key Stage 3 is experiencing difficulties in her mathematics work and this is preventing her from moving on to the next stage of the work. The teacher looks at the work the student has done and finds that she is consistently applying an incorrect algorithm for the matter in hand. The teacher points out the problem with the student's algorithm, makes it clear what the problem is and how to address it in another algorithm. He then sets the student the task of applying the new, correct algorithm, but the student's success is still sporadic. The teacher then checks with the student that she understands the principles behind the new algorithm, i.e. that it is not simply being applied unthinkingly and procedurally. The teacher finds that the student's understanding of the concepts behind the algorithm is at best fuzzy, so he clarifies these, only to find that the student still experiences problems. The teacher checks further, and finds that the child has been discussing the matter with her parents and that they have taught her a different way of working from that which the teacher is suggesting, so that there is cognitive conflict.

The teacher then assesses the explanations the child has received from her parents and finds them to be faulty. He clarifies the problems with the explanations that have been received at home and ensures the student understands why those were faulty and why the new ones are an improvement. To ensure the new concepts are fully understood the teacher sets them in a range of contexts and problems so that the student has learnt to apply them in new and varying situations, thereby cementing the understanding (echoing the issue of 'refreezing' from Chapter 2).

What can be seen in this example is the twin notion of persistence in diagnosing problems and the movement from symptomology to real causes. In this the teacher exercises his professional judgement both in diagnosis and subsequent teaching. He ensures that the new, correct version is in place before the student moves on.

Figure 3.4　An example of *poka yoke* in schools

educational terms *poka yoke*, then, translates into the need for substantial training, for rapid and effective support mechanisms and for the accountability of each individual in the educative process – answerable to the groups of other professionals as well as to the consumers. For *poka yoke* to work in education requires the devolution of responsibility for aspects of the school, teaching, learning and achievement on to the teachers; in this respect it goes hand in hand with flat management and collegiality.

Poka yoke in education as error prevention also exposes the weaknesses of the inspection system in education – the *post hoc*, bolt-on, quality-control model – as it tolerates and allows waste and faults to exist, rather than building in perfection and supporting the development of perfection (the notion of 'right first time' that will be discussed in Chapter 4). In the *poka yoke* model quality is built-in (quality assurance) rather than bolt-on!

Flexibility and teamwork

The thrust in Japanese companies is for consensus-based decision-making and involvement, high efficiency, continuous improvement and error

A school for students with moderate learning difficulties is seeking to further the integration of its students into mainstream education. This is a major change, for until now it has deliberately operated a policy of non-integration because most of the students had come into the school having 'failed' in mainstream education and the staff did not want to risk further loss of self-esteem by placing the students back into a situation in which they felt themselves to be failing. Most of the staff are in favour in principle of the new move, though some influential staff are against it in the way that it is being introduced as what they see as an almost blanket piece of dogma. They argue that they are able to meet the students' learning, emotional and social needs far more successfully by not mainstreaming the students, that mainstreaming will only be tokenist, that the necessary resources will not be available in mainstream education, and that the students will very likely be negatively labelled by staff and mainstream students when they go into those schools.

To address these concerns, the senior management team conducts a SWOT analysis (Strengths, Weaknesses, Opportunities and Threats) and a force-field analysis of the proposal, in which the strengths of the arguments, issues and practicalities are set alongside the weaknesses and disadvantages of the proposal. The intention here is to anticipate all the strengths and weaknesses of the proposal, to identify problems that might be encountered and to see how these problems can be addressed. Having undertaken these analyses the senior management, informed by the majority of the staff, decides that instead of opting for an overall movement towards integration at all costs, a trial will be conducted and a review undertaken to evaluate the success of the project, and that, if at any time any of the problems become insurmountable, then the well-being of the students must prevail without hesitation.

In this example, akin to action research in some respects, two deliberate strategies have been utilized to identify possible problems in the implementation of the substance of the innovation. Further, by adopting a genuinely consultative, collegial and democratic approach, the management has also defused a potential problem of hostility and resistance to the change *per se* by some of the staff; the management of change with the people involved has been effective. The senior management team was answerable to the staff of the school.

Figure 3.5 *Poka yoke* in the management of change

prevention; the corollary of this is an emphasis on flexibility and teamwork. Indeed Wickens, in describing Nissan, identified the centrality of a 'tripod' of three key principles at Nissan, all of which are person centred though one of which is also product centred: quality consciousness, flexibility and teamworking (Wickens, 1987: 38).

Flexibility and teamworking as examples of *genba kanri* (workshop management) are taken to considerable lengths in Nissan. Flexibility can take many forms (Wickens, 1987: 56; 1995: 147), for example: structural, organizational, financial, numerical and functional (e.g. labour and time). At Nissan (Wickens, 1987) there are no job descriptions,[10] restrictive practices and demarcation lines are absent; employees undertake the full range of tasks within a team and are provided with the support necessary in order to develop the skills needed for them – indeed training is given in specific task-focused skills, computing skills and 'people' skills (e.g. teambuilding, management, appraisal, presentation, communication). The team meets daily and this is scheduled into the everyday activities rather than being 'snatched' time, with this time being used for *kaizen* activities and for communications, echoing the Japanese view that if something is worth saying then it is best said face to face. Teamworking is regarded not necessarily as everyone working in a group but as everyone working in the same direction towards the same aims and objectives (hence the need for a careful vision and mission statement so that everyone knows where the organization is going). Teamwork – particularly as teams overlap – ensures effective communication and the integration of research, development, practice and operations (Clegg, 1992: 165–6). Teamwork is designed to encourage flexibility, versatility, quick thinking, multiskilling, promoting the motivation of workers not only through rotating the jobs to be done but by involving each team member in the decisions about how the programme of rotation will be decided.[11]

Concomitant with teamworking at Nissan is the notion of parity in the organization, for example: everyone works under the same conditions and terms of employment; there are no numbered grades; everyone is salaried; all employees and their families have the opportunity to covered by a medical insurance that is paid by the company; all overtime is paid; there is no reserved or privileged parking; canteen services are single status; there is no 'clocking on'. Wickens (1995: 115) makes the point that one cannot expect a first-class response from employees who, themselves, are treated as second-class citizens. The final comment from Wickens is perhaps apposite in a climate where the recent experience of teachers is of public vilification and institutionalized bullying by autocratic senior managers. An educational example of teamwork is presented in Figure 3.6.

What is being advocated in the Japanese management style is flatter, team-based approaches with devolved responsibilities. In turn these are premised on open and extensive communication. The policy of *hoshin kanri* (policy deployment) is based on the requirement that discussions will be held with all those who are affected by decisions and planning.

Criticisms of the Japanese model

The picture of Japanese industry that has been painted so far is decidedly 'upbeat' and suggests several reasons why Japanese business has become the envy of many businesses, towering in importance. However, this is not to say that the 'Japanese model' is without its critics. Indeed there have been trenchant criticisms of the practices at Nissan (by Garrahan and Stewart, 1992). Indeed Brandon (1992: 108) uses terms such as 'devious' and 'underhand' to describe some Japanese practices. Whether these criticisms apply to all Japanese manufacturing companies or, rather, only to the automobile industry, is a moot point. However, serious concerns have been raised, questioning whether, for example, the model can be applied outside Japan because of the differences in culture between Japan and other countries (Harvey-Jones, 1988: 17).

A secondary school science department is seeking to improve investigational science Key Stage 4. The department comprises six full-time 'dedicated' staff, two part-time staff with particular specialisms, two technicians and three staff who also teach in areas of the curriculum other than science. It has recently appointed a new head of department and three newly qualified teachers. The head of the department chairs the opening full departmental meeting, with one member present from the senior management team of the school who has responsibility for curriculum matters, the school's examinations and assessment co-ordinator, the Key Stage 4 co-ordinator, and two student representatives from the school's student council.

At this meeting three main tasks are addressed. First, the need for this development is agreed, together with the commitment of everyone for it to be addressed substantially and developed in practice. Secondly, the priorities for development are established, viz. 1) the need to conduct an in-depth audit of current practice and needs assessment of investigational work throughout Key Stage 4 in order to define the problem (e.g. as lack of investigational work, or poor investigational work, or uneven attention to, or experience of, investigational work, or investigational work being covered adequately by some teachers but not others, or investigational work being covered adequately in some aspects of science but not others; 2) to identify an agenda for change/development, setting tasks, roles and responsibilities of team members, time frames etc.; 3) to identify implications that might affect other aspects of the school, e.g. timetabling (investigational work might require long blocks of time), assessment and examinations, homework policy, staffing, staff development funds.

The head of science has overall responsibility for the development; heads of each science subject have responsibility for the audit and needs assessment; it is agreed that all the science staff will be involved in the development exercise, subject by subject; the head of science and/or subject leaders will liaise with the senior management and other non-science parties to discuss implications of the development that have been identified that go beyond simply the science department (e.g. for resourcing, budgeting, timetabling, assessment and examinations). The meeting decides that it is unnecessary for the whole group to meet together until the end of the first term, by which time smaller subgroups and activities by individuals will have been undertaken.

Comment: The decision to bring everybody in the team face to face is an attempt to: 1) create involvement in and ownership of the development; 2) save time through subsequent tracking down of important individuals and repeating discussions with them; 3) recognize that the development impacts on the department and beyond; 4) ensure that everybody has named tasks; 5) recognize that newly qualified staff need to have a voice as they have recent up-to-date knowledge of developments and practice; 6) operate a needs-driven policy; 7) recognize that, because the problem is multifaceted, it will involve several 'key players' who all have something separate but important to contribute – notion of the multiskilled team; 8) keep to a minimum the demands on time that are made by having the whole-team meeting constantly together as a whole group, bringing the advantages of a division of labour.

Figure 3.6 An example of teamwork in a science department

The concerns about the vulnerability of just-in-time systems to small problems and faults have been noted above (Beale, 1994). Beale also argues that the just-in-time system at Nissan is a form of management-by-stress, for example those workers who are not giving 100 per cent are very conspicuous as their failure affects everyone. He argues that there is considerable staff turnover at Nissan, though Wickens (1987) disagrees with this.

Many of the criticisms of the 'Japanese model' concern the human cost of work. For example, Kamata (1983) comments on the fact that employees are required to work so fast that they are exhausted and that there is not even enough time for personal needs to be met, a view shared by the Japan Auto Workers Union (1992). Nomura (1992) argues that workers at Toyota are paid too low, that their work is too intense, that the shift system is too onerous, that many workers sacrifice their holiday to overtime work and that personnel practices are unfriendly. That this resonates almost exactly with the nature of teachers' work is a salutary indicator not only of the 'intensification thesis' (Hargreaves, 1994) but that there is also a danger that teachers are regarded as exploitable operatives.

Roth (1993) regards teamworking and lean production and management as over-riding the human aspects of work, low staffing levels leading to permanent overtime and high stress and the denial of life outside work. Parker and Slaughter (1988) regard teamwork as management-by-stress – the down side of teamwork. Lincoln and McBride (1987) comment on the poor levels of job satisfaction of employees (though Cole, 1979: 238, suggests that this might be because Japanese workers expect a lot from their employment). Certainly teachers need no reminding of the stress that currently exists in their work, regardless of whether they are working in a collegial or hierarchical organization.

There are several other criticisms of the Japanese model. For example Beer *et al.* (1990), Clegg (1992), Keys and Miller (1994) and Burnes (1996), argue that their record on equal opportunities in employing women is not strong; women's representation is low and their work is temporary. Both these features resonate in education, where the number of senior women appointments is out of balance and where the system generally has seen the rise of part-time employment, fixed-term employment and underpaid employment of newly qualified late entrants into teaching who secure positions at a salary level lower than that to which they are entitled.

There is an immense social cost to employees in the Japanese model in terms of long hours and participation in work-related social events. There is limited job satisfaction. Management practices are authoritarian and oppressive and, in fact, single status is not a reality, there being, in effect, a two-tier system in which the minority have good conditions but the majority do not; indeed the lack of trade unions leaves workers defenceless in the face of management pressure. Workers become slaves to the company because they do not have skills that can be applied outside the company.

Further, there is evidence (Cole and Tominaga, 1976; Keys and Miller, 1994: 382–3; Burnes, 1996: 104–6) that some aspects of the Japanese model are breaking down, for example: the concept of lifetime employment is being eroded; the youth of Japan are experiencing low job satisfaction because promotion is restricted in a seniority-based organization and the 'promotion of years' (*nenko garrets* as outlined earlier); there is a realization that more fundamental research and development activities must replace the perfecting of existing technologies; there are skill shortages in companies.

Some of the criticisms of the Japanese model are exemplified at Nissan. Beale (1994: 173–5) argues that, at Nissan, despite the celebration of participation and consultation, in fact power still resides squarely with managers and, because much of the workforce is deunionized, limited power and authority reside with shop stewards (see also Garrahan and Stewart, 1992), and that workers' compliance for management initiatives and everyday operations is actually what is being sought. This is a familiar picture, too, in education, where compliance rather than questioning or constructive criticism are frequently the order of the day from governments and senior managers.

Beale argues that there are weaknesses in incremental, piecemeal/add-on approaches to initiatives that are proposed by management (discussed above in connection with 'downstream' innovation), and that this leads to short-termism, rather than the espoused long-termism of Japanese companies. He questions whether management is sufficiently willing to change itself (echoing the industrialist Senge (1990) who argues that the hardest people to change are senior staff).

Both these latter points are echoed in education, where: 1) the recent bureaucratic pressure on school has led to a stifling of creativity and where any long-term planning has taken second stage to short-term survival and coping; 2) faced with pressure for change, many senior managers, despite a rhetoric of collegiality, have resorted to autocratic approaches in order to respond rapidly, hierarchical approaches being more effective for short-term decision-making and action (discussed in Chapter 6) though perhaps counterproductive for longer-term change that is rooted in an open and collegial organizational culture.

Garrahan and Stewart (1992) argue that Nissan's practices are essentially exploitative, expropriating workers' creativity and ideas as well as employing cheap labour in areas of high unemployment (a charge that Wickens (1987) has refuted, demonstrating that salary levels are very attractive). They argue that, far from being the virtuous circle of flexibility, teamworking and quality consciousness, the experience of many workers at Nissan is of dehumanization, a vicious circle of control, exploitation and surveillance. This is exactly the experience of many teachers, whose working and personal lives are taken up with trying to keep abreast of innovation demands (e.g. Pollard *et al.*, 1994) and the coupling of these with inspections, audits, tight prescription and mandatory development plans.

Flexibility and teamworking conceal the fact that workers are being taught a range of low-level, non-transferable skills that, in effect, require employees to remain in the company because they are unskilled to work outside it. Flexibility means that workers can do whatever they are called upon to do in the production of surplus value and that the standard operation is exhausting and does not condone necessary recovery time. In educational terms, this has its direct parallel in 'cover' arrangements for absent colleagues, where schools are not permitted to 'buy in' cover for illness until several days have elapsed.

For Garrahan and Stewart the extended role of supervisors and teamwork acts as constant surveillance of workers, and this is reinforced by the quality control mechanisms that, in fact, require workers to become self-surveilling. Employees only have autonomy and decision-making over minor matters and major issues are decided for them. Consensus is imposed rather than agreed and the 'Nissan' way of doing things (the Nissan family in which even outside interests and welfare are taken care of by Nissan), coupled with its recruitment and appointment mechanisms, reinforces 'group-think', lack of challenge and a strongly paternalistic management structure and mentality. Teamworking is a euphemism for group consent to subordination and produces intensification of demand through peer group pressure – the continuous treadmill of work. Most workers, they aver, experience autocratic rather than democratic line management. Continuous improvement, in their model, is little more than the collusion of workers in their own exploitation and subordination because it is about rendering more effective a given, rather than negotiated, system (the standard operation). If this were a model for education, then, surely this would be the death knell of effective teaching, which, at heart, is creative, negotiatory, debated and interactive.

Summary of implications of the Japanese model for education

It has been noted above that the 'standard operation' drives much of the organization of work in Japanese production; whether this is a model that one would wish to import into education is perhaps questionable. Further, the transferability of the assembly-line mentality is suspect, for example teachers do not have control over the 'raw materials' – the children – (nor indeed over the funding of resources), nor might they wish to regard education as the delivery of non-negotiable processes (the separation of conception and execution). Indeed students do not learn in the singular, standard and programmable ways that the assembly line connotes (if only students would be so then education would be so much easier!).

Clearly, then, it would be advisable to be aware of the potential dangers of embracing Japanese practices. Nevertheless, given their success and their resonance with many other positive practices in the management of change, it would be hasty to dismiss the positive aspects of the Japanese model. Despite the concerns about the potential negative side of some Japanese business practices nevertheless there are very many important implications for education in many fields.

Consensus, consultation and involvement

Widespread consultation, negotiation and involvement in advance of change; the development of a corporate and shared vision, mission and philosophy; the drive for consensus in collegial decision-making; the importance of co-ordination and communication; responsiveness to the customer.

Motivating staff

The respect for the professional judgement and autonomy of the people closest to the job; the importance of job satisfaction and an involved, committed workforce; support and development from within the organization in order that promotion from within is effective; the obligation of the organization to address the all-round welfare of participants; the replacement of coercive styles of management by enabling, facilitating and empowering styles of management, releasing the creative energy of staff; the importance of catching and developing motivation in the planning, implementation and evaluation of change; the commitment to bottom-up decision-making and improvement; the visibility and public celebration of success.

Continuous improvement

The importance of long-term planning; the commitment to, and importance of, small-scale continuous improvements through the involvement of all staff; the importance of continual openness to change, modification and improvement; the importance of research, development and problem-solving; high investment in technology, resources and ongoing training.

Efficiency

Single-mindedness in keeping to an agenda and philosophy; the emphasis on efficiency and the elimination of waste; the efficient use of resources – e.g. time, space, materials, people, money; the importance of being organized and co-ordinated; the practice of lean production – focusing on essentials and doing them expertly; the emphasis on quality assurance rather than quality control; the need for consistency and efficiency (the acceptable educational equivalent of the 'standard operation' rather than the non-negotiable nature of the National Curriculum, discussed above).

Error prevention

The concern for quality and total quality management; the need to provide continuous training, education and development; prevention of failure and problems rather than *post hoc* correction; the replacement of inspection with support for self-monitoring and development; the significance of 'right first time' and 'zero defects' after extensive trialling and discussion prior to implementation; the provision of immediate support when problems arise; the keeping of paper and 'bureaucracy' to an absolute, essential minimum.

Teamwork and flexibility

The push for collaboration and co-operation and teamwork; the need for flatter management organization and the recognition that leadership is not the monopoly of senior managers; the benefits of not having lengthy and precise job descriptions; the emphasis on flexibility and versatility and the appropriate training for flexibility; the importance of single status, regardless of the task being undertaken – respect and parity of esteem; the importance of group and team development, rewarding and supporting groups in their practices of improvements through group projects and 'group-think'; the programming of time for team activities; careful monitoring of individual and team development; the interpretation of individual progression in terms of its contribution to the improvement of the whole team; the importance of taking seriously and working with the multiple perceptions and circumstances of participants in change; devolving responsibility to all members; the importance of the role of middle managers; the careful selection and recruitment of staff within the context of their contribution to the team (however defined).

Many elements of the Japanese model commend themselves to education. Many of the issues outlined here are represented significantly in the educational as well as the business literature about the management of change.

Notes

1.   Some of the literature used here is written by the former Chief Executive of Nissan, Peter Wickens, who is clearly sympathetic to Japanese practices. The Japanese car manufacturer Honda captures much of the 'Japanese ethos' in its advocacy of: a) respect for theory and fresh ideas; b) effective use of time; c) enjoyment of work and the development of a stimulating working environment; d) harmonious relations at work; e) the value of research and the spirit and practice of endeavour.

2.   See Cool and Lengnick-Hall (1985), Beale (1994), Collins (1994), Keys and Miller (1994), Wickens (1987; 1995), Burnes (1996: 100–4), Herbig and Palumbo (1996), Porter (1996).

3.   Clegg (1992: 164–9) argues that retention of staff is achieved through internal promotion and salary increases to match – the 'golden chains' for commitment.

4.   Stringfield (1997: 154–5) notes that the Toyota company receives over two million suggestions for improvements each year.

5.   Wickens (1995: 134) estimates that up to 90 per cent of improvements to production at Nissan stem from the people who are doing the job. He argues (*ibid*.: 141) that many workers spot low-cost solutions to problems that are often overlooked by 'professionals' (who tend to go for expensive and complex solutions) (see also Clegg, 1992: 165).

6.   Reynolds and Farrell (1996) report that up to 80 per cent of time is spent in whole-class interactive teaching in some Pacific Rim countries.

7.   McGregor's work resonates with expectancy theory (Vroom, 1964). Wickens (1995: 27) argues that the amount of effort that people expend on a particular activity is a function of the degree of expectancy they have that the activity will lead to better performance, rewards and meeting their own desired objectives. If the activity is expected to lead to the desirable

outcomes and benefits then people will work towards them; if it does not, then they will not.

8. Because the just-in-time philosophy requires the immediate supply of high-quality parts, many companies who themselves have international quality marks (e.g. ISO 9000 – see Chapter 4) will only deal with suppliers who themselves carry such 'charter' marks of quality, thereby attempting to guarantee assured high quality levels throughout. The National Economic Development Council (1991: 215–16) indicates that the practices at Nissan impacted significantly on their suppliers, for example: the emphasis on teamwork and flexibility; the drive for preproduction quality assurance and error prevention; the creation of customer-orientated teams; the development of management styles that are based on openness and widespread communication; the drive towards continuous improvement.

9. Wickens (1987) reports that if a worker spots a problem and needs advice he or she activates a blue flashing light for immediate assistance so that the progress of the assembly never actually stops.

10. Hammer (1996: 109) observes that at Mutual Life Insurance job descriptions and departments were replaced by a new position of 'case manager'.

11. The commitment to teamwork, coupled with continuous improvement in the charting of each individual worker's skills, is evidenced in five incremental levels of development (Cowling and James, 1994: 94). The incremental and broadening levels and types of skill here equip employees to progress to supervisors' roles and beyond, echoing the comments about the tradition of recruitment and promotion from within the organization in lifetime employment. Further, at Nissan, the monitoring of personal and team improvements is very public. Charts of performance abound both visibly and in profusion. The achievement of success is a matter for public celebration. Indeed salary increases are aligned to group performance (Kenney and Florida, 1988: 135).

4
Change and the push for quality

Introduction

One of the major areas of change in industry over the last two decades has been in the push for quality. Value for money, accountability, the impact of market forces, questions about public and private services, international competition all join to push for quality. Further, the rise of a consumerist mentality and the service sector within emerging and developed countries and democracies have given rise to the need to meet the demands of quality. Industry is constantly changing and transforming itself in order to improve quality. Dean and Evans (1994) use the example from the Polaroid company in the 1980s and research by the MIT Commission on Industrial Productivity that indicated five basic reasons why companies were failing:

1) outdated strategies (a failure to invest in human and material capital);
2) short time horizons (short-termism);
3) weaknesses in the technology needed to meet the requirements of development and production;
4) a neglect of human resource management and development;
5) lack of co-operation.

Companies had to change to focus on quality or else they would simply cease. Producer capture (where producers dictate the products and terms) had to give way to consumer orientation. Much of the educational debate on quality is inspired by the principles of quality and quality development in industry and business. For example, addressing the points raised by Dean and Evans (*ibid.*) in an educational context suggests the need for schools to:

- build in quality at all stages of planning, implementation and evaluation;
- keep close to the requirements of 'stakeholders', e.g. parents, children, the economy;
- be proactive in setting its quality development and assurance requirements;
- ensure that the senior management of the school are committed to quality development;

- ensure that everyone is trained to meet the demands of quality assurance;
- ensure that stakeholders are kept informed about the quality development and control measures in operation;
- ensure that quality is maintained through continuing professional development;
- ensure that they have a sense of direction and longer-term aims;
- develop quality co-operatively – within the institutions and by linking to other agencies and support networks.

Defining quality

Many and varied are the definitions of quality.[1] For example:

1) excellence;
2) a product or service that is distinctive and that confers status on owner (i.e. high quality);
3) conformance to specification or standards;
4) fitness for purpose;
5) effectiveness in achieving institutional goals;
6) meeting customer's stated or implied needs and specifications;
7) understanding what the consumer values and needs – proof of needs;
8) providing a highly reliable product/service;
9) improving the specification of a product/service – product development;
10) being better than competitors;
11) identifying and excising weaknesses and failures – identifying root causes;
12) accentuating the positive, eliminating the negative, i.e. controlling the process and the product;
13) identifying and meeting critical success factors;
14) high customer/consumer satisfaction – delighting customers;
15) high employee satisfaction;
16) managing a strategic and period plan;
17) managing general finance;
18) allocating funds effectively;
19) ensuring effective delivery;
20) providing effective support and development of staff capabilities;
21) initiating, designing and undertaking research projects;
22) effective recruitment and staff stability;
23) managing employees' welfare;
24) effective communication (internal and external);
25) effective resource management;
26) effective information systems;
27) serviceability;
28) maintainability/serviceability;
29) meeting minimum standards of acceptability;
30) adaptability;
31) availability and convenience;
32) fitness of purpose;

33) durability;
34) up-to-dateness.

The significance of this breadth of embrace is that the notions of quality and quality development can meet several agendas simultaneously. The multifaceted nature of quality and effectiveness suggests that the search for simplistic or reductionist views of quality and quality development is fruitless. In the definitions above one can detect several contrasting views of quality:

• quality as that which the consumer defines as quality;
• quality as reliability;
• quality as excellence;
• quality as the extent to which predefined objectives have been met;
• quality as fitness for purpose;
• quality as conformance to specifications;
• quality control;
• quality assurance;
• total quality management (TQM).

These might coexist comfortably; alternatively they might exist in tension with one another. For example consumers might not wish to have a reliably excellent product because it costs too much; schools might wish to be reliable, if mediocre, maintaining the raised performance of less able students whilst supporting the 'high-fliers'; quality might turn out to be something that was not anticipated in objectives. Schools seeking to develop their quality have to reach an initial agreement on exactly what version of quality they are seeking to develop.

Quality as that which the consumer defines as quality

This derives from Feigenbaum's (1991) advocacy of staying close to the customer; quality is what the customer says it is. Bank (1992) argues that customers are the most important people in any business and that the company depends on them rather than *vice versa*; people do the company a favour by buying their products rather than the company doing them a favour by serving them.

What is being advocated here is a break with 'producer capture' – where producers produce what they want to produce and where customers are simply compliant. If a company is not responsive, then consumers will simply take their custom elsewhere. This has its direct parallel in education where the Adam Smith Institute (1984) criticized education for its 'producer capture', i.e. that schools were self-serving, meeting the needs of teachers rather than students, parents and the wider society.

This view of quality does not necessarily mean high quality – the customer may not wish to have, or be able to afford to have, a Rolls-Royce. Hence meeting customers' needs may not ensure that a high-quality product is provided; customers may be perfectly happy or have to put up with mediocrity and low cost. Whether this is a view that one would want to promote in education might be questionable.

A secondary school in an urban area experiences serious problems with a small but significant number of disruptive students who have rejected the curriculum. These students are performing poorly in most areas. The school is committed to mixed-ability teaching, arguing that it brings benefits to students of all abilities being taught in the same classes. The school is faced with a series of dilemmas, for many parents want the disruptive students removed from the class as they are impeding the development of a high-quality education for their children, and the parents are unimpressed by the argument that to remove the disruptive students from the class might be preventing them from learning the social habits necessary for life outside and beyond school. Further, many vocal parents argue that mixed-ability teaching is hindering the progress of their children who are bright but who are becoming demotivated by having to wait for the teachers to attend to the disruptive students. The school is losing 'bright' students to other schools and its rate of exclusions in increasing.

The school communicates with parents through a series of open meetings, written communication and one-to-one discussions with parents of disruptive students. Evidence is discussed about 1) the educational achievements of all ability ranges in mixed-ability groups in the school; 2) the level and types of disruption of difficult students; 3) the arguments (with evidence) for and against mixed-ability grouping, setting and banding, removal of disruptive children from the class (temporarily or permanently), teaching disruptive children separately. Four items are identified for decision-making:

1. Should the school move away from mixed-ability grouping and move towards banding and setting by subject?
2. What is the level of disruption that teachers and other students should have to tolerate?
3. Where should disruptive students be placed in the school's teaching arrangements?
4. What resources and actions are required to address the answers to the first three questions?

Having heard evidence, argument, opinion and preferences the school takes a democratic decision with its parents that 1) setting by subject will be implemented; 2) low-level disruption will be addressed by a range of consistently applied and graded sanctions (e.g. time out, working separately, being kept in school at break times); 3) high-level disruption will be addressed in the first instance by parental contact and/or longer-term exclusion from classes, with teaching being conducted – within resource constraints – within the school; 4) more extensive involvement of outside agencies for disruptive students will be practised (e.g. psychological services, social services, the police and legal services). In the example the school is seen to be addressing needs which both it and its customers have identified.

Figure 4.1 Quality as that which the consumer defines as quality

A dilemma is raised, for example if the views of quality between producers (teachers) and consumers (parents) disagree, if the parents require a form of education with which teachers do not agree, or if parents' values systems are discordant with those at school. A common example here would be the parents in a difficult school who advocate their child punching another in self-defence whereas the school has a ban on physical violence. The question here is whether quality is compromised if one stays too close to the customer. The link between quality and values become very clear when values are discrepant. An example of this version of quality is provided in Figure 4.1.

Quality as reliability

The literature on high-reliability organizations indicates some important features of quality as reliability – consistency – and the support systems that have to be ensured for such industries and organizations to function effectively. High-reliability organizations and industries involve high-risk operations that are not permitted to fail, for fear of disastrous consequences, for example nuclear power plants and operatives, electricity supply companies and controllers, the gas industry, air-line traffic controllers. They must have 100 per cent reliable functioning, trial and error is not permitted. Bierly and Spender (1995), Reynolds (1995) and Stringfield (1997: 152–7) define some of their characteristics:

- they invest massively in training, both before service and during service, in order to eliminate any failures and weaknesses in the operation;
- the operation has a limited number of explicit goals;
- operations, procedures and practices are laid out in regularly reviewed standard procedures that are intended to cover all operations and contingencies, ruling out human judgement;
- considerable attention is devoted to identifying and rectifying minor flaws and errors, in the belief that, unchecked, these could escalate into huge failures at a systems level (echoing the view of chaos theory outlined in Chapter 1);
- the practice of simulation is used extensively in order to identify problems and weaknesses so that action can be taken (i.e. focus is given to the 'trailing edge' of weaknesses rather than to the successful aspects of the organization and operation);
- the organization has high-quality resources and equipment, kept in optimum condition;
- the close interaction of technical, bureaucratic and cultural systems that are all geared to producing high reliability;
- a high degree of centralization that is combined with a high degree of delegation;
- such delegation is controlled strongly and culturally by extreme care in selection and training and by mutual monitoring, feedback, support, advice and criticism;
- communications are extremely efficient, enabling the system to absorb problems, surprises and damage and, thereby, to deliver consistent high reliability;
- there is an acceptance that failure is likely to be catastrophic in its results;
- they hold powerful databases on those aspects of the running of the organization that enable it to achieve its mission, with built-in triangulation, monitoring, and updating;
- they place great emphasis on performance appraisal in order to build out

weaknesses in professional judgement;
- hierarchical structures give way to collegial decision-making and interdependence at peak times;
- they are highly supported by their supervising organizations;
- short-term gains take secondary importance to high reliability.

The high-reliability organization renders itself immune to damage and failure through heavy investment in training, support, monitoring and singularity of task. The characteristics of the high-reliability organization match very closely indeed the characteristics of successful Japanese companies, e.g. Nissan.[2]

In educational terms, the development of the school as a high-reliability organization requires attention to several features:

- investment in effective initial and post-initial training and continuous professional development;
- the clarification of a limited number of core tasks and purposes, with agreement on how these will be addressed;
- whole-school policies for all major operations and contingencies, together with strong adherence to these;
- attention is placed on the best means for ensuring that these operations (however defined) are practised;
- there is agreement on the major ways of working/teaching/learning etc., in the school, and staff adhere to these;
- constant identification of the possible weaknesses of the school in order to solve them;
- open discussion and agreement of actions to be taken in problematic areas, so that consistency is ensured;
- resources and technology are as high quality, well kept and up to date as possible;
- a school identifies all its major networks and systems (discussed in Chapters 6 and 7) and ensures that they are in harmony with one another (pulling in the same direction) to improve consistently high standards of education and achievement;
- information is centrally held and there is clear leadership from the senior management;
- appointing and recruitment practices to the school are rigorous so that the most appropriate staff are appointed;
- monitoring, evaluation, performance indicators, databases and appraisal systems are used constantly and demonstrate a high fitness for purpose;
- standards are made clear and operational;
- there are support networks and systems for developing effective education both within and outside the school;
- communication is extensive, formally and informally;
- staff are aware of the seriousness of, and accountability for, their responsibilities;
- staff are accountable to each other as well as to outside bodies;
- short-term innovations and improvements are set in the context of the school's longer-term development and improvement;
- immediate interventions and backup strategies are in place in case problems occur.

The extent to which these are realistic is problematical as the examples of fail-safe organizations cited above require massive ongoing investment and a recognition that there is a minimum requirement in order to ensure that the system is effective. That is not the case in an education system that is starved of resources. Further, schools do not have the highly singular and specific purposes and tasks that characterize many high-reliability organizations.

High-reliability organizations take care to build out human frailty and any differences that are contingent on human characteristics; schools develop the personalities and abilities of individuals. The prospect of schools as stifling or sacrificing humanity, individualism, creativity, personality, relationships and emotions in the instrumentalism of high reliability is disquieting. This is not to say that schools should not be reliable, it is to say that steps to make schools reliable might have to be careful not to be so intrusive that they make schools simply impersonal, task-orientated teaching shops. Should a school be like an air-traffic control room, an electricity generator and supplier? Possibly not! An example of a school addressing issues of high reliability is provided in Figure 4.2.

A secondary school is seeking to ensure high reliability in its operations. It addresses this through a series of strategies:

- it collects and keeps ongoing publicly available data on student performance across a range of abilities from the time of each student's entry into school;
- it subscribes to a public 'value-added' project on measuring school and individual achievements;[3]
- it has a full range of policies to ensure consistency where consistency is deemed important (e.g. 1) curricular – planning, teaching, learning, marking, monitoring, assessment, record-keeping, quality assurance, homework, records of achievement, review; and 2) whole-school issues – equal opportunities, special educational needs, language, discipline (including sanctions and rewards, assertive discipline), pastoral care, bullying, truancy, parental communication, continuing professional development), work experience;
- it has operationalized its policies into concrete performance indicators, detailing specific, measurable practices, minimum acceptable practices and success criteria;
- it has detailed and agreed strategies for dealing with critical events (e.g. disruptive students, irate parents, lateness, accidents and emergencies);
- it uses appraisal and mentoring for professional development and action planning;
- it has set action plans for departments, faculties and the whole school, set within the school's overall development plan, aims and objectives.

The school is striving to ensure that a minimum required level of consistency of practice and philosophy is addressed in order to ensure the smooth functioning of the school whilst enabling acceptable variability to meet individual autonomy, professional judgement and differentiation for students' differing needs.

Figure 4.2   A school as a high-reliability organization

Quality as excellence

This is the 'Rolls-Royce' model of quality, where high quality and exclusiveness are the order of the day. This version of quality is usually expensive; exclusiveness has to exclude. Taking Feigenbaum's (1991) view, quality and cost are a sum rather than a difference, evidenced in private élite education. The highest-quality materials lead to the highest-quality products; care is lavished on the production of the product and the work is very labour intensive (e.g. small classes in schools), often highly specialized and time-consuming. The analogy carries into education straightforwardly in the exclusive private school for the privileged. However, the school effectiveness and improvement movements suggest that high-quality education can be and should be available to all children, regardless of background.

Attached to this view of quality as excellence is the question of status; high-quality products have status; some cars attract praise that is close to reverence whilst others are the target of derision. Some would argue that the car you own is a marker of who you are and what kind of person you are. In educational terms Young (1971) indicates that high status attaches to academic subjects, curricula that are organized into subjects and taught to the most able students in homogeneous ability groups, unrelated to everyday life (mental) and vocational work, and formally assessed. On the other hand low-status knowledge, he argues, is interdisciplinary, taught to mixed-ability groups, is related to everyday life (practical) and vocational (manual) work, and is not formally assessed. The link between academic curricula and formal examinations is rehearsed frequently in the tenacity with which the A-Level 'gold standard' examination resists modification.

Peters and Waterman (1982), Goldsmith and Clutterbuck (1984), Peters and Austin (1985), Kanter (1989) and Peters (1989) identify several elements of the excellent organization:

- clear, vision-driven management and effective leadership;
- keeping the goals of the organization limited and ensuring that these are addressed ('sticking to the knitting');
- making standards explicit and operational;
- continuous change, improvement and innovation;
- building in high involvement, commitment, participation, ownership and empowerment of all colleagues;
- loose–tight organizations;
- scrupulous attention to customers;
- informed and proactive leadership;
- devolution of responsibility to autonomous teams;
- the use of management information systems to monitor and measure activities and outcomes;
- the development of creativity through problem-solving approaches and rewards systems.

An example of a school seeking to develop a 'quality-as-excellence' model is presented in Figure 4.3.

An infants (Key Stage 1) school is seeking to ensure that it provides an excellent education for its children. The school has identified its key – core – tasks and proposals, and these have been encapsulated in the mission statement and aims and objectives of the school. The school has consulted very widely with parents to ensure that it represents the priorities parents hold for their children's education, and these have been identified as: 1) the development of effective learning habits and strategies in all its children; 2) the thrust towards high standards of numeracy, literacy and communication in all its students; 3) the provision of a wide curriculum which is motivating and educationally significant; 4) the early identification of children with learning difficulties, followed by rapid intervention; 5) furthering already effective involvement of parents.

The headteacher has booked one of the school's in-service days to inaugurate a term's focus on the standards of literacy and numeracy, and the school has decided to operate on six fronts. First, it will undertake baseline assessment of all children upon entry to the school. Secondly, year teams, with the curriculum co-ordinators, will develop and set concrete targets for achievement across the ability range, making concrete the statements in the relevant school's policy documents. Thirdly an action research model will be operated to try to raise the standards of literacy and numeracy in the school. Fourthly all the teachers will review how they address literacy and numeracy across the curriculum, so that consistent practice can be developed. Fifthly, teachers will be asked to identify children who present problems with literacy and numeracy and to bring to team and staff meetings sufficient case details of these so that effective interventions can be discussed; this will also include an identification of strategies that have been used to identify such children. Sixthly, ongoing communication with parents will be undertaken through individual meetings, parents' evenings, newsletters in a range of languages and specially convened public meetings for the whole school. Part of the school's in-service budget is spent on providing supply cover so that teachers can be released during school time to undertaken the developments.

What can be seen in this example is 1) leadership that sets the tone and direction, and devolves responsibility and tasks; 2) an identification of core tasks and purposes (sticking to the knitting); 3) involving everyone in the organization; 4) adopting a problem-solving strategy in combination with other development tasks; 5) the generation of actual data to inform planning; 6) close communication with parents; 7) seeking improvements and changes that are concrete; 8) ensuring that goals and standards are explicit; 9) trying to make the development situation as attractive as possible by building into school time rather than by regarding it as out-of-hours work.

Figure 4.3   Developing a quality-as-excellence model

Quality as the extent to which predefined objectives have been met

The introduction of ideas and terms such as target-setting, action planning, specification of intended learning outcomes, target-orientated curricula, outcome-based education and attainment targets combines to place the notion of objectives-based views of quality high on the educational agenda. The organization sets out its mission statement, operationalizes it into targets and procedures, and then, at a suitable time, assesses their achievement (see Frazer, 1994). As Wickens (1987) argues in connection with the value of mission statements and vision, at least they provide a direction and something to return to if one senses that one is being blown off course. The school development planning movement (e.g. DES, 1989; Hargreaves and Hopkins, 1991) is predicated on effective target-setting.

The use of an objectives model states the importance of using Stake's (1976) 'countenance' model in evaluating educational change, as it charts the degree of congruence or distance between objectives and actuality in respect of antecedents, transactions and outcomes. This model – as with most objectives models – is useful in two ways. First it requires users to specify the success criteria in operational terms – the actual concrete practices or evidence – that will be used to judge the extent to which objectives have been met (Morrison, 1993). Secondly it can be used as a springboard to development if teachers then ask for explanations of, or causes for, the extent of the congruence (or its lack) between intentions and actuality, i.e. if the results are used formatively.

A second example indicates how schools can address a view of quality as the extent to which predefined objectives have been met, through the use of a review (Figure 4.4).

Quality as fitness for purpose

Quality as fitness for purpose (see BS 5750 and ISO 9000, discussed later) focuses on the operations, processes or procedures that lead to the achievement of the purpose. The company's purposes are heavily informed by the customer's requirements.

Quality as fitness for purpose (as with the preceding model of quality as the achievement of objectives) is comparatively silent on considerations of the worthwhileness of the purposes. If the purposes are faulty then even the best fitness for the purposes will not guarantee a high-quality outcome. 'Fitness *for* purpose' should be complemented by 'fitness *of* purpose'.

Despite the possible reservations about the view of fitness for purpose, nevertheless the call to evaluate existing practices, to consider and evaluate alternatives and to adopt a piecemeal, incremental and carefully piloted approach to education is perhaps desirable. An example of fitness for purpose is given in Figure 4.5.

Quality as conformance to specifications

This model requires the detailed specification of the operating standards, not simply on the production line but also on several other aspects of the organization (e.g. health and safety, and personnel matters).[4] Crosby's (1980) view of quality is that there should be 'zero defects'; it is always cheaper to do the right thing first time (error prevention was a feature of Japanese industry, Chapter 3).

The practice of 'zero defects' is seen as industry's rejection of the notion of acceptable quality levels (AQLs). AQLs suggest that companies will

REVIEW OF HALF-TERM/TERM*	
Year groups: **Dates:**	**Class:** **Topic (if appropriate):**

Please comment on the following and add any other points you feel are important:

1) the extent to which your intentions and objectives for the term have been successful and reasons for this;
2) the extent to which the planned content and PoS have been covered and reasons for this;
3) the degree of children's success in achieving intended learning outcomes and reasons for this;
4) particularly successful activities and reasons for this;
5) resource availability and use;
6) the extent to which differentiation, progression and continuity have been successful and reasons for this;
7) particularly effective and less effective teaching strategies, experiences, content, and reasons for this;
8) assessment arrangements and results;
9) standards of children's progress and achievements, and reasons for this.

Please comment on the following and any other points you feel are important:

1) implications and recommendations for the future (e.g. objectives, contents, resources, teaching and learning, assessment);
2) what you would modify for the future with reasons for this;
3) how this can be followed up and how subsequent work can build on this (short and medium term);
4) implications for other staff;
5) implications for future action plans, targets and curriculum planning.

* = Delete as appropriate

Signed:
 Date: _____

Figure 4.4 A school's review document

A secondary school has consulted widely about parents' and employers' views of what is required from students leaving school at age 16. One main concern was expressed – the raising of the employability of lower-achieving school leavers, through functional literacy and information technology (IT) skills. The language and IT teams reviewed their written policies in order to address six main tasks. To:

1) translate the policies into activities, experiences, curriculum content, knowledge, skills, processes, assessment criteria, identification of students 'at risk' of not meeting specified lower limits of functional literacy and IT;
2) determine specific, concrete outcomes of programmes of IT study;
3) identify resource needs (e.g. materials, people, equipment, time, space, administration, professional development, involvement of other staff) in order to meet the requirements of (1) and (2);
4) identify key decisions that will need to be taken by senior managers and governors if (1) to (3) are to be effective;
5) set time frames and success criteria for the achievement of (1) and (2) above;
6) communicate and disseminate objectives, processes, outcomes and achievements to all relevant parties.

This example demonstrates how the purpose has been identified through open consultation with different parties of 'consumers', how tasks, processes, resources, decisions, responsibilities and success criteria have been defined, so that it becomes possible to identify and perhaps measure those elements of the process that might or not demonstrate 'fitness', including criteria such as suitability, adequacy, appropriacy, conformity, controllability, adaptability, readiness, competence.

Figure 4.5 Fitness for purpose

allow some degree of imperfection or variance in their performance, in effect tolerating imperfection (*ibid.*: 146). This violates the notion of elimination of waste, discussed in Chapter 3. AQLs build in waste and inefficiency, with potentially devastating results. Bank (1992: 24) indicates that tolerating 99 per cent acceptable quality levels, rather than zero defects – 100 per cent performance – could result in 200,000 incorrect prescriptions annually, 30,000 babies being dropped by nurses and doctors, one word being misspelt on each page. Would one really want to travel on an aircraft where only 99 per cent of it was working correctly (see the discussion above of high-reliability organizations)?[5]

The 'zero defects' movement implies total control and replicability of products, materials and processes. That sits uncomfortably with the processes and practices of education, where what is taking place is more than mere technology, and where they are decidedly – and thankfully – diverse, non-controllable, non-standard and non-standardizable. Further, one has to question how realistic a zero defects policy can be in education.[6]

For education the notion of conformance to specification goes wider than zero defects, for it suggests the need for:

- identification of whose specifications/requirements are to be involved;
- identification of what those specifications are (operational procedures, policies);

- careful monitoring, assessments, reviews and measurements of the contents, the process, the students, the outcomes;
- delineation of the limits of acceptability of variability in performance and processes (e.g. 1) how many students might fall below an acceptable lower limit of GCSE grades; 2) how strict is the adherence to the school's marking policy, what are the minimum resources that will be necessary – e.g. textbooks, people, time, equipment space; 3) what are the main teaching and learning styles that will be adopted; 4) recording and reporting).

It can be seen here that: 1) elements of education (the aims, objectives, contents, processes, outcomes, achievements) have to be specified in concrete, specific, operational terms so that they are susceptible to evaluation, review, monitoring and measurement; 2) criteria for ensuring that conformance is addressed are made explicit; 3) performance indicators (the kinds of data) are established that will give evidence of the achievement of the criteria; 4) decisions will need to be taken on what constitutes non-conformance (i.e. what are the limits of conformance/ acceptable performance).

Quality control

Quality control attempts to create quality by identifying and eliminating those products which do not conform to specifications or requirements; it inspects-in quality and inspects-out mistakes. Quality control is essentially a *post hoc* matter, it is product focused, inspectorial and regards quality as a 'bolt-on' rather than as a 'built-in' matter, i.e. it is reactive rather than proactive. It seeks reliability of a standard outcome, and is designed to ensure that products and outcomes meet minimum defined (threshold) standards and to ensure that substandard products are rejected.

Feigenbaum (1991) argues that this view of quality emphasizes reliability, serviceability and maintainability. In his view quality control has four steps:

1) setting standards;
2) appraising performance;
3) acting when necessary;
4) planning for improvements.

The quality control model – where it operates correctly (see the discussion below of OFSTED) – is good for reliability and accountability; the standards are the same and are applicable to all; standards are public and are known and easily measurable; products and outcomes can be compared easily; the use of outsiders as inspectors might be desirable as they should have an unbiased and clear view; minimum acceptable standards are necessary (see the discussions of ISO 9000); it enables rankings and monitoring of rejects; it builds in high reliability (see below).

On the other hand the quality control model contains several potential weaknesses. For example, it is a council of perfection; it is too coercive; it puts too much pressure on people so that they 'perform' unnaturally; inspectors might be subjective; it only controls products, neglecting processes; it builds in failure; it fails to catch the developmental nature of an organization/person; it runs on short timescales; it can be superficial and only, therefore, enable the superficial to change; it undermines continuous improvement; externals might fail to catch the real meaning and character of a unique situation; it causes resentment; it lacks validity – a quick tour of inspection; it is unfair and undesirable to judge outcomes by uniform criteria; it stifles innovation; it is mechanistic; it is too 'top down'. This is the model that is castigated quite severely by the 'quality gurus' of business (see below). It resonates strongly with McGregor's Theory X, which is a view of management from which Japanese (and other) companies have moved away very considerably.

Quality control in education can be seen in the work of OFSTED and inspections, themselves premised on the assertion of 'improvement through inspection' (Office for Standards in Education, 1993). It is possible to glean from the OFSTED documents a series of criteria by which effective teaching and learning can be judged in the press for quality control. These can be converted into statements for rating scales, together with an indication of the kinds of evidence that might be used in making the judgements (Figures 4.6–4.8). Used formatively, these same checklists can be used for quality assurance purposes (see below: quality assurance). Quality control and quality assurance overlap – an overlap which is present in the industrial and business literatures themselves.

Quality assurance

Quality assurance echoes McGregor's Theory Y. It attempts to build in quality (Deming, 1982) and to prevent failure from arising at all. It is essentially a 'process' matter that is active before the product is complete; it avoids mistakes occurring and plans proactively for quality to be 'built-in' rather than inspected-in ('bolt-on' – Wickens, 1987: 93). It adopts the 'right first time' view from Crosby (1980), arguing that it is cheaper and more efficient to build out waste and error rather than to correct them.

This model avoids having 'rejects' and failures; it focuses on prevention; it is more humanistic and collegial; it enables people to understand their work better, therefore it is empowering; it can make for flexibility. Whereas quality control is aimed at a single need, quality assurance is aimed at diverse needs; it encourages innovations and development; it has long-term benefits; it is more supportive and less coercive; it is rooted inside an institution; it builds in the practice of *kaizen* – continuous improvement, particularly through teamwork and the notion of small-scale incremental change; it makes for high motivation; it respects professionalism and professional development; it looks at strengths and builds on these – not simply focusing on negatives; it is a continuous, rather than 'one-off' process; it promotes teamwork and people are more accepting of advice and criticism; it is a 'bottom-up' process; it replaces the reporting/ description of successes and failures with the explanation for successes and failures.

Quality assurance has three elements (e.g. Dean and Evans, 1994: 15):

QUALITY OF LEARNING	
The effectiveness with which children:	
1) are paced through the lesson	1 2 3 4 5
2) use skills and understanding	1 2 3 4 5
3) progress appropriately in knowledge, understandings and skills	1 2 3 4 5
4) experience a variety of learning contexts	1 2 3 4 5
5) develop learning skills, including observation and information seeking, looking for patterns and deeper understanding, communicating information and ideas in various ways	1 2 3 4 5
6) are willing to ask questions, to try to find answers, to solve problems	1 2 3 4 5
7) apply what has been learned to unfamiliar situations	1 2 3 4 5
8) evaluate the work that they have done	1 2 3 4 5
9) foster and utilize inquiry skill	1 2 3 4 5
10) offer comments and explanations	1 2 3 4 5
11) demonstrate motivation, interest and the ability to concentrate, co-operate and work productively	1 2 3 4 5
12) persevere and complete tasks when difficulties arise	1 2 3 4 5
13) undertake practical activity which is purposeful and which encourages them to think about what they are doing	1 2 3 4 5
14) respond to the challenge of the tasks set	1 2 3 4 5
15) are willing to concentrate	1 2 3 4 5
16) can adjust to working in different contexts	1 2 3 4 5
17) appear to be committed to and enjoying learning	1 2 3 4 5
18) experience achievement that matches their abilities	1 2 3 4 5
19) remain on task	1 2 3 4 5
20) listen attentively to the teacher	1 2 3 4 5
21) participate in the lesson	1 2 3 4 5
22) can work independently	1 2 3 4 5
23) can work co-operatively	1 2 3 4 5
24) take responsibility for their own learning	1 2 3 4 5
25) select appropriate resources	1 2 3 4 5
26) demonstrate their learning both orally and practically	1 2 3 4 5
27) understand the purposes of learning	1 2 3 4 5
28) learn from their mistakes	1 2 3 4 5
29) behave well in lessons	1 2 3 4 5
1 = very little; 2 = a little; 3 = quite a lot; 4 = a lot; 5 = a very great deal	

Figure 4.6 Quality of learning

1) everyone in the enterprise has a responsibility for maintaining and enhancing the quality of the product or service;
2) everyone in the enterprise understands, uses and feels ownership of the systems that are in place for maintaining and enhancing quality;
3) management (and sometimes the consumer) regularly checks the validity and reliability of the systems for checking quality.

QUALITY OF TEACHING	
The effectiveness with which:	
1) teachers promote effective learning	1 2 3 4 5
2) teachers' expectations of children are high and appropriate	1 2 3 4 5
3) teachers develop skills and understanding in children	1 2 3 4 5
4) lessons are planned, their imaginativeness and links to ATs	1 2 3 4 5
5) progression and continuity are planned and appropriate	1 2 3 4 5
6) matching, differentiation individual needs are addressed	1 2 3 4 5
7) the objectives of the lesson are appropriate	1 2 3 4 5
8) the objectives are clear	1 2 3 4 5
9) children are made aware of and understand the lesson objectives	1 2 3 4 5
10) expectations of the outcomes are appropriate	1 2 3 4 5
11) the approach, methods and materials match the lesson objectives	1 2 3 4 5
12) teachers have a secure command of their subject knowledge	1 2 3 4 5
13) the lesson content is appropriate and suitable	1 2 3 4 5
14) the activities are chosen to promote the learning of that content	1 2 3 4 5
15) the activities are engaging, interesting and challenging	1 2 3 4 5
16) teachers motivate children	1 2 3 4 5
17) teachers communicate their high expectations of the children	1 2 3 4 5
18) focus on high attainment and good progress is maintained	1 2 3 4 5
19) teachers support and encourage children	1 2 3 4 5
20) resources are used: their availability, accessibility, quality	1 2 3 4 5
21) teachers assess children's progress and provide constructive feedback to them	1 2 3 4 5
22) the lesson is conducted at an appropriate pace	1 2 3 4 5
23) the range of teaching techniques (e.g. individual, pairs, small group, large group, whole class) demonstrates fitness for purpose	1 2 3 4 5
24) teaching methods are varied, appropriate and promote learning	1 2 3 4 5
25) all children are encouraged to participate	1 2 3 4 5
26) positive relationships are developed with children	1 2 3 4 5
27) classroom organization and resources (time, space, people, materials) promote learning	1 2 3 4 5
28) strategies for consolidating and accelerating learning are used	1 2 3 4 5
29) regular and positive feedback is given to children to enable them to become aware of their achievements and progress	1 2 3 4 5
30) teachers explain matters clearly	1 2 3 4 5
31) teachers use questions	1 2 3 4 5
32) teachers use instructional talk	1 2 3 4 5
33) teachers conduct discussions	1 2 3 4 5
34) teachers engage in procedural talk	1 2 3 4 5
1 = very little; 2 = a little; 3 = quite a lot; 4 = a lot; 5 = a very great deal	

Figure 4.7 Quality of teaching

- documents related to the planning of the work: forecasts, lesson plans and individual notes;
- teachers' records of work done by children
- the nature and contribution of homework
- the use of special support assistants
- input from visiting specialist teachers
- individual plans for children with special educational needs
- lesson observation
- discussion with teachers and children
- samples of children's work, including homework
- assessments and records of children's work
- marking, comments and follow-up
- results of formal assessments
- discussions with children

Figure 4.8   Evidence of quality

However, quality assurance requires a long 'lead-time' before gaining the payback (see the discussions of the Japanese model), which may not accord with the short timescales of decision-makers; many people cannot handle and do not want empowerment and responsibility (Jaques, 1990); they might still be externally imposed; for quality assurance processes to operate efficiently it assumes that all inputs/suppliers into the system will have the same quality assurance systems (see the discussion in Chapter 3, Note 8 of the fact that ISO 9000-bearing companies, e.g. Nissan and ICI, will only accept products from other companies that have the ISO 9000 charter); it is very – and continuously – exacting; it requires similarities of systems of quality assurance for efficiency in order for a company not to have to retest products and parts it receives; it adopts a singular view of human nature – that people want to improve – which misrepresents reality and is too simplistic a view of humans and institutions.

Quality and effectiveness are concerned with harnessing and developing the inbuilt potentials and qualities people in an institution possess. Change, development and effectiveness come from within rather than from without, leading to and building on the empowerment of all participants in an institution. Indeed it can be argued that quality control concerns structures, systems, norms and roles whilst quality assurance is about people and individual needs. This is represented in Table 4.1.

The reductionism for the sake of clarity in this table oversimplifies matters, for example it is not the case that the quality assurance model does not seek reliability, nor is it the case that quality control does not focus on processes. Rather, the table seeks to highlight emphases, in the knowledge that there is considerable overlap between quality assurance and quality control. One would wish a quality assurance system, for example, to be both reliable and valid and to use reliable instruments.

In education, quality assurance has a very wide embrace, taking in other conceptions of quality discussed in this chapter, for example (West-Burnham, 1997): total quality management, conformance to specifications,

Table 4.1 Elements of quality control and quality assurance

Quality control	Quality assurance
Reliability (consistency, comparability, transparency, fairness, objectivity, standardization to norms)	Validity (meaningfulness, specificity, utility, individualized, meeting diverse needs)
Systems determined	Agency/person developing
External use (e.g. accountability)	Internal use (development purposes)
Externally imposed (e.g. inspections, people as technicians)	Internally established (developmental, people as professionals)
Inspecting-in quality	Building-in quality
Technicist	Interactionist, emancipatory
Coercive	Supportive
Authoritarian and directive	Collegial and participatory
Summative	Formative
Product focused	Process focused
Describing and reporting success/failure	Explaining and seeking causes of success/failure
Pathological (looking for failures)	Optimistic (*kaizen*)
Reactive and *post hoc* – after the products are produced	Proactive and *ante hoc* – planning to produce high-quality products

a consumer-driven view of quality, fitness for purpose, meeting defined objectives, reliability. The emphasis on prevention that is characteristic of quality assurance itself is devolved on the adequate preparation of staff – of people. For example a series of government circulars (DFE, 1993a; 1993b) specified the preparation of newly qualified and serving teachers in respect of 12 main areas: 1) subject knowledge; 2) subject application; 3) planning the curriculum; 4) class management, 5) pupil learning; 6) teaching strategies and techniques; 7) assessment and recording of pupils' progress; 8) further professional development; 9) relationships with children; 10) pastoral care; 11) departmental management; 12) leadership. It is being suggested here that effective quality assurance requires high-quality and highly trained staff. Clearly that has resource implications.

Total quality management (TQM)

The section introduces TQM rather than provides a full review. TQM catches much of the contemporary thinking about the successful management of change. It emphasizes people, ethos and culture as well as quality systems. TQM places the whole company high on its agenda (Ishikawa, 1985: 103), being premised on the development and harnessing of the commitment of all members to continuous improvement (Walsh, 1991). Here products, processes and people are mutually potentiating. It emphasizes the creation of a quality culture and quality development (Collins, 1994); such a quality culture is premised on ownership of responsibility for quality and achieving goals by everybody.

In the creation of a quality culture the emphasis is on sharing values (Judd and Winder, 1995), the connectedness of all aspects of the organization, the importance of relationships and systems, the need for measures of quality to be established, the need to draw on and develop participants' experience of quality, and shared responsibility for quality development and problem-solving (e.g. Senge, 1990: 78).

Poor quality arises from bad systems rather than bad people (Wickens, 1987; Smith, 1990). The product is not defective because the worker is stupid or lazy but because he or she is inadequately trained, has poor tools or has insufficient time to do the job. This view is essentially optimistic, arguing that people are naturally motivated to achieve that to which they are committed and that the task of management is to create conditions that harness this motivation and potential (McGregor's Theory Y rather than Theory X). This echoes Senge's (1990: 95) view that one should not push growth but, rather, one should attempt to remove the factors that limit growth.

In terms of focus, nothing in the organization escapes the searchlight of quality, purposes, processes, resources (e.g. human, material, spatial, temporal, administrative), customer focus, organizational structures, management and leadership styles, success rates and productivity, costs and so on. In terms of processes TQM espouses several principles of operation, for example (e.g. Mortiboys and Oakland, 1991; Bank, 1992; Murgatroyd and Morgan, 1993; Goffin and Szwejczewski, 1996):

- the all-pervasiveness of quality – from processes into interpersonal relationships;
- the focus on the processes of quality development and maintenance;
- the openness to breaking with existing practices;
- the breakdown of compartmentalization;
- the development of a culture or ethos of quality in an organization, regarding everything through the lens of quality and evaluating everything on the criterion of its potential contribution to quality;
- a commitment to the shared vision or mission of the organization;
- teamwork, synergy and the involvement of everybody in an organization for quality;
- everyone pulling in the same direction towards the same goals;
- the importance of openness;
- a search for root causes of problems rather than symptoms (see the discussion of cause-and-effect diagrams below);
- the importance of ownership and self-management;
- a concern for the well-being and motivation of everybody in the organization;
- valuing all the staff of the organization;
- the valuing of creativity, challenge, empowerment and thirst for change;

- the recognition and reward of positive achievement;
- effective leadership and managers as role models;
- the move from middle managers as bosses to becoming facilitators and coaches;
- the development of flatter management hierarchies;
- extensive and effective communication throughout the organization.

Teamwork for TQM recognizes that most processes in business, industry and the services are of such an order of complexity that this places them outside the control of any single individual; hence teamwork is a necessity (Mortiboys and Oakland, 1991: 25). Miyashiro (1996b) cites Sun Microsystems as an example of effective TQM. The company states its commitment to quality thus:

1) quality commences with the satisfaction of employees (e.g. in the working environment, enabling employees to take pride and satisfaction in their work; the work is suitably challenging and provides career development opportunities);
2) the ultimate proof of quality is the satisfaction of the customer;
3) improvement of quality requires the capability of quality to be measured;
4) everybody has a responsibility for quality;
5) quality development and outcomes are deliberate – planned – rather than accidental.

Kanji (1996) draws out the links between TQM and planning change:

- innovation concerns a product (the need for customer satisfaction in TQM);
- innovation concerns processes (the need for employee satisfaction in TQM);
- innovation concerns application (in TQM all work is part of the process of quality development);
- innovation affects a system, i.e. is systemic (the need in TQM for effective measures of quality);
- innovation requires appropriate technology (teamwork in TQM);
- innovation requires core competencies to be identified and developed (people are the creators of quality in TQM);
- planned innovation must be transferable to the real situation (the TQM notion of prevention of error).

However, Collins (1994: 41–2) suggests that the TQM approach is mechanistic and regards an organization as a system – 'an apparatus' – rather than as a vibrant culture of sentient humans. He argues that the philosophy of TQM is fundamentally naive for it neglects issues of power, hierarchy and micropolitics and the micropolitical, time-wasting games in which those who hold power often engage. West-Burnham (1997: 11) summarizes criticisms that suggest that the managerialist tone of TQM undermines teacher professionalism, collegiality, democracy and the debate over values. Indeed he questions whether educational outcomes are susceptible at all to being 'managed'. Managerialism (Everard and Morris, 1990) is at heart manipulative and hence anti-educational.

Criticisms of the TQM approach suggest that it is far too 'activity centred' rather than 'results centred' – replacing the standard practice of 'Ready, Aim, Fire' with 'Ready, Fire, Aim' (see Fullan, 1991). Schaffer and Thompson (1996: 141) suggest that there is a rhetoric about TQM programmes – whilst they might make managers feel good, in fact they contribute little 'bottom-line performance'. That these programmes might improve morale is not questioned, but Schaffer and Thompson cite a 1991 survey that indicates that, of 300 electronics companies surveyed, although 73 per cent of them had costly TQM programmes, 63 per cent of them had failed to improve quality defects by even as much as 10 per cent (*ibid.*: 142).

They are suggesting that the 'payoff' for companies involved in TQM activities is unproven and suspect, as these programmes tend to disregard results, are too diffuse, non-specific and large scale, and operate under the fallacy that the number of TQM activities correlates with improvements in performance. Rather, they suggest 'results-driven' activities, related to specific, measurable, short-term, rapid, action-orientated, outcome-focused, impatiently pursued, expert-supported, energetically advanced goals, were much more successful in achieving improvements (*ibid.*: 143–8), usually with far less investment. Innovations here are responsive to real need, focusing on activities that yield results, that work, thereby being economical, efficient and avoiding wasting time and effort.

The views of quality that have been discussed so far are diverse. They place differential emphasis on aims and purposes, worthwhileness and values, processes and procedures, products and outcomes, measurement, control and assessment. The message here for education is perhaps one of eclecticism. The previous discussion has attempted to indicate some of the strengths and weaknesses of each of the versions of quality; hence educationists should be driven by the notion of 'fitness for purpose' and decide the versions and elements of quality on which to focus. For education, it is probably true to say that at some time all the preceding views of quality will be necessary.

The quality gurus

The quality agenda and process of development have existed in industry for much longer than in education. Merli (1996) has identified three 'generations' of a total quality approach. The first generation emphasized continuous improvement of operations and the elimination of waste. The second generation focused on the organization itself, on the continuous improvement of the organization of the business, leading to an increased attention to 'managerialism' and 'management by policy' (the *hoshin kanri* of Japanese companies). The third generation, the 'mature phase', emphasized total quality, the identification of priorities and policy implementation. Bendell (1991) identified three groups of 'quality gurus' since the 1950s:

1) Americans who disseminated their views of quality to the Japanese (e.g. Deming on management philosophy, Juran on the costs of quality, Feigenbaum on total quality control);

2) Japanese who developed their own concepts of quality in response to the Americans' views (e.g. Ishikawa on the values of simple tools for quality and quality circles, Taguchi on minimum prototyping, Shingo on error prevention and zero defects);

3) the more recent gurus from the west who build on and extend the Japanese practices (Crosby on raising awareness of quality, 'right first time', conformance to standards and zero defect, Peters on customer satisfaction; Møller on personal qualities and personal management).

Deming

Deming's work is already disseminated widely in education. He articulates his 14 well-known points for developing a quality company (Deming, 1982: 23–4):

1) create constancy of purpose towards improvement of product and service;
2) adopt the new philosophy;
3) cease dependence on inspection to achieve quality. Eliminate the need for inspection on a mass basis by building quality into the product in the first place;
4) end the practice of awarding business on the basis of price tag. Instead, minimize total cost;
5) improve constantly and for ever the system of production and service;
6) institute training on the job;
7) institute leadership;
8) drive out fear;
9) break down barriers between departments;
10) eliminate slogans, exhortations and targets for the workforce asking for zero defects and new levels of productivity. Such relations only create adversarial relationships, as the bulk of the causes of low quality and low productivity belong to the system and thus lie beyond the power of the workforce;
11) eliminate work standards (quotas) on the factory floor. Eliminate management by objectives and numerical goals. Substitute leadership.
12) remove barriers that rob the hourly worker of success and pride;
13) institute a vigorous programme of education and self-improvement;
14) put everybody in the company to work to accomplish the transformation. The transformation is everybody's job.

The ramifications in the sphere of education are massive. Inspection is castigated for building in failure, coming too late and for being ineffective and costly. The thrust towards system-wide improvement and responsibility has implications for the funding and resource levels of education, moving culpability for poor quality away from teachers and towards the funding providers. The emphasis on breaking down barriers and the advocacy of teamwork recognizes the value of synergy and the complementarity of skills and abilities. The emphasis on partnerships and continuity of contact is, perhaps, a salutary message in an age where the customer and competition are supreme.

Deming's perceived demoralization of the workforce and the disrespect to employees by the use of slogans and general exhortations to work harder have their exact parallel in education in the 1980s and 1990s when the then government orchestrated widespread suspicion of teachers and blamed them for the perceived failure in standards of education and coupled this with the Parents' Charter and the legal requirements to bring in a range of new curricula, assessment and management bureaucracy. In Deming's view management by appraisal and evaluation is counter-productive, building in fear, stress and low self-esteem, and demolishing teamwork. He uses harsh phrases when discussing this matter (*ibid.*: 102), talking of making people feel bitter, bruised, depressed, crushed, battered, desolate and dejected – an experience familiar perhaps to many teachers.

In education Arcaro (1995a) suggests that Deming's work has significant implications for support for participants and prevention of failure rather than failure detection, whilst Greenwood and Gaunt (1994) translate Deming's 14 principles into education very clearly:

1) undertake a commitment to constant learning and curriculum development;
2) adopt Deming's system of profound knowledge as the major tool of management (appreciation of the system; knowledge of statistical theory; theory of knowledge; knowledge of psychology);
3) build in quality in teaching and learning (rather than inspecting-in quality);
4) develop partnerships within schools and between schools and the communities they serve (e.g. parents, employers, districts);
5) improve constantly the system in which teaching and learning occur;
6) support ongoing learning and staff development;
7) lead effectively, rather than drive or manipulate;
8) promote enjoyment in learning rather than fear (e.g. of being punished);
9) collaborate and develop crossdepartment teams;
10) communicate openly, widely and honestly;
11) create an environment that is free from grades and rank ordering;
12) encourage students to take a pride in their work;
13) develop the whole person (students and staff);
14) negotiate learning.

Though Deming's work was in the first wave of quality gurus, nevertheless his message for education is as contemporaneous as it is powerful.

Juran

Juran (1988; 1993) argues that the pursuit of quality should be continuous, an ongoing process rather than an event, that it needs 'hands-on', practical leadership by senior staff together with considerable investment for support and training of all participants. Juran's important contributions to the quality issue are in outlining a process of quality development and in articulating quality in terms of fitness for purpose, conformance to specifications, and a trilogy of quality planning, control and improvement. For fitness for purpose to be addressed (Bendell, 1991) an organization needs to identify its purposes (and purposes for quality development – West-Burnham, 1992), implement its plans to meet these purposes, monitor and evaluate the progress towards their achievement, ensure that responsibility for achieving the goals is assigned clearly and appropriately, ensure that participants are motivated, and ensure that rewards are based on results.

Feigenbaum

Feigenbaum (1991) adopts a view of quality as that which the customer says it is (not necessarily the best but the best for the customer) and that quality and cost are a sum rather than a difference. Quality development is premised on teamwork and individual diligence. He argues that there are several benchmarks for total quality control in business organizations and industry: in his view quality is company wide and a total way of managing – 'an ethic', quality is mutually dependent on innovation and requires continuous improvement, it needs to connect with customers and suppliers.

Feigenbaum argues that quality control for reliability and maintainability has to take account of the notion of conformance to specifications or standards. An institution or company should set out its quality standards, undertake an appraisal of the degree of conformance to these standards, take action if the standards are exceeded and plan to improve the standards. He advocates the centrality of human relations as the fundamental issue in quality control activities, with an emphasis on participation and effective communication.

Ishikawa

Ishikawa is perhaps best known for the development of quality circles and the 'fishbone' cause-and-effect diagrams (also known as the Ishikawa diagram) (discussed below). For Ishikawa, quality has several dimensions (Ishikawa, 1985; Bendell, 1991). For example:

1) improved, standardized, defect-free, reliable products;
2) costs are kept to a minimum and processes are rendered lean;
3) elimination of waste;
4) equipment and other facilities are kept at a high standard;
5) reduction of inspection;
6) positive relationships between departments and people are developed;
7) accurate records and data are kept;
8) discussions are open and democratic, and meetings are arranged to run smoothly;
9) quality control is everyone's responsibility and is premised on teamwork.

In order to bring out the best in people and their active participation in quality Ishikawa (1985) suggested the use of quality circles. A quality circle has several characteristics:

- it is a group of up to ten people from the same workshop area and at different levels of seniority who meet regularly; group activity is emphasized;

- participation is voluntary, with an emphasis being placed on personal and mutual development; participation by all employees is highly desirable;
- it values group activity;
- it values self-development very highly;
- it is intended to improve and develop the enterprise in question;
- the activity links very closely with operations;
- it respects humanity and strives to make the working environment positive;
- originality, vitality, continuity, creativity are all welcomed;
- openness is encouraged;
- conflict and disagreement should be open but courteous and productive;
- each member must have good credibility in the organization;
- it is intended to promote positive relations, satisfaction and personal motivation;
- it uses agreed and standardized quality control techniques (discussed below);
- the profile of quality and overcoming problems to improving quality are major goals;
- it is intended to maximize and develop continuously the potential of all participants.

Quality circles, argues the Department of Trade and Industry (1994b), recognize that it is people who create systems and processes and who oversee their operation; therefore utilizing people's resources is an essential ingredient to quality development. As a concomitant to quality development, Ishikawa (1985: 37–9) strongly advocates the need for ongoing, permanent, long-term education for quality control. For him quality control starts and ends with education. At best, he argues, formal education before work can contribute only one-third of the total education a worker requires.

Ishikawa is noted also for his view that there is a comparatively limited range of useful and easy-to-use techniques and tools for improving quality. For example:

- the *Pareto chart* (a device that enables trivial and important variables in improving or preventing quality to be identified). Pareto (an Italian economist) discovered the 80/20 ratio – where 80 per cent of any problems (e.g. road accidents, staff absence), are attributable to only 20 per cent of their causes – the vital few causes are separable from the trivial many causes. For example, 80 per cent of traffic accidents occur on only 20 per cent of roads, or 80 per cent of a product is purchased by only 20 per cent of the population. Through simple measurement techniques and tally marks a form of cumulative line graph is constructed easily, with the largest causes being graphed first and the smaller ones following, thereby portraying large and small causes. An example of a Pareto chart for an educational innovation is given in Figure 4.9.

  In this chart the vertical axis represents the percentage of the scores for a particular problem; hence it can be seen that the first two problems with the innovation account for 80 per cent of the overall problems (the vital few

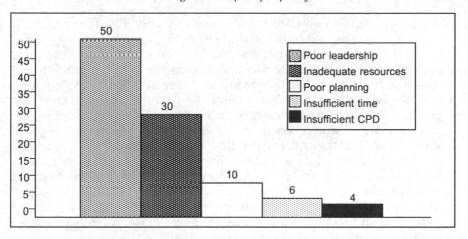

Figure 4.9 Pareto chart of causes of poor innovation

causes) whilst the remaining causes account for only 20 per cent of the problems in total (the trivial many). These scores can be obtained straightforwardly, for example by frequency counts and aggregated rating scales;

- a cause-and-effect ('fishbone') *Ishikawa diagram*, in which organizations identify as many causes of problems as possible in the area (e.g. using brainstorming) they wish to study, in order that improvement can take place, and draw these on to a chart that, when complete, resembles a fish's skeleton (see Figure 4.10). Minor elements and major elements make up the skeleton (e.g. in business this might appear under the headings of equipment, people, resources, environment, methods,

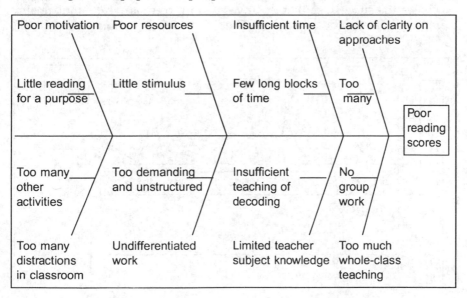

Figure 4.10 The Ishikawa cause-and-effect chart

resources, whilst in education the major elements might be resources, teaching methods, communication, leadership, policies, staffing). Lines out to the main headings become the fish's ribs, and lines off the ribs (subcauses) become the interstices. The intention is to unearth genuine causes of problems rather than symptoms (see also Senge, 1990: 104);

- the *histogram*, where data (e.g. examination scores, absentee rates) are grouped (bounded) and presented in histograms, thereby enabling the nature of the distributions to be observed (e.g. positive or negative skewedness) and the variability of the results (the range) and variations in performance to be seen, such that participants can then seek to explain the frequencies for each category and the causes of the dispersal (range) and degree of variability;

- the *scatter diagram*, where two sets of data are mapped on to a graph in order to identify whether there is any degree of association (correlation) between them (for example, between a class's success rates in formal assessments and their attendance rates);

- the *control chart*, where, for example, a series of data is collected over time, techniques are applied to identify the means of groups of results over time and then upper and lower action lines – acceptable limits of variability – are established (through straightforward statistical procedures), outside which action is deemed necessary for remediation (Greenwood and Gaunt, 1994: 99–106). A system or process is in control if its range of variability lies between calculated upper and lower limits of acceptability. It can be seen that the variability falls between acceptable upper and lower limits (Figure 4.11).

- *benchmarking*, where a company looks to the leaders in its field (or other related fields) – the best in the class (Weller, 1996) – to examine what makes them so successful and what the leader company is doing to achieve the success, so that the investigating company can emulate and improve on the best practice. The focus for benchmarking can be

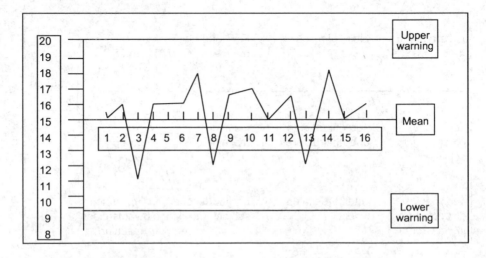

Figure 4.11 A control chart

whatever the company wishes it to be, for example the products, the processes and operations, the organizational structure, management and leadership styles, the culture of the organization, the services to customers and employees. West-Burnham (1991) identifies a four-step process for benchmarking: *review* (e.g. the product, service or process identified, deciding which organizations on which to focus); *analysis* (of factors contributing to success, their applicability to the company's own practices and the implications of changing); *planning* (identifying what to achieve and how to achieve it); *action* (implementation, monitoring and review of achievement of targets, making recommendations for further improvements). Weller (1996) argues that it is important that the company being benchmarked has sufficiently similar characteristics to those of the investigating company so that observations will be transferable (comparing like with like) – an important message in comparing and benchmarking schools and in assessment of performance and the 'value-added' component of schools.

It is beyond the scope of this book to examine these techniques, but they are discussed in an accessible style in, for example Bank (1992), Kanji and Asher (1993) and, in the field of education, Greenwood and Gaunt (1994). Ishikawa's practical recommendations for developing quality control are discussed more fully later in the chapter. Ishikawa's work (see also Mizuno, 1988) suggests that quality should and can be measured.

Taguchi and Shingo

Taguchi (1986) was a strong advocate of the building-in of quality, routinely optimizing the processes and products before manufacture is undertaken rather than inspecting-in quality. Quality (e.g. reliability, fitness for purpose, maintainability) had to be addressed at the design – the planning – stage. Therein is a salutary message for education. Shingo (1986; 1988) is a principal advocate of the *poka yoke* (error prevention) system. Shingo is, thereby, a protagonist of the notion of zero defects and mistake-proofing.

Crosby

Crosby's work (1980: 111) is notable for its emphasis on a quintet of concerns in quality:

- quality is conformity to requirements, and not excellence or elegance;
- problems must be identified by the individuals or the departments that are causing them; prevention rather than cure is the key to quality;
- it is always cheaper to do things right first time;
- the only worthwhile performance measurement is the total cost of quality and the price of non-conformance;
- the only worthwhile quality performance standard is that of zero defects.

Crosby's (1980; 1984) view is that it is the cost of non-conformance that dissipates a company's profitability.[7] Crosby uses the term costs in its twin interpretation, first in terms of how much it costs to achieve the quality product or service, and secondly in terms of the cost of failure.[8] The costs of quality, for Crosby (1980), come in the areas of prevention, appraisal and failure, all of which, he stresses (p. 15) come about because insufficient attention is paid to doing it right first time. For Crosby the ideal organization is one in which:

- people do things right the first time as a matter of routine;
- change is planned proactively and used to the advantage of the company;
- growth is sustained, consistent and yields profits;
- new products and services are developed in time for when they are needed;
- people are happy to work in the organization.

Crosby is insistent on the 'people' aspect of the organization in meeting change as quality development. He emphasizes motivational factors (surely a message for educationists!), arguing that simply paying people more will not guarantee change, quality and improvement. In a passage that echoes Maslow's work on the hierarchy of needs (p. 218), Crosby suggests that, whilst money may be an initial attraction, people require more than money out of their employment, e.g. by having their contributions recognized and appreciated. Motivation exerts a powerful influence on employees – surely a key message for policy-makers in education.

Peters

The work of Peters is particularly useful because of the close links that it draws between quality and the management of change and innovation. Peters (1989: 27) identifies several hallmarks of successful companies, for example: flatter management; an identification of – and targeting towards – niche markets; quality and service consciousness; responsiveness to consumers and employees; an ability to maintain rapid innovation; the recognition that the main way to add value is to use highly trained, versatile and flexible staff (see Chapter 3).

For Peters, to cope with change means to be proactive, in particular by being obsessively responsive to customers – an essential feature of quality. To do this, he argues, requires building blocks for capability. He identifies 13 attributes of a revolution for quality (*ibid.*: 70–80):

1) an obsession with quality by the management (the emphasis on the emotional commitment is deliberate);
2) the need to adhere closely to one system (echoing his comments from his 1982 work that an organization needs to 'stick to the knitting');
3) quality is measured and should be both visible and undertaken by the participants. Peters insists (1989: 480) that we can introduce and simplify systems by ensuring that they measure exactly what they are designed to measure, a feature that Fitz-Gibbon (1996) suggests should lie at the heart of many indicators of school effectiveness;

4) the achievement of quality should be rewarded;
5) all participants require training in the techniques for quality development;
6) multifunctional teamwork is the main way to promote a quality organization;
7) small, niche products and marketing are desirable;
8) constant simulation is undertaken to sustain the ethos of innovation and quality;
9) the process of quality improvement is undertaken through an organizational structure that parallels the operational structure;
10) everyone is touched by, and is a participant in, the quality process;
11) simplification is a key to quality;
12) quality improvement is continuous.
13) effective leadership is central to the quality improvement process.

Møller

Møller's (1988) work also emphasizes the significance of the development of personal self-esteem as an essential ingredient of high productivity. The opportunity to make gains in productivity arises more in the field of administrative and interpersonal relations than in production processes. Møller identifies several key features of planning for increased self-esteem, for example: 1) setting personal goals for quality and establishing one's own 'personal account' for quality; 2) checking how far one is satisfied with one's efforts; 3) effective personal management, e.g. stress management, being committed to the task and enterprise, demonstrating self-discipline and perseverance, behaving with integrity and ethically; 4) regarding contacts as potential clients and valued customers; 5) avoiding errors and utilising resources efficiently; 6) performing tasks and activities effectively and efficiently; 7) demanding quality of self and others.

Møller's work echoes the need for human resource development within a context of quality development. It also argues for the need for appraisal, target-setting, continuing professional development, participatory approaches to planning and innovation, the importance of incentives and rewards, careful identification of the locus of decision-making and responsibility, action planning and problem-solving approaches to change and innovation, and a recognition of the importance of the school in the community.

Kitemarks and charter marks of quality

International companies are seeking the 'charter' marks of quality, not least because many will only deal with other charter-mark-bearing companies. The Department of Trade and Industry (1994a) and Wickens (1995: 178) noted the worldwide trend towards companies seeking accreditation as an index of more stringent customer demands for quality. One can view the acquisition of charter marks as an approach to the management of the change process through the use of a bureaucratic device, through a set of procedures. There are two important distinctions in quality certification and accreditation agencies: some of them set substantive standards of achievement, i.e. move towards guaranteeing high standards (quality as excellence), for example the Investors in People award. Others are concerned that a company adheres to a set of procedures and processes that are designed essentially to guarantee that a company has a mechanism for examining issues of quality. Examples of the latter include the BS 5750, EN 29000 and ISO 9000. These latter procedures themselves do not guarantee high standards, they only guarantee a certain thoroughness of documentation and review. For example the Department of Trade and Industry (1995: 10) explicitly states that it is possible to gain the ISO 9000 whilst making an inferior product, i.e. that the standard offers no guarantee of the excellence (or indeed of the competitiveness in a price war) of the product or the service being provided.

BS 5750

The early charter mark was BS 5750; this was superseded from 1992 by ISO 9000 and EN 29000. BS 5750 is a set of 20 clauses that are designed to ensure that each stage of production is subject to quality audit and development in order to ensure fitness for purpose and conformance to requirements. The clauses are:

1) *management responsibility* (management must document its commitment to, and policies and goals for, quality, identifying personnel and responsibilities for quality, providing adequate resources for training in quality verification, appointing a named management representative for quality and reviewing its quality system);
2) *quality system* (a documented quality system will be used to ensure conformance to requirements);
3) *contract review* (each contract will be reviewed to ensure that the requirements are defined, documented and able to be met by the company);
4) *design control* (procedures will be in place to ensure that requirements and specifications are met);
5) *document and data control* (all documents relating to BS 5750 will be kept, reviewed and updated);
6) *purchasing* (the product will conform to specified requirements and suppliers or subcontractors will be chosen on their ability to meet these);
7) *control of purchaser-supplied product* (procedures will be in place for the verification, storage and maintenance of products and components);
8) *product identification and traceability* (procedures will be in place to enable the product to be identified from specifications and drawings during each stage of the production, delivery and installation);
9) *process control* (the processes of production and installation, including 'special' processes, will be subject to quality documentation and practice);
10) *inspection and testing* (products received will be subject to inspection to ensure conformance to requirements, in-process inspection and

monitoring will be undertaken, postproduction inspection will be undertaken (including inspection of previous inspections), records of inspections will be kept);

11) *inspection, measuring and test equipment* (equipment used for inspection and monitoring will be tested regularly and calibration checked);

12) *inspection and test status* (the test status of a product will be identified);

13) *control of non-conforming product* (the use of non-conforming products will be prevented, and responsibility for disposal of such products will be identified);

14) *corrective and preventive action* (procedures will be in place for identifying non-conforming products, their causes and their correction);

15) *handling, storage, packaging, preservation and delivery* (procedures to prevent damage in handling, storing, packaging and delivering products will be in place);

16) *control of quality records* (records will be kept on all required aspects of quality, including quality records of suppliers);

17) *internal quality audits* (documented internal audits will be undertaken to establish the effectiveness of the quality procedures and system);

18) *training* (the company will provide appropriate training needs in quality for all participants);

19) *servicing* (procedures will be in place to ensure appropriate servicing);

20) *statistical techniques* (these will be adequate to ensure the acceptability of the process capability and required characteristics of the product).

The pedigree of this list in industry is immediately obvious. Hence quite whether one would wish to use it in the human sector of education might be questionable. However, the notion of careful audit of all stages (including baseline – entry – assessment of students) is a move which currently appears unstoppable. One can see the emphasis being laid on responsibilities, systems, documentation, responsiveness to customer requirements, resources and personnel required for quality, training requirements for quality, and audit and review. One can see that specific standards are not laid down; these are set by the company itself. Only specific procedures are specified that are designed to ensure reliability as consistency.

In the field of education West-Burnham (1992: 148–9; 1997: 70–1) has argued that the introduction of BS 5750 into education will ensure that

• management takes responsibility for the quality policy, with quality objectives being operationalized and responsibilities identified;
• appropriate training, incentives, rewards, resources and communication for quality are guaranteed;
• emphasis is laid on quality as prevention (i.e. quality assurance);
• the processes are in place to ensure responsiveness to customers.

The arguments both for and against the adoption of BS 5750 in industry are several, and serve as a cautionary note in considering their application to the world of education. One can identify several claims that are made in favour of BS 5750:

• the development and communication of a quality policy and practices are unavoidable;

- quality improvements are made and market share is improved (e.g. Green, 1992);
- external credibility, publicity and recognition are gained;
- complaints are reduced because responsiveness to customers is a high priority;
- effectiveness is improved;
- procedures for quality are documented (e.g. Green, 1992);
- documentation is straightforward and helpful for inducting new staff (O'Brien, 1992);
- team spirit, high morale and participation are developed;
- management is required to consider systems for quality assurance;
- continuous improvement is facilitated;
- the costs of quality are kept to a minimum;
- training is guaranteed;
- consistency of work is ensured because everybody knows the agreed standards.

On the other hand there are several difficulties with BS 5750. For example:

- it is costly and time-consuming to install and implement (e.g. up to 12 months for the mechanism to be in place and up to three years (Ishikawa, 1985) for management to understand fully the implications of quality management). It often requires the use of consultants and it requires additional expenditure on 'getting the system up-and-running';
- it is not cost-effective in some sectors (e.g. the service sector) because it neglects employee motivation, involvement, time commitment and incentives;
- it creates massive paperwork – it is a bureaucratic approach to ratcheting up standards through procedures;
- it is all form and no content;
- the emphasis on documentation of procedures might result in simply documenting inefficiency;
- it is demanding to set up and benefits are not immediate;
- the requirement of sustainability can place immense pressure on staff;
- it requires considerable motivation, commitment and a positive attitude to quality development from all participants;
- it is easy for quality to become the preserve of a cabal;
- there is insufficient guidance on leadership, management and the creation of a culture of quality;
- it is an inappropriate model for the service sector and human services.

Bowring-Carr and West-Burnham (1994) make many useful suggestions for how BS 5750 can be used in education. For example:

- management responsibility will entail the formulation of a policy on quality and procedures for its operation;
- quality system will entail the writing of a manual for quality;
- contract review might entail review of the management of contracts with teachers, parents, governors and local authority;
- design control will entail the keeping, implementation and updating of policy and planning documents and records;

- purchasing might embrace appointment procedures (both full-time and supply teachers), the upkeep of the fabric of the building as well as buying resources;
- purchaser-supplied products might include procedures for attending to the needs of all students and staff, matters of health and safety and visits;
- product identification and traceability might include the full documentation of a student's progress, attendance, assessment results, other areas of development (akin to the Record of Achievement);
- process control implies attention to pedagogy, curriculum delivery, motivation and punishments, provision for students with special needs, transfer to a subsequent educational establishment;
- inspection will be both formal (external) and informal (internal) assessment, testing and examinations, and will include baseline assessment;
- inspection, measuring and test equipment will address moderation procedures, consistency of actions (for example in policies for the curriculum and for behaviour);
- inspection and test status will require the maintenance of an effective record-keeping system;
- control of non-conforming product might focus on underachievement, relationships with parents, course review, removal of damaged or out-of-date materials;
- corrective action will include mechanisms for improvement, prevention of problems and procedures for handling complaints;
- handling, storage packaging and delivery will refer to matters of health and safety of staff and students;
- quality records will require the school to document the steps it is taking to achieve quality;
- internal quality audits will require the review of the extent to which what is intended to happen in the quality system is actually happening;
- training might refer to staff development, induction and identification of needs;
- statistical techniques will require schools to keep and process data on all aspects of the school.

ISO 9000

The ISO 9000 (incorporating ISO 9001–ISO 9004) is modelled on BS 5750; hence much of the preceding discussion applies here, particularly in connection with the 20 clauses of BS 5750 as, in very many respects, these are the same in ISO 9000.

ISO 9000 (Department of Trade and Industry, 1995: 33–40) requires several features of a quality system for industry that translate clearly into education:

- a quality policy that demonstrates a commitment to quality;
- a statement of how arrangements for quality will be maintained (together with a statement of the people, tasks and resources involved in maintaining and improving quality);

- a management review of the system to ensure that customers are satisfied;
- a straightforward statement of how the quality system operates;
- a plan that indicates how the quality of the product is maintained;
- a clear understanding of customer requirements and an ability to meet them;
- an ability to convert customer requirements into concrete specifications;
- ensuring that people receive all the information they need and that this is updated;
- a procedure to ensure that suppliers match the quality required and deliver it on time (a very difficult area for education as schools largely cannot ensure the quality of the products – the students – who come to the school);
- careful checking and care for materials provided by customers (assessment and monitoring might be the order of the day, and teachers have a legal 'duty of care' for children respectively);
- careful tracking is kept of the product from the point of entry to the organization to the point of exit;
- work is carefully planned and controlled;
- checking the quality of the goods, from the point of receipt to the point of delivery, is continuous;
- appropriate and accurate checking instruments are used;
- review of checking procedures is undertaken;
- error prevention and correction are constant;
- avoiding the repetition of problems is a major priority;
- care is taken to look after the product whilst it remains in the company;
- monitoring of quality performance is undertaken;
- confirmation is addressed that the intentions of the quality system are being realized;
- adequate training for quality is provided;
- after-sales repair and servicing are addressed adequately;
- statistics are used to ensure quality control and to solve problems.

The Department of Trade and Industry (*ibid.*) notes that a company seeking the ISO 9000 kitemark will need to possess certain features that have their direct parallel in education (see Table 4.2).

The complex list of bullet points above makes much of assessment and ongoing monitoring, themselves central – and developing – features of education.[9] The previous conceptions of quality are addressed in ISO 9000, e.g. fitness for purpose, efficiency, conformance to requirements, meeting customers' requirements, zero defects, right first time, conformance to standards and procedures. With regard to education, Healy (1994) summarizes the attractions as including: 1) a delineation of key process variables – how a system is working in practice and what the elements of that system are; 2) identifying tasks and responsibilities in ensuring quality; 3) establishing and using data and monitoring systems; 4) identifying the central purposes of the school and the procedures needed to meet those (i.e. to establish criteria for fitness for purpose).

However, ISO 9000 requires, rather than develops, commitment

Table 4.2 The DTI requirements for quality in industry applied to schools

Industry	Schools
A written policy for quality	A policy on quality assurance
A manual for quality	Documentation of quality development foci, procedures and indicators
Instructions for work and procedures for quality	Documentation of quality assurance procedures
A recording system to deal with and document all failures in quality and customer complaints	An agreed procedure for handling complaints together with a register of all complaints received from outsiders/parents together with a record of action taken. Statistical data on students' assessment results and achievements (e.g. value-added data)
A nominated person who is responsible for the quality system	A senior member of the school with responsibility for all quality matters
Regular management reviews of the quality system and audits of its operation	Regular management reviews of the quality system and audits of its operation

(Wickens, 1995). Though the disciplined approach of the processes might be helpful one ought not to lose sight of where the processes are leading – the purposes and aims of education. At heart let us not overlook the fact that the thrust of ISO 9000 and BS 5750 is towards standardization and control through the implementation of a *system*. Whether that is a model one either wishes to or is able to espouse in education is highly questionable. Will BS 5750 and ISO 9000 guarantee excellence in the human services? No.

Investors in People

The Investors in People project, established in 1991 by the Confederation of British Industry, is much more prescriptive in its programme, contents and standards for quality development. The Investors in People kitemark is premised on four principles:

1) *making the commitment*: senior managers make a public commitment to develop all staff to achieve the objectives, mission, vision of the organization and a plan is drawn up for this to occur; needs are identified and communicated to all participants;
2) *target-setting*: training and development needs of all staff are reviewed and plans are made to meet them within the overall goals of the organization;
3) *action planning*: action is taken to train and develop staff throughout their employment;

4) *monitoring and evaluation*: these are undertaken to assess the impact of the investment in training and development, to assess achievements and to build on further development planning in order improve effectiveness.

One can detect here a commitment to involvement, participation and the continuous professional development of staff; that resonates loudly with education (Barker and Bell, 1994).

To gain the Investors in People award the institution must:

• develop, document and communicate its objectives and expectations;
• ensure that necessary staff development is provided in order to enable the objectives to be met;
• implement the plan for meeting the objectives;
• assess the impact of the programme and staff development on the performance of the institution;
• review this assessment in order to plan subsequent developments.

Schools seeking the Investors in People recognition need to have clear objectives: they must have school and individual development plans in place, together with documentation of training needs, job descriptions and appraisals (with associated reference to action planning). They must have established their success criteria and indicators of achievement (kinds of evidence). Schools must also provide evidence that these procedures are being successfully utilized.

The link between Investors in People for education and effective practices in business is clear. Both

• require learning and continuous improvement;
• are people focused;
• concern the delivery of the vision/mission of the organization;
• concern developing in the organization the capability (capacity and ability) for change and improvement;
• stress the significance of partnership, involvement, commitment and ownership;
• involve a view of quality management as total quality management and development.

The implication here is that the Investors in People programme will impact significantly on the schools' development planning and mission statement. An example of this is reported in Figure 4.12.

Two other awards are perhaps worth mentioning here. In the USA the Malcolm Baldridge National Quality Award (Kanji and Asher, 1993; Arcaro, 1995a) has several requisites that echo BS 5750, ISO 9000 and issues in TQM, for example: 1) quality as defined by the customer; 2) effective leadership; 3) evidence of a commitment to continuous improvement; 4) widespread participation; 5) rapid response; 6) quality of design and error prevention; 7) a long-term view; 8) using facts and data to inform effective management; 9) the development of partnerships; 10) responsibility to the public and community.

Secondly, the European Quality Award, which was developed by the European Foundation for Quality Management, resonates with the key

As part of its school development plans a secondary school is extending the notion of appraisal to the non-teaching staff of the school, to ensure that the overall aims of the school can be realized through the identification of development needs of everybody in the organization and through the extension of collegiality to all kinds of staff in the school. It further ensures that desirable consistent practices are developed and understood with all the staff involved. Job descriptions are reviewed as part of this process, together with an identification of further development needs to meet the changing requirements of the school and curricula. The target-setting and action planning that are part of the individual appraisal are in line with the overall direction and policies of the school, so that there is a degree of harmony between individual and organizational practices, needs and developments.

Such a step reinforces the four principles of the Investors in People award: commitment of all and for all for the good of the institution; target-setting for development and training needs; action planning – interventions and the implementation of policies and programmes in order to meet the targets that have been set; monitoring and evaluation in order to assess the effectiveness of the developments and to establish future needs and programmes.

Figure 4.12   An example of the Investors in People process

features of TQM (Mortiboys and Oakland, 1991), e.g. that it is through processes that the organization harnesses and releases the creativity and talents of its members towards improving performance. Processes and people are the twin enablers of quality. The emphasis in the European Foundation for Quality Management Award is on: 1) effective leadership; 2) a policy and strategy for continuous improvement; 3) effective management of people; 4) effective management of resources; 5) attention to the processes of continuous improvement; 6) customer, client and employee satisfaction; 7) impact on the community and society; 8) business results (and their relationship to projected results). The award also lays emphasis on the importance of mission, vision and declaration of values.

Strategies for developing quality in education

Problem-solving approaches

A major feature of quality development, particularly for TQM, is the significance it gives to problem-solving approaches, thereby rooting the development of quality in real issues and building in ownership and involvement. For example, Arcaro (1995b: 60) argues for the adoption of a seven-stage process of problem-solving for TQM:

1) defining the problem;
2) analysing the problem;
3) collecting data to inform analysis of the problem;
4) analysing the data collected;
5) developing a solution to the problem;
6) implementing the solution;
7) evaluating the implementation of the solution and its outcome.

Greenwood and Gaunt (1994) suggest a nine-stage process of quality development (see also Dean and Evans, 1994: 157; Smith, 1996):

1) presented symptoms;
2) team brainstorming of underlying problems;
3) establish important causes;
4) brainstorm possible solutions;
5) evaluate solutions;
6) choose one;
7) plan to implement;
8) implement;
9) monitor.

Staged approaches

Deming (1982) suggests a four-stage approach of plan, do, study, act:

- *plan*: here participants identify opportunities for improvement in the organization, process, product, etc. They document and audit the present situation and create a vision of the new, improved situation, in doing so defining the nature and scope of the improvements required;
- *do*: the plan for improvement is implemented, if possible on a small scale or a pilot;
- *study*: the results of the pilot are studied and feedback and discussion take place to discover what has been learned about improving the process;
- *act*: the process for improvement is adjusted in light of the preceding stage, the revised plan is operationalized and then implemented.

Juran suggests that an organization defines its goals for quality, devises plans for reaching those goals, and assigns responsibility and rewards for their achievement. Echoing Crosby (1984), Ishikawa (1985) sets out a ten-stage process of quality development:

- *step 1*: raise awareness of need for quality improvement, where it might be needed;
- *step 2*: set targets for continuous improvement;
- *step 3*: establish an appropriate structure in the organization in order to steer and push the process of quality improvement;
- *step 4*: provide training, staff development and support;
- *step 5*: ensure that problem-solving approaches are managed through the establishment of projects;
- *step 6*: report progress towards the achievement of the targets for improvement;
- *step 7*: celebrate success;
- *step 8*: communicate the progress, activities and outcomes;
- *step 9*: document successes, improvements and changes;
- *step 10*: institutionalize improvement through the establishment of an annual cycle of improvement.

Buchanan and Boddy (1992) report the quality development project of British Telecom that fuses a staged approach with a problem-solving approach. Stage one was a quality improvement proposal; stage two was an analysis of problems and planning to address them; stage three was the communication of the plan and its implications; stage four was the drawing up of detailed activities; stage five was the implementation (see also Kanji and Asher, 1993: 14; Wickens 1995: 198–204).

The message that comes through the writing of the quality gurus on the management of quality improvement is of the need to identify needs and to set targets and goals. In educational terms this is the Tylerian (1949) model of curriculum planning, where aims and objectives determine content and processes. This is an objectives-driven model of quality development. Mortiboys and Oakland (1991) summarize some key factors in developing effective total quality management that impact significantly on the management of change. They argue for the need to

- promote positive relations between customers and suppliers;
- manage the process of quality development effectively and efficiently;
- establish a cultural change towards a quality culture;
- ensure effective communication;
- show commitment from everybody, including the senior managers;
- use tools for quality assessment (see the discussion of Ishikawa above).

Bank (1992: 53–7) suggests a ten-step sequence for the delivery of quality:

- *stage 1*: devise a mission statement (focusing on the target rather than the process);
- *stage 2*: evaluate the extent to which the outputs (the products) match the mission statement;
- *stage 3*: identify and agree the target customers;
- *stage 4*: for each product identify the customers' requirements which must be met;
- *stage 5*: establish the production specifications of the product;
- *stage 6*: establish the operational procedures for producing the required product at the lowest cost;
- *stage 7*: devise the measures to assess the actual against the desired quality of the product;
- *stage 8*: identify problems caused by a shortfall or excess of the products;
- *stage 9*: establish a team whose purpose is to solve the problems of the gap between desired and actual products;
- *stage 10*: evaluate customers' satisfaction in terms of the customers' stated requirements.

In the process of quality development key importance is given in the industrial literature to mission statements and vision as being goal and direction-setters, and as establishing priorities (e.g. Belasco, 1990: 12). In educational terms Murgatroyd and Morgan (1993: 81) argue that vision statements should be challenging, clear, memorable, involving value-driven, visual, mobilizing guidelines, and linked to students' needs. Of course, whether a mission statement will ever galvanize people into action is a measure not solely of the properties of the statement but of a whole range of contextual factors in the organization and individuals. That may be ludicrously optimistic.

Training for quality development might be extensive, involving, for example (Greenwood and Gaunt, 1994) problem identification and problem solution, knowledge and expertise in using statistical technique and 'quality tools' (outlined earlier), skills of communication and teamwork, brainstorming and lateral thinking.

Burridge *et al.* (1993) set out ten principles for effective quality development in Birmingham LEA that address the significance of the management of teacher development and that resonate with the preceding discussions of quality and quality development in industry and business:

1) its impact on learning and teaching should be as direct as possible;
2) it should be built on actual school needs and built into its processes of development planning;
3) it should involve a collaborative and participative way of working on monitoring and evaluation;
4) it should be based on school responsibility and school ownership;
5) its effective introduction into a school entails appropriate training;
6) it flourishes best in a responsive organizational structure with an open management style and a whole-school commitment;
7) it requires the allocation of roles and responsibilities which are both clearly designated and carefully articulated;
8) it must be appropriately resourced – particularly with respect to the allocation of time to undertake monitoring and evaluation;
9) it should involve as wide a range of stakeholders as possible;
10) its methodology should be agreed and understood and should include:

   - building both formative and summative review mechanisms into development planning;
   - consulting widely on the selection and use of techniques of data gathering and methods of establishing criteria;
   - negotiating access to information;
   - generating both qualitative and quantitative information;
   - substantiating judgements made about worth or effectiveness by collecting evidence and setting this against open, agreed criteria;
   - interpreting evidence in context;
   - ensuring that the findings of monitoring and evaluation are used, that they inform decision-making and lead to action;
   - documenting the systems and procedures developed for monitoring and evaluation and subjecting them to internal review and external moderation and validation.

In a total quality school, Arcaro (1995a) suggests:

- there is room for improvement in every educational process;
- every improvement, however big or small, is worth while;
- small improvements add up to significant change;
- mistakes are treated as opportunities to improve.
- everyone shares responsibility for trying to prevent problems and for fixing problems when they do occur;
- everyone in the school or district is committed to continuous improvement.[10]

Burridge *et al.* (1993) provide six statements about quality development:

1) quality development is a process of development planning;
2) quality development centres on systematic monitoring and evaluation;
3) the type of evaluation central to quality development is self-evaluation;
4) the kind of self-evaluation central to quality development is supported self-evaluation;
5) supported self-evaluation serves three purposes summed up as: Proving (to fulfil accountability demands), Improving (to improve learning and teaching) and Learning (to support teachers as learners and schools as learning communities);
6) the core process of QD can be represented as a six-stage cycle of development planning comprising:

   • Where are we now?
   • Where do we want to get to?
   • What do we need to focus on?
   • How do we get there?
   • How are we doing?
   • How have we done?

Quality development, then, resides in several features (*ibid.*):

• the learning organization;
• success through people;
• excellent communication;
• preventing failure (see the comments earlier about quality assurance and control);
• concern for customers – internal and external;
• leadership and vision;
• participation;
• training a priority;
• mutual accountability;
• a quality 'mind-set';

In practical terms Burridge *et al.* (*ibid.*) identify a six-stage process of quality development in response to posed questions:

1) Where are we now (audit, stock-taking, establishing baseline, identifying strengths, weaknesses, needs)?
2) Where do we want to get to (vision building, mission statement, aims, objective setting)?
3) What do we need to focus on (establishing priorities for action – with criteria – target-setting, key issues)?
4) How do we get there (identifying tasks, roles and responsibilities, steps, timescale, action planning, staff training/support/resources/information)?
5) How are we doing (progress checks – monitoring, evaluation, action research, formative evaluation, process evaluation, reflection on progress, collaborative inquiry)?
6) How have we done (success criteria, success check, final review, summative evaluation, how far have we travelled from the baseline, what have we achieved, what has been the impact of our changes, do

we need to rethink our vision/aspirations)?

At the end of this sixth stage one returns to stage one for the next cycle of planning and implementation.

Such staged approaches are common to action research, which adopts a multistaged approach: needs analysis/problem identification → planned intervention → implementation → monitoring/evaluation → new needs analysis/problem identification (e.g. Kemmis and McTaggart, 1981; Hopkins, 1985). This echoes the work of Hargreaves and Hopkins (1991) who suggest that an action plan for change should identify preparations (initial tasks), routes (tasks) and destinations (targets). Action planning, argue Dalin *et al.* (1993), should indicate goals, a sequence of activities, tasks that can run in parallel, time frames, resources and decision points. An example of an approach to quality development is presented in Figure 4.13.

To be able to cope with quality development, Burridge *et al.* (1993) suggest that participants need the necessary understandings, attitudes, skills and procedures for quality development.

Understandings

- The extent of the research base and theoretical framework for QD;
- the value of an outsider acting as supporter and moderator;
- the way in which QD is related to national changes and the capacity to manage them;
- the role of development planning in achieving continuous improvement;
- the relationship between quality development, quality assurance and quality control;
- the potential of collective self-evaluation to improve learning and teaching.

Attitudes

- Being optimistic about the potential for improvement;
- a commitment to engage in a continuous process of reflection and analysis;
- taking collective responsibility for the task in hand;
- being constructively critical of practice and performance (of self and others);
- a willingness to give and receive support with colleagues;
- able to acknowledge the intrinsic educative value of evaluation;
- being open about what is actually happening in school;
- willingness to try out new ideas and learn from mistakes.

Skills

- Identifying success criteria;
- giving and receiving negative and positive feedback;
- breaking down a large goal into do-able targets and tasks;
- thinking clearly about the allocation of roles, responsibilities, tasks, times and resources;

A secondary school is seeking to address its quality assurance procedures. It has undertaken a review of its practices and its planning for quality proceeds in one respect as follows:

1. specification of the problem: one of the major issues the school faces is the sustainability of the consistency of its high standards of achievement over time, subjects and year groups for the high-ability students;
2. evidence of the problem: the senior management team (SMT) has noticed some variability across such student groups, evidenced by assessment and examination data on performance in a range of subjects, over time and over year groups. The SMT has convened a series of meetings with subject heads in which control charts (discussed earlier) have been studied to ascertain the levels of acceptability of variability;
3. management of the problem diagnosis: the SMT has agreed with departmental heads that each department will undertake: a) a diagnosis of the extent and causes of the problem; b) the devising of a development plan to address the issue;
4. causes of the problem: each department undertakes an Ishikawa cause-and-effect diagram (discussed earlier) and complements this with a rating exercise to ascertain the extent and the relative size of the causes of the problem (see the discussions earlier of the force-field and Pareto analyses). In the science department the staff decide that limited material resources, mixed-ability grouping in the Key Stage 3 teaching groups, perceived irrelevance and poor diagnosis of abilities are the four major causes, as they lead to unstimulating teaching, insufficient differentiation and matching, and an inability to 'stretch' the brightest students consistently, and problems of low motivation. In the mathematics department four major causes are identified as: i) mixed-ability grouping at Key Stage 3; ii) insufficient 'instruction' (direct teaching); iii) an overemphasis on students working through the work book in an attempt to cope with different abilities and stages reached; iv) the pressures from disruptive students. This type of analysis, when conducted across all departments, indicates that there are four major causes of the problem in the school in this respect: mixed-ability grouping at Key Stage 3; too little direct teaching; too few material resources; poor diagnosis of abilities and hence poorly matched work;
5. possible solutions: each department undertakes a brainstorming of possible solutions in respect of its own problems. The SMT, with heads of department, undertakes a brainstorming of possibilities at a whole-school level. The ideas are evaluated for their cost/benefit, ability to address the causes, practicability, effects on the target student population, potential gains and losses to targeted and non-targeted groups, importance (i.e. what would happen if the suggestions are not followed). In short a needs assessment is undertaken (see Chapter 2). Departmental solutions/interventions are identified that are in harmony with whole-school solutions, viz.: a) setting at Key Stage 3; b) increased whole-class instructional and interactive teaching; c) targeted resources for the high-ability students;
6. planning for implementation: school and departmental development plans are drawn up in conjunction with the SMT (in respect of resourcing issues). The development plans are to include: a) the aims, objectives and targets for the innovation/intervention/curriculum/students; b) an indication of how these

aims, objectives and targets will be met (the main features of the intervention); c) the time frames for introduction; d) the resource matters; e) an identification of tasks, responsibilities and the sequence of tasks; f) the criteria to be used in monitoring and judging the effectiveness of the implementation and stages of the intervention, together with the kinds of evidence required; g) the success criteria for judging the effectiveness of the intervention and achievement of the aims, objectives and targets, together with the kinds of evidence required; h) the staff development needs to implement the programme, together with a plan for how these will be met. The SMT plans how feedback sessions, ongoing monitoring and formative evaluations will be undertaken.

In this example the global issue of quality development has been segmented into manageable chunks to render it operational and manageable. The strategy is a combination of problem-solving and action research: clear steps are taken to build in involvement and ownership within an 'aligned organization' (Wickens, 1995) that is agreed at a whole-school level. Development planning proceeds in response to a needs assessment that tackles causes rather than symptoms and that addresses priorities (i.e. 'needs' is interpreted as the priority problems and the priority solutions). Clear monitoring and success criteria have been established, and the whole setting of the intervention is evidence based at all stages.

Figure 4.13   Quality development in a secondary school

- teamwork, team-building, team maintenance, team membership, team leadership;
- collecting information, analysing and interpreting it, using it to make decisions;
- designing instruments for gathering data.

Procedures

- Involving the whole community in development planning;
- building monitoring and evaluation into routine school life;
- making time to decide on priorities for change and development;
- creating space for action research during the working day;
- establishing systems for collecting information, for making sense of it, for passing it on and for using it to influence decisions.

This reinforces the need that was emphasized by the 'quality gurus' for training, staff development and support.

The preceding discussion sets a vast agenda for educational change for improving quality. This has been organized into three areas: 1) addressing definitions of quality; 2) addressing people and institutional/organizational issues; 3) addressing quality development issues. One cannot under-estimate the current significance of the quality issue in education. It requires schools and educational institutions to change, sometimes drastically, and indicates what those changes might be and how they might be managed and implemented. What is very clear in the discussions of quality is the significant impact of the features of Japanese companies and their management that were discussed in the previous chapter, and how the changes needed for quality development embody the features and processes of change that were discussed in Chapter 2. The whole is a seamless web.

Notes

1.   Deming, 1982; Peters and Waterman, 1982; Crosby, 1980; 1984; Ball, 1985; Ishikawa, 1976; 1985; Shingo, 1986; Taguchi, 1986; Møller, 1988; Peters, 1987; Feigenbaum, 1991; Juran, 1988; 1993; Department of Trade and Industry, 1994a; Finch, 1994; Green, 1994; Raisbeck, 1994; Vroejenstijn, 1995.

2.   The high-reliability organization matches very closely the excellent business organizations and industries that were identified by the study of leading companies undertaken by Peters and Waterman (1982). These characteristics/prescriptions are: (i) a bias for action; (ii) keeping close to the customer; (iii) developing autonomy; (iv) developing productivity through people; (v) using hands-on, value-driven management; (vi) sticking to the knitting (reducing the tasks to those that are necessary and those that the company does well); (vii) simple forms and lean staff; (viii) simultaneous loose–tight properties (having a few non-negotiable rules and principles within which there is room for much personal autonomy). High-reliability organizations exhibit strongly features (1), (4), (6), (7) and (8).

3.   An example of this is the A-Level Information Systems (ALIS) and the Year 11 Information Systems (YELLIS) project at the University of Durham.

4.   ISO 9000 breaks down into four additional subelements (ISO 9001–9004), the operations required to produce the outcome so that each subelement can be measured.

5.   Galbraith and Lawler (1993) argue for the need to avoid the acceptance of mediocrity as mistakes will be compounded over time.

6.   For a discussion of the failure of the zero defects movement in the USA see Ishikawa (1985: 151).

7.   Bank (1992) suggests that between 20 per cent and 30 per cent of a company's revenue is lost on the costs of quality, and Mortiboys and Oakland (1991) suggest that between 15 and 30 per cent of a company's average sales revenues is lost to the costs of quality, rising to up to 40 per cent in service organizations, with these costs being caused, they aver, by weak management.

8.   Bank (1992) charts the costs of the disaster of the space shuttle Challenger, where lives were lost, opportunities were lost, the costs of prevention and appraisal were huge, the loss of image was immeasurable, and the costs of recovery and correction were huge.

9.   Lieberman, 1990; Buxbaum, 1993; Street and Fernie, 1993; Askey and Dale, 1994; Corrigan, 1994; Endrijonas, 1994; Healy, 1994; Bettes, 1995, Department of Trade and Industry, 1995; McLachlan, 1996; Morrison, 1997a; West-Burnham, 1997. ISO 9000 has several claimed attractions, many of which echo those of BS 5750 and hence will not be rehearsed here, e.g. it: ensures that management take quality seriously and themselves take

responsibility for quality; ensures consistency; eliminates waste, reworking and the costs of quality; establishes a disciplined approach to quality and internal audit; facilitates the supply of higher-quality goods to customers; enables participants to know what is required, what to do and what their responsibilities are; enables progress to take place in manageable steps, with 'chocks' or 'ratchets' to prevent backsliding; enables an organization to examine its business and improve its systems, its methods and procedures; involves and motivate staff in the quest for improved performance; promotes continuous improvements; enables a company to do things right first time; identifies and defines key roles and responsibilities; identifies accountability and authority, and promotes leadership; ensures that orders are delivered consistently and on time; exposes faults in the product or service and develops systems to investigate, improve, rectify these rapidly and prevent their recurrence; documents customer complaints and failures in the product or service; sends clear messages to customers about the concern for quality; improves communication; certifies the product or service, thereby furthering customer confidence; provides a system for identifying and documenting staff training needs; promotes positive relationships and partnerships with suppliers; provides a basis for ongoing development; is applicable to small, medium and large organizations; provides a value-for-money service; makes for responsiveness to the customer and the community; improves recording systems; fosters the development of an ethos of quality; creates codes of conduct and a complete package; pools experience for mutual benefit and improvement.

Criticisms of ISO 9000 are that it: is too expensive to install, implement and administer; fails to address the needs of small businesses; is heavily biased towards manufacturing companies; is an irrelevance; still enables a company to produce rubbish; is a massive paper trail, standards are paper driven; only concerns conformity to standards, being silent on the desirability of those standards, i.e. it neglects the significance of 'vision' and constancy of purpose; is too formalized and impersonal; has insufficient focus on the customer; documents failure rather than improving quality; can be undesirably coercive (failing to address Deming's criterion of 'driving out fear'); requires total involvement if it is to meet the claims that are made for it – which is unrealistic; neglects comment on the significance of teamwork and leadership; does not make clear how barriers between groups and tasks will be eliminated; is something to which many employees might be resistant; only concerns standardized, uniform procedures and products, i.e. it misconceives the nature and purposes of education and the significance of important and desirable variability; cannot guarantee the resources (e.g. the students); might lift the 'trailing edge' companies though bureaucratic procedures, but suppress excellence; ties down processes rather than opening them up; understates the significance of continuous improvement. West-Burnham (1997) argues that ISO 9000 does not fully meet the demands of TQM. One should, therefore, perhaps exercise considerable caution and circumspection before deciding to opt into the ISO 9000 award.

10.   Hopkins (1994) argues for the need to address ten principles in

developing quality for effective schools: 1) the main focus should be on teaching and learning in classrooms; 2) ongoing staff development is vital; 3) leadership should empower everyone to achieve individual and institutional goals; 4) all members of the school should build and share the visions and purposes of the school; 5) the school's priorities should reflect those purposes and vision; 6) concrete planning should address the priorities; 7) the substance of staff development should be teaching skills as well as subject knowledge; 8) collaboration is essential for staff development; 9) monitoring and reflection are integral to the process; 10) policy implementation must be sensitive to contextual and professional needs.

Part II
Microcontexts of Change

5

Individual motivations for and against change

Introduction

The previous chapters have all signalled the fact that effective change in many respects hinges on the people in the organization, their involvement and development (Harvey-Jones, 1988: 249). This entails taking seriously the fact that most individuals have some considerable personal and emotional investment in an organization. Change is inescapably and intensely personal, because it requires people to do something different, to think something different and to feel something different (Duck, 1993: 109).

The recent spectacular growth of workplace counselling (e.g. Carroll, 1996; Carroll and Walton, 1997) attests to the significance of this aspect of managing change (discussed later). As Duck (1993: 113) argues, it is not simply whether people feel positive or negative about a change but how they handle this. The company has a responsibility to manage its people appropriately and effectively in change. The advocacy of empowerment of employees means involvement and support for people in change rather than abandonment.

People react to and cope with change in a variety of ways, from complete rejection to complete acceptance. Senge (1990: 219–20) establishes a continuum for this, which moves from apathy (no enthusiasm or energy) to non-compliance (not being forced into change), grudging compliance (being forced to change against one's will), formal compliance (doing the basic minimum in the change), genuine compliance (doing everything required but no more – staying within the letter of the law) and enrolment (doing whatever is required within the spirit of the law) to commitment (complete involvement to make it work).

Judson (1991) suggests a similar continuum of reactions to change, including: 1) acceptance (being enthusiastic and co-operative, through acceptance under pressure to acceptance through resignation); 2) indifference (apathy, loss of interest in work, doing the minimum to get by); 3) passive resistance (doing as little as possible without 'breaking the rules'); 4) active resistance (a 'go-slow' or periods of absence); 5) sabotage. This echoes Harris (1987) who identifies five responses to change: antagonistic, no commitment, the feeling of 'let it happen', the feeling of 'help it to happen' and the commitment to 'make it happen', i.e. from antagonism, through indifference to compliance and on to positive commitment.

People's reactions to change vary in accordance with their perceptions of the change – whether they find it attractive, revolutionary – and whether they themselves are comfortable with change. Some people are more naturally committed to change (the innovators and extended professionals – Hoyle, 1975); others are more traditionalist; others do not want anything to do with change (the abdicators). Some – if not all (Harvey-Jones, 1988: 107–8) – fear change, others wish for it, others are cautious about whether it is possible, others struggle to ensure that it works.

Central to the discussions of change is the analysis of the personal motivation for change and how personal motivation can be developed. People must be motivated to change, to face novelty, to cope with the disequilibrium that change brings. People's motivation to change is often a function of whether they regard the change as an improvement; if they do not then some resistance can be anticipated. This chapter considers resistances to change and reports from the business literature on how motivation for change can be fostered and motivation to resist change can be reduced.

Resistance to change

Resistance is natural and perhaps unavoidable. Dalin (1978) and Dalin *et al.* (1993) argue that there are four significant barriers to change:

1) value barriers, where the proposed change challenges one's values system or if one does not agree with the proposed values;
2) power barriers, where people may accept an innovation if it brings them greater power, or they may resist it if it diminishes their power;
3) psychological barriers, where people resist the challenge to security, confidence, emotional well-being and homeostasis that change brings;
4) practical barriers, where people will resist change if it threatens to deskill them, if the investment in reskilling is too daunting, or if resources (e.g. materials, people, time, money, space, administrative support, expertise) are insufficient to support the change.

The first three, if not all four, of these factors are devolved on personal factors. Leigh (1988) suggests four sources of resistance: 1) cultural factors in the organization; 2) social factors; 3) organizational factors; 4) psychological factors. In the field of business Bowman and Asch (1987: 233–4) argue that people will resist change for fear of inadequacy and admission of weaknesses and for fear of loss of present status and current job satisfaction.[1] Katzenbach and Smith (1993a) suggest that resistance to change can stem from lack of conviction (the value barrier) and personal risk and discomfort (the psychological barrier). With regard to the latter, the theory of cognitive dissonance argues that if a change is proposed that is very dissonant with the attitudes, practices and beliefs of those affected, then resistance should be expected unless those affected are prepared to change their attitudes (Burnes, 1996: 320). Working on change, then, is not solely working on the content of the change, nor solely on the organization of the change, but also on the personal dimensions of the change.

There can be several reasons for rejection of a change proposal (Clarke, 1994). For example rejection might be the result of ignorance (insufficient information about the change); if this is the case then overcoming rejection might be achieved by the fuller provision and dissemination of information. Rejection might be the result of doubt (people are unsure of the value of the change); if this is the case then the case for the change needs to be made more compelling – it needs to be argued. Rejection might be the result of situational factors (what is being proposed is not seen as an improvement on existing practice); if this is the case then clearly motivation will have to be increased through the provision of support for the change. Rejection might be the result of personal concerns – anxiety, alienation, stress, etc.; if this is the case then personal and psychological support should be forthcoming. Rejection might be the result of previous experience – 'we've tried this before and it didn't work'; if this is the case then the possible causes of failure or the perception of failure need to be examined and the new case made for the change.[2] An example of the usefulness of identifying the types of barriers to change is given in Figure 5.1.

Reducing resistance is a key factor, therefore, in the successful management of change. Watson (1966) recognizes this and suggests that resistance is less if

- ownership of change is high (i.e. the change is devised by participants rather than outsiders);
- the project has clear and complete support from senior managers;
- participants see the change as reducing and streamlining – rather than increasing – their current tasks;
- the project is consonant with the values and ideas of participants;
- the programme promises new and interesting experiences for the participants;
- participants feel that their security and autonomy are safe;
- participants have been party to problem diagnosis and agree the priorities;
- the project is agreed by the groups concerned;
- objections are taken seriously and argued out in full;
- care is taken to avoid misunderstandings and misinterpretations, through the provision of feedback, clarification and discussion;
- participants experience mutual support, trust and confidence;
- the project is open to review, revision and modification.

Markus (1983: 430–4) suggests that there are four main types of resistance:

A secondary school has recently appointed a headteacher. She has decided to move towards a 'target-orientated' curriculum in which key targets for students' achievements at ages 14, 16 and 18 have been set within each subject. She has required faculty heads to submit plans for such a curriculum by the end of a half-term, including: 1) a delineation of the targets to be reached in each subject; 2) a development plan from each subject department, indicating how it intends to meet the targets; 3) a time frame for planning, introduction, monitoring and review; 4) an indication of resources needed by each department.

Within a fortnight the project encounters difficulties: 1) there are widespread complaints about insufficient information about the innovation; 2) department heads object to management by diktat both by the headteacher and faculty heads; 3) time frames effectively prohibit discussion, development and team planning; 4) objections are received both to the objectives-driven nature of the proposed innovation and to the requirement to set targets; 5) there is a widespread view that the exercise will not improve standards of achievement in practice; 6) the backwash effect of teaching to targets is generally seen as deleterious to a broad, motivating, pedagogically creative curriculum; 7) staff see little incentive for the change and they feel ill-equipped to handle the new expertise required. To address these matters the headteacher brings in an 'outside expert' to explain the rationale and to answer concerns voiced. This only serves to heighten the problem as it is generally viewed as 8) the headteacher avoiding taking responsibility and effective leadership and 'people management' herself. The headteacher is viewed as 9) overloading staff with too many innovations too quickly, and this is exacerbated by the fact that many of them are structural – affecting deep-seated practices in the school.

The example indicates the four barriers from Dalin *et al.* (1978; 1993): value barriers (staff disagree with the rationale and principles – concerns (4) and (6)); power barriers (staff object to the misuse of power and the upset of power – concerns (2) and (8)) psychological barriers (staff feel ill-equipped to handle the change, are unconvinced as to its practical efficacy, are unmotivated and feel that they are simply being pressured into change, over-riding their personal concerns and personal, professional judgements – items (5) and (7)); practical barriers (staff have insufficient information, inadequate time, are suffering from innovation fatigue and see the headteacher as risking 'bandwagoning' – concerns (1), (3) and (9)).

Being able to crystallize the *type* of barrier enables the appropriate type or approach to its solution to be identified, dealing with real causes rather than symptoms (see Chapter 4 on the Ishikawa diagram). A more effective strategy might have been to have introduced the innovation at a staff meeting for which briefing papers had been circulated previously, to have taken questions and concerns, to have identified how the innovation builds on the best of existing practice, to have involved departmental heads much earlier in the discussions, giving them autonomy to set time frames, priorities and practices they had agreed within their departments, to have allowed time for problems and concerns to be discussed and 'argued out', to have identified development needs and costings, to have agreement between all parties and levels of the organization (e.g. senior management, faculty heads, department heads, subject teachers) about how each department would proceed, and to have located another innovation within a context of other ongoing innovations. The over-riding concern here would be to elevate the personal, interpersonal and collegial aspects of the innovation into a much more complete management strategy than the 'steamroller' effect the headteacher has adopted. Staff need to be persuaded that the innovation is worth undertaking and they need to be motivated to change; there need to be incentives.

Figure 5.1   Identifying barriers to change

people focused, system focused, organization focused and politics focused. He argues that if resistance is encountered in the first two of these (people and systems) then solutions might be relatively straightforward, for example: improved training, better staff; improved designs and designers. If resistances in the latter two (organization and politics) are encountered, then these are much more difficult to solve (discussed in Chapter 6). Buchanan and Boddy (1992) suggest that people will be most likely to resist changes that affect adversely their power, influence, responsibility, autonomy and, indeed, access to information. They argue that to handle change effectively necessitates taking careful account of minimizing loss of power and influence; offering new opportunities; offering an attractive trade-off for potential losers; undermining or marginalizing the potential power of those who will lose in the change – perhaps rather a manipulative set of strategies!

Judson (1991) argues that change affects behaviour, psychological states and social relations, and these are devolved on predispositions and feelings about change; feelings of security and insecurity; potential for conflicts between existing and proposed norms; the degree of trust in colleagues, senior managers and unions; recent events; the perceived degree of threat; particular anxieties about aspects of the change; concerns about how the change will be implemented. Within these he suggests that there are several factors that tend to correlate with feelings of resistance. Resistance is higher and more intense the higher are

- people's predispositions towards apprehension and fear;
- conflicts between existing and proposed values and beliefs;
- the number and significance of apprehensions there are about how one is affected by the change;
- the number and significance of recent events that might bring stress and anxiety about the change;
- the number and significance of perceived threats to basic needs;
- the threats to self-esteem.

Conversely, resistance is lower and less intense the greater are

- feelings of security;
- the extent of trust in the management, colleagues and unions;
- the number and significance of recent events that might promote positive feelings about proposed changes;
- the number of positive expectations about the change that are confirmed;
- the possibilities for enhancement of self-esteem.

Judson's analysis suggests some critical dimensions of resistance, i.e. those factors which will maximize or minimize resistance (*ibid.*: 66–70), which might be fears or anticipations. For example:

- potential economic losses and gains;
- personal security and insecurity;
- personal convenience and inconvenience;
- job satisfaction and dissatisfaction;

- interpersonal relationships – improved or worsened;
- satisfaction and dissatisfaction with the management of the change;
- change to beliefs and values.

To address these factors, Judson suggests several techniques that can be used by managers of change: compulsion, persuasion, offering security and reassurance, demonstrating empathy and understanding, managers becoming personally involved, being open to criticism of the change and being prepared to make modifications.

Plant (1987: 18) identifies the most frequent sources of resistance:

- fear of the unknown
- lack of information
- misinformation
- historical factors
- threat to core skills and competence
- threats to status
- threat to power base
- no perceived benefits
- low-trust organizational climate
- poor relationships
- fear of failure
- fear of looking stupid
- reluctance to experiment
- custom bound
- reluctance to let go
- strong peer group norms.

Possible ways of addressing resistance in educational change are outlined in Table 5.1. There are certain key features that recur from Table 5.1:

- communication;
- involvement and ownership;
- prevention of problems;
- clarity at all times and in all things;
- clear focus;
- encouraging success;
- looking at causes of problems and difficulties;
- providing evidence of benefits;
- using outsiders where appropriate;
- using evaluation and self-evaluation;
- involving and addressing personal responses;
- being sensitive to people;
- identifying the kinds of threat/problem posed;
- working on and with people's perceptions;
- building trust;
- looking at cultural factors in the organization;
- providing support (including personal support);
- addressing issues of timing;
- playing to people's strengths;
- offer compensation;
- undertaking a task analysis.

Table 5.1 Addressing resistances to educational change

Source of resistance	Ways of addressing resistance
Perceived loss of status and control	Ensuring early involvement; much consultation; providing assurance; empowering participants and sharing decision-making; identifying facilitating factors and worries and addressing them; extensive communication; compensation; setting new goals; addressing self-esteem
Fear of the unknown	Providing extensive information and communication; giving examples of where it has worked; benchmarking; identifying the exact concerns; clarifying aims; providing support
Lack of clarity of purpose	Visible leadership and commitment from senior managers,[3] ensuring early involvement of staff; extensive communication; having clear and achievable objectives; creating a clear vision (and using lay terminology)
Uncertainty and ambiguity	Extensive communication and sharing of information; providing evidence of past successes of this innovation; clear roles and responsibilities; identify exactly of what people are uncertain; bringing in an 'expert'; providing support as people 'live through it'
Feelings of vulnerability	Ensuring and communicating appropriate resource commitment, support and empathy; encouraging staff; reassurance; identify exactly why people feel vulnerable; teamwork; praising past successes; create win–win situations; 'buddying' and mentoring
Lack of clarity on the benefits of the change	The provision of information; 'talking it out'; the presentation of logical and compelling benefits; finding benefits and making them personal; sharing the benefits; making the case clear; cost-benefit analysis; give examples of where the change has worked (with visits); compensation; evaluation by the senior management team
Reluctance to let go of the present	Establishing the need for change (i.e. circumstances have changed); providing support for new practices; undertake 'rites of passage' to mark the end of an era; offering counselling upon request (discussed below); encouraging early retirements; changing the organizational culture (see Chapter 6); convincing people that the change is an improvement and providing evidence of this; keeping what is best of existing practice; providing opportunities for staff to see new practices elsewhere; providing training; teamwork; being realistic in the new demands; encouraging constructive criticism
Threats to expertise and established skills	Providing appropriate training; raising awareness that many new skills build on existing skills; providing opportunities for staff to use existing skills in new situations; moving people around; reskilling; visiting sites where the innovation is working elsewhere; shadowing; building self-esteem

The feeling of having surprises sprung	Careful timing; advance notice of change together with the provision of adequate information about the change; being proactive; identifying people's agendas; involvement; communication and progress reports
Fear of failure and threats to self-esteem	Providing adequate training and support; communicating that blame is off the agenda and communicating this in advance; identify areas of vulnerability; involvement; identify why people feel threatened; clarification that the change builds on existing expertise
Admission that the present situation is unsatisfactory	Making it clear that situations were perfectly acceptable when the existing practices were introduced and in operation but that circumstances and requirements have changed; recognize and accept that the situation is unsatisfactory; use unfreezing strategies; recognize the consequences of not moving; generate possible solutions and means solving problems; conducting an audit
Concern about ability to cope	Support, trust, positive feedback and communicating confidence in participants; reskilling; mentoring; removing other demands; providing learning time/opportunity/resources
Fear of loss of control	Ensuring a realignment of control, i.e. providing new areas of control; communicating how autonomy and control will be addressed in the changed situation; being perceptive to what people are thinking and feeling ('nipping problems in the bud'); shared ownership of the project; praise, support and confidence building; devolving clearly defined roles and tasks that suit people's strengths; teams and paired work; involvement; shared planning of the process of change; identify possible areas of loss of control; be proactive; provide opportunities for people to voice concerns and fears in a non-threatening environment; engage people in discussing the reasons for the change; pointing out the benefits of the change
Stress	Stress management and reduction (discussed below); time management and self-management; enabling people to be more assertive and to avoid being 'put on'; having a sense of humour; keeping matters in proportion; trying to keep tasks manageable; be aware of the 'critical point' – where stress ceases to be positive; giving praise and valuing people; ensuring hospitality at meetings; avoiding duplication of work; keeping meetings to a minimum; communicating extensively; ensuring enough people are doing necessary tasks
Increased workload	Avoiding overload; maintaining some existing and familiar practices and routines; recognizing and rewarding extra efforts made; teamwork and a division of labour; divide up tasks and delegate; use technology; compensation; review the necessity of existing practices; time management; be selective on tasks; using expertise from within and outside the institution; extensive communication to reduce paucity of information; being sensitive to others' roles in the organization; providing incentives (discussed below); trying to move from reduction of dissatisfaction to positive motivation and rewards

The use of pressure and force to induce and sustain change has long been recognized as perhaps unattractive but necessary in organizations (i.e. the use of power-coercive strategies). Kanji and Asher (1993: 35) suggest that force for change can come in various forms: top-down pressure, peer pressure, bottom-up pressure, pressure from customers, pressure from competitors, data on performance (the quality measurement tools discussed in the previous chapter) and the setting of required targets.

Of course, one has to be extremely cautious about using the tactic of force for, as Senge (1990: 58) notes, the harder one pushes, the harder the system pushes back. Rather, Senge argues (*ibid*.: 95), it is a much more conciliatory and productive stance to adopt the view that, rather than pushing growth, it is more fruitful to remove the factors that are impeding it. Similarly Everard and Morris (1990) argue that it is much more productive to seek the virtuous circle of a win/win situation than the vicious, zero sum circle of a win/lose situation (I win but you lose, or you win if I lose) because win/lose situations very frequently become lose/lose situations – everyone and everything loses.

The danger of using the tactics of force is well exposed by Kanter (1983). She argues that change will often be seen as a threat when it is done imposed or done *to* employees, regardless of whether they like it or not. Rather, she suggests, change is regarded much more favourably if it is done *by* and with employees, thereby building in involvement and making it an opportunity rather than a threat, cemented if rewards are attached to it.

Strebel (1996) argues that employers should put themselves in the shoes of the employees if they want to understand why change might be resisted, as this will enable them to manage perceptions – a central issue in managing change. He suggests (*ibid*.: 88) that employers take very seriously the question 'are the rewards worth it?' for employees.[4] Employers, too, need to be prepared to change (Hunt and Carter, 1995: 136).

What one can see in the business literature is not only a range of degrees of resistance but also a range of strategies for overcoming them. The earlier discussion identified a continuum of resistance (e.g. from rejection to commitment); these suggest a continuum of strategies for overcoming resistance (Macmillan, 1978; Thompson, 1993) that can be arranged in order from overt coercion to support, facilitation and empowerment: 1) explicit and implicit coercion; 2) obligation; 3) manipulation and co-optation; 4) inducement; 5) negotiation and agreement; 6) facilitation and support; participation and involvement; 7) communication and education.

Motivation, incentives and facilitating factors

Robertson *et al.* (1992: 137) argue that effective performance is the product of ability, training and motivation. If incentives are to be used as a way of motivating staff for change and for overcoming resistance then the nature of the incentive is important (O'Brien and Jones, 1995). Wickens (1995: 115–16) makes the telling point that reward systems must motivate *everybody*, rather than the select few, as to reward a few is to give out the message that some people are more valuable than others (see also Harvey-Jones, 1988: 57). One does not receive a first-class service from people whom one treats as second-class citizens (Wickens, 1995).[5]

The International Job Survey Research Ltd (1992) identified six major factors in securing employee satisfaction: 1) job security and stability; 2) safe working conditions; 3) satisfactory working conditions; 4) the involvement of employees; 5) the style of management adopted; 6) staff development. Developing staff is a key motivational feature. Turner and Lawrence (1965) suggested that the task had to provide opportunities for people to exercise variety, autonomy, knowledge and skill, and responsibility. Further, Robertson *et al.* (1992: 153) suggest that a motivating environment has to be present, which includes the need for employees to

- know how much effort is needed to perform appropriately;
- have competence and confidence in their abilities;
- have concrete and specific performance goals;
- have regular feedback;
- have good performance acknowledged;
- be part of a fair incentive scheme;
- have their psychological and physical needs met;
- be involved in negotiating changes to their work;
- have variety, clarity, significance, autonomy and opportunities for development in their work.

Carnall (1995) argues that the incentive and motivation structures and systems one adopts depend to some extend on the premises and beliefs one has of people's nature. For example, the view of people as rational economic (*ibid.*: 95) argues that employees are primarily motivated to change by financial incentives. The view of people as essentially social beings (*ibid.*: 96) argues that they are motivated strongly by social needs and the need to realize their own identities through interpersonal relationships (often because the very work processes themselves have become dehumanized, meaning destroying and alienating). The corollary of this view is that peer pressure can exert a more profound influence than management control; managers need to look at people's social needs and their need for acceptance.

People are variable, unique and have differing needs and motivations; their needs vary in content, priority and importance, and interact with each other to produce new needs. Needs and motivations change over time and context, and at any one moment there will be a combination of motivations and needs at work – rejecting the essentially simplistic, unifactorial view of people in the rational-economic, social and self-actualizing perspectives. Evenden and Anderson (1992: 208) argue that people will be motivated by a sense of belonging to the organization, by excitement at the prospect of change and by their confidence in the management of change.

Wickens (1995: 66), echoing Maslow's hierarchy of needs and Crosby's view of needs changing over time (see Chapter 4), argues powerfully that motivations change over time, for example once a person has a secure job then the motivation for security is replaced by the need for involvement and ownership (e.g. in identifying problems, making recommendations, implementing plans to solve problems), and thence onwards to be able to exercise responsibility and autonomy. Ultimately, if one adopts Maslow's hierarchy, it might be the case that the motivation is for self-actualization.[6]

The view of people as essentially self-actualizing, akin to McGregor's Theory Y, argues that people are inherently self-motivated and self-motivating and that they do not need extrinsic incentives and rewards. They are not necessarily resistant to the goals of the organization and, given the opportunity to exercise autonomy, appropriate responsibility and self-development, will work happily towards the achievement of the organization's goals – a win/win situation in which the individual and the organization both benefit.

Herzberg's 'two factor' theory (1968) suggests that it is intrinsic factors that give satisfaction to employees (e.g. meaningfulness, interest of the job, challenge, responsibility, achievement, recognition, personal and career development) and that these are higher-order qualities (similar in some respects, therefore, to Maslow's hierarchy). On the other hand it is extrinsic factors (e.g. pay, administration, company policy, status, supervision, relationship with peers, accountability, job security, working conditions and surveillance) – 'hygiene factors' (so named because, as with the human body, hygiene matters have to be addressed before other aspects of physical fitness can be developed) – that give rise to dissatisfaction and that reside in lower-order qualities. The gratification of lower-order needs does not, in itself, produce satisfaction, it simply removes dissatisfaction. Further, the satisfaction of the hygiene factors is only short term whereas the satisfaction of the higher-order motivators lasts longer.[7]

The ramifications of Herzberg's work are important, for they suggest that if we want to stimulate motivation it is important to address the characteristics of the job itself and to ensure that it is satisfying higher-order motivations. It is not enough simply to provide extrinsic rewards for employees; job satisfaction begins when basic hygiene factors are correct. These are important messages for motivation.

Bartlett and Ghoshal (1995: 136) suggest that people naturally want to learn and that they are both satisfied and motivated to learn further and participate when they do learn. The importance of motivation through involvement and personal development has not been lost on industry.[8] Peters (1987) argues that there is no limit to the possible achievements and accomplishments of the average person if he or she is completely involved in the organization.

One of the keys, then, to motivation, appears to be empowerment; as Kanter (1983) argues, it is powerlessness which corrupts, not power. This resonates with Adair's reporting (1987: 92) of the manager who said that he never had so much authority as when he began to give it away! Not only is building commitment important for organizational successes (indeed Wickens (1995: 117) argues that absence from work is due more to lack of commitment than to sickness) but also genuine empowerment is a massive motivator. Peters (1987: 283–6) advocates the development of empowerment through widespread involvement in decision-making, listening, celebrating, recognizing achievement, training and developing people, providing incentive pay for everybody, providing security of employment, and eliminating humiliating and unsatisfactory working conditions and management styles. He argues (*ibid.*: 480) that, at heart, trust is the 'glue' that binds the company together, keeping it stable, and this strengthens the company in its constant change and experimentation. Wickens (1995: 188) adds to this the importance of trying to avoid personal criticism if someone makes a mistake (see below: change and conflict management).

Wickens (*ibid.*: 29–30) summarizes a range of factors that both identify resistance and suggest how they might be tackled:

- people and groups that receive special attention respond positively to it (the Hawthorne effect);
- once lower-order needs have been met higher-order needs take a higher profile;
- management needs to make optimum use of individuals' talents;
- people's goals differ and their response to change varies according to the degree to which they see their effort as worth while;
- if people are not trusted they will behave as though they are not trusted;
- if people are involved in goal-setting they will be more likely to be committed to them;
- pay and conditions of work have to be right but, on their own, will not bring job satisfaction;
- physical, emotional and mental satisfaction at work is crucial;
- empowering everyone frees senior staff to undertake other tasks;
- recognizing and celebrating achievement are essential;
- the social dimension of work (both formal and informal groups) is highly significant;
- employees will be more satisfied if they are engaged in tasks they see as important;
- change which is imposed from outside almost guarantees resistance.

Two 'theories' which from business can illuminate the notion of resistance and ways of overcoming it – expectancy theory and exchange theory. Expectancy theory (discussed in Chapter 3) argues that people will involve themselves in change if they expect it to be worth while and to lead to personal benefits; the higher the perceived benefits are the greater will be their willingness to be involved in the projects of change. Lawler (1991) cites these perceived benefits as including: financial benefits, job security, promotion opportunities, training and development opportunities, public recognition, feelings of accomplishment and more interesting work.[9] The importance of communication, involvement and incentives in order to achieve motivation is stressed in expectancy theory.

Harvey-Jones (1988) suggests the need to address: 1) how motivation will be sustained in a flatter organization which minimizes promotion; 2) how the expectations of new blood in the organization can be met; 3) how horizontal career development can be created and managed; 4) how individual responsibility for self-management of career development can be facilitated; 5) how people are advanced in the organization and whether the appropriate role models are promoted. The issue here is that career development, as a powerful incentive and motivational strategy, needs to be planned and managed. Together incentives, motivation, rewards and opportunities for development provide an important context for expectancy theory.[10]

A more politicized – or micropoliticized – view of motivation derives from exchange theory, or social exchange theory (Blau, 1964; Homans, 1971). Here an individual will undertake an activity or change if something is offered in return ('give and take'). It is akin to bartering or bargaining; I have something you want; you have something I want. The basis of exchange theory is obligation, often unspecified obligation (Carnall, 1982), creating a sense of responsibility and mutual obligation, and premised, to some extent, on trust or confidence in both parties that obligations will be honoured.[11]

Exchange theory offers a powerful explanation of the micropolitics of an organization (see also Charan, 1996: 19). In the field of education the significance of micropolitics cannot be overstated. Hoyle (1986: 125–49) argues that micropolitics comprises several elements: *interests* (professional as well as personal, e.g. status, promotion, working conditions, empire building, deskilling, upsetting power bases), *interest sets* (formal and informal cliques, cabals and coalitions), *strategies* (e.g. bargaining, dividing and ruling, co-optation, displacement, controlling information, controlling meetings – 'rigging' agendas, 'losing' recommendations, 'nobbling' members, invoking outside bodies, 'interpreting' consensus, 'massaging' minutes) and *power* (influence). In the UK Bowe's *et al.'s* (1992) work suggest that the introduction of the National Curriculum and local management of schools has led to an increase in the significance of micropolitics as departments are put in a state of competition with each other for scarce resources.

Hoyle (1986) suggests that micropolitics are more concerned with interests rather than goals, influence rather than authority, coalitions rather than departments, groups rather than the whole institution and strategies rather than procedures. Hoyle's account adopts a Foucauldian, postmodernist tone in suggesting that a significant theoretical underpinning of micropolitics is exchange theory, i.e. there is no single locus of power. For example, whilst headteachers have many properties to exchange, influencing, for example, material resources, promotion, esteem, autonomy, application of rules, teachers, too, have valuables that can be exchanged, for example, esteem and support for the headteacher, opinion leadership, conformity, reputation.

Power is relative rather than absolute, power is plural, mobile, fluid, negotiated, constantly distributed and redistributed, and fragmentary (Foucault, 1980: 98; Layder, 1994: 102–4) and it manifests itself in the network of social relationships (Usher and Edwards, 1994: 89). We might regard the process and dynamics of change, then, as a series of trade-offs.

Exchange theory for the management of change suggests the need to take very seriously the view that: 1) trade-offs will have to be made in the management of change; 2) the micropolitics of the organization will have to feature in the planning of change; 3) individuals and groups have a legitimate expectation of something to be gained by the change.

Force-field analysis

Inhibiting and facilitating factors can be presented through force-field analysis. In force-field analysis the range, nature, quantity and intensity of inhibiting and facilitating factors can be identified. A force-field analysis can proceed in four stages.

First, ask staff to generate a range and nature of facilitating and inhibiting factors – the good points about the innovation and the troublesome points about it (this can be done, for example using nominal group technique (Morrison, 1993), Delphi technique (*ibid.*), focus groups, discussion groups or simply by brainstorming). Secondly, for each of the factors either identify how many colleagues feel these to be inhibiting or facilitating factors (i.e. ascertaining the frequency/quantity of identification) or ask colleagues to rate these factors on a five-point scale of how strong/important they feel these factors to be, either as facilitators or inhibitors (i.e. ascertaining the intensity the responses). Thirdly, plot these on to a force-field chart. Fourthly, interpret this chart to identify significant facilitating/inhibiting factors. An example of this is given below.

A primary school of 20 teaching staff is considering adopting a highly structured approach to the teaching of reading, with an emphasis on phonics and tightly framed sequential programmes. The headteacher conducts a force-field analysis (Figures 5.2 and 5.3) to identify how to proceed with this innovation and this generates two charts.

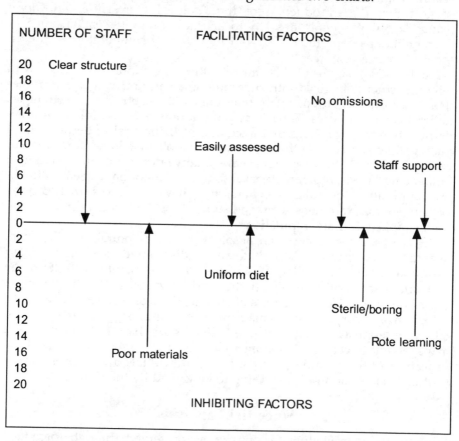

Figure 5.2 Force-field analysis of an innovation in school reading

Here one can see that generally there is stronger support for the innovation in two main ways – because the facilitating factors have a greater number of 'votes' (54) than the inhibiting factors (46) and because the strength of the most powerful facilitating factor 'clear structure' (20) is greater than the strength of the most powerful inhibiting factor 'poor materials' (16). This example is based on simple frequencies.

The second chart (Figure 5.3) is more sensitive and subtle, because it replaces a simple frequency count with a rating scale. Staff are asked how strong is the particular factor in facilitating or inhibiting the innovation (1 = very weak; 2 = weak; 3 = a little strong; 4 = strong; 5 = very strong) and the results for each position on the rating scales are totalled across staff, e.g. 5 staff voting 'strong' = 5 × 4 = 20. The results for the same factors are presented below.

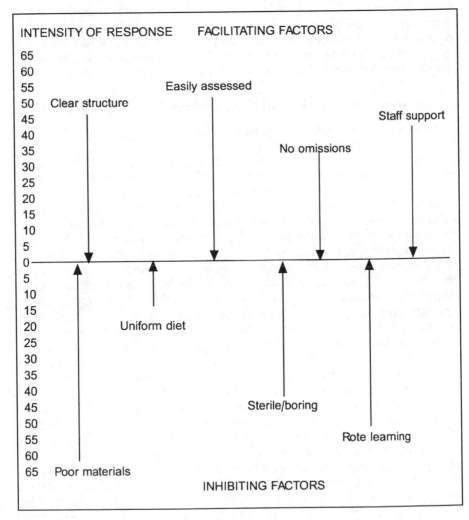

Figure 5.3 An alternative force-field analysis

The second chart is strikingly different from the first, reflecting the intensity of the factors rather than the number of people who felt like this. In this example the overall intensity of inhibiting factors (185: 65 + 20 + 45 + 55) is higher than for facilitators (175: 50 + 45 + 35 + 45). Further, the factor 'poor materials' (65) is seen to outweigh the strongest facilitator 'clear structure' (50) and is seen to be a very strong factor indeed. This second chart is useful for assessing the size of the factor rather than the number of people. It is not that one chart is better or worse than another; they simply do different things. The first shows how widespread is the factor whilst the second shows its strength; both feature in the planning of the management of change.

Force-field analysis is useful also in examining issues in the management of change, for example the facilitating and inhibiting strengths of leadership, staff support, collegial working, organizational health, ability to utilize existing expertise, clarity of the innovation, communication, morale, personal commitment, ability to cope with overload and deskilling, ideological commitment, motivation, support structures, resources, effectiveness of target-setting and development plans, etc. Each of these factors could become the elements for simple frequencies and ratings in force-field analysis.

Change as loss and gain: the emotional aspects of change

Though something might be gained by a change, something will also be lost in it. The rise of workplace counselling recognizes the importance of looking to this very personal aspect of change. If change deskills (which is inevitable) then loss of self-esteem and self-knowledge may follow in its wake, both for employers and employees. Self-esteem and performance are linked, perhaps through stress, in a curvilinear relationship: as stress is heightened performance is increased and self-esteem is raised. If stress becomes too high and the required performance becomes too high (the 'intensification thesis' discussed earlier in the book) then stress becomes counterproductive, leading to questioning of self-worth ('I am not up to the job') and lowering of self-esteem. As Walton (1997) argues, whilst change can release energy and engender feelings of accomplishment, encouragement, empowerment and transformation, it can also engender feelings of loss, grief, despair, fragmentation, stress, disruption and regression. In many senses change invalidates many of the experiences people have had to date (Marris, 1993) and the search for a new identity can be painful. Letting go is very hard because of the emotional involvement one has in existing practices (Clarke, 1994: 53–4).[12]

Fink *et al.* (1971) chart a range of reactions to change: shock and threat (often producing denial), defensive retreat (often producing a defence of the status quo), acknowledgement (often a feeling of discomfort and unease but preparedness to undertake the change), and adaptation and change (a growing sense of security in, and positive feelings towards, the change). Similarly Arrobo and James (1987: 116–18) suggest that people will engage in a 'loss cycle' of denial, trauma, uncertainty about understanding the change, uncertainty about how change will affect them, depression and then moving towards acceptance and finally hope (see also Kubler-Ross,

1990). This is echoed by Adams *et al.* (1976) who indicate seven stages of reaction to personal change:

1) immobilization (frozen and shocked);
2) disbelief;
3) depression;
4) acceptance of the reality of the change (letting go of the existing situation);
5) testing (new practices, behaviour, lifestyle);
6) searching for meaning (rationalizing the change);
7) internalization of the change.

Carnall (1995: 144) identifies the stages of: denial (of the need for change); defence (of the status quo – territories, practices and jobs); discarding (of existing and old behaviours); adaptation (to new behaviours); internalization (of the change and new practices). Personal change (Clarke, 1994: 50) is the hardest thing to manage in a change, a paradox as it is probably the thing over which one can exert the greatest control.

The business literature stresses the need to take very seriously the emotional aspects of change.[13] Whether one wishes to argue that problems experienced are often work induced does not negate the issue that there is a problem that may not be soluble but only manageable. Counselling can help people to manage their problems, and feeds into the win/win situation advocated above (see also Carroll, 1996: 43), where the individual and the organization benefit (profit?) from satisfied employees. Indeed Carroll (*ibid.*: 38) argues that counselling can create a new culture of caring, empathy and the need to take people seriously in an organization that is very beneficial in managing change, for example by:

- providing a humanizing workplace through being a mechanism and forum in which people are respected, listened to, believed, trusted and helped to make decisions;
- setting up training to address problems caused by ineffective or underdeveloped management practices;
- advising managers about effective and human ways of working with people in the organization and in the management of change, spreading understanding of personalities, emotions, psychological states and needs.
- helping with the management of individuals and organizational change, using their expertise to advise about coping with change as loss, confusion and problems of readjustment;
- helping people to cope with bad news (particularly in a climate of redundancy, career change and organizational change), and making it clear to people that the organization is ready to face up to bad news and handle it as effectively as possible;
- following up those who have been made redundant and those who are left in the organization after redundancies have been made (who, too, will experience a sense of loss);
- providing role models and models of behaviour and effective professional relationships in a humanistic organization;

- seeking to empower people in the organization (echoing the comments earlier about the need for self-actualization);
- creating the need to take seriously individual differences;
- facilitating the growth and development of the organization by improving the context of their work, e.g. by recognizing that change in one area of the organization impacts on other areas of the organization;
- improving and understanding of organizational behaviour and dynamics in managing change.

Many companies are setting up systems for workplace counselling. Egan and Cowan (1979) discusses this in terms of 'upstream' and 'downstream' counselling. In 'upstream' counselling the counsellor tries to tackle issues that are significant to participants *before* those issues turn into problems, whilst in 'downstream' counselling the counsellor works with employees who have already experienced some form of emotional damage, stress or trauma.

There is a clear recognition in the business literature that emotions play a significant part in an organization, for example feelings of excitement, delight, fear, enjoyment, jealousy, admiration, etc. However, there will be some emotions which are dysfunctional and hence it is advisable – for everybody's good – that they are handled effectively. Ostell (1996: 533–6), for example, indicates how anger, anxiety and depression are usually dysfunctional. He suggests a range of strategies for handling these, including practising empathy, and an examination of 1) thought patterns, 2) initial palliative strategies, 3) corrective and adaptive strategies, 4) the opportunity for 'time out', and 5) the provision of support strategies.

To ease the stress of personal transition Clarke (1994) advocates:

- accepting that something has finished;
- grieving for its loss and keeping in mind the best memories;
- allowing and creating time to think about the change and the new situations it will bring; if change is planned and, to some extent, predictable, then it might be seen as manageable;
- deliberately planning and managing the transition, accepting that progression and regression will occur, coupled with re-experiencing of regret for the past;
- examine how negatives might be turned into positives.

Arroba and James (1987: 26) argue that change alters people's expectations and relationships and hence will be very disruptive; therefore people's expectations need to be 'sounded' as part of the support processes for change. Change, they argue (*ibid.*: 99–104), is inevitably stressful and can be observed in four areas – the physical, behavioural (what we do and say and how we do and say things), mental and emotional. To cope with change and innovation Marris (1993: 219) argues that it is important that people are given the opportunity to react to change proposals and work out their own feelings about it and meanings autonomously. The creation of time and space for this to occur is accompanied by the patient acceptance that people will have different perceptions of the change and will attach different feelings towards it.

Though this section has suggested a role for counselling, few schools have formal counselling mechanisms. However, the rise of mentoring, collegiality, teamwork and collaborative enterprises in schools is perhaps the less formal – though equally important – equivalent of counselling, though, of course, it would not have the psychotherapeutic base of some counselling approaches. What is being advocated here is the use of several elements of counselling in the workplace, for example effective and active listening, empathy, reflection, support, clarification, probing, planning, considering and reconsidering, choosing and deciding.

Change and conflict management

Whether one chooses to change attitudes before behaviour or *vice versa* in managing personal change is a moot point in the business literature.[14] Nevertheless it seems that conflict is inevitable in change; one has to assume that it will occur (Fullan, 1991), and maybe even encourage it (Marris, 1993). One of the tasks of managers, therefore, is effective management of conflict. Conflict management is a vast field and clearly justice cannot be done to it in the space available here. However, certain features of it can be noted here (that link closely to stress management). Arroba and James (1987) suggest that people will react to potential conflict in one of four main ways: fight (dealing with it aggressively); flight (being unassertive and fleeing the change); freeze (doing nothing and, therefore, remaining passive); being assertive (talking through the situation). They indicate that both verbal and non-verbal behaviours feature strongly in conflict management and therefore, by implication, both feelings and cognitions will be the focus of the management of change. Everard and Morris (1990) suggest a five-fold way of coping with conflict:

1) avoiding (side-stepping or postponing the conflict in the hope that it will go away or does not really exist). They do not advocate this view as it simply buries rather than solves the problem; the problem will resurface;
2) fighting (standing up for one's rights and fighting one's corner);
3) smoothing (placing a high priority on other people's feelings and viewpoints);
4) compromising (seeking solutions that will satisfy all parties although the outcome may not be to anybody's complete satisfaction);
5) problem-solving (where everyone works towards a collectively owned problem solution).

They suggest that 'concern for relationships' and 'concern for results' can be used as two axes in plotting people's styles of managing conflict. Low concern for relationships and results will lead to the adoption of avoidance strategies; high concern for relationships and low concern for results will lead to the adoption of smoothing strategies; low concern for relationships and high concern for results will lead to fighting strategies; high concern for both relationships and results will lead to the use of problem-solving strategies; strategies of compromise are located, as one would expect, in the mid-point between high and low concern for both relationships and results.

The management of conflict, then, involves both cognitive and affective dimensions (values, attitudes, emotions, reasons, etc.). It is possible to identify some general principles for conflict management which can be applied to education. For example:

- separate the rational from the emotional;
- try to regard conflict as an opportunity;
- be a good listener;
- look for trade-offs;
- recognize that conflict resolution is not a unilateral decision;
- try to focus on issues rather than on *ad hominem* arguments;
- try to replace a win/lose situation with a win/win situation;
- try to move towards a problem-solving strategy where everybody owns the solution;[15]
- maintain as much communication as possible;
- avoid postponing the conflict;
- talk *with* others rather than *about* them;
- work with people's expectations.

An example of conflict management is given in Figure 5.4.

Change as creativity

The argument so far has suggested that change will encounter resistance in several forms. This could be accepting a very negative stance on change, regardless of whether it is being realistic or not. An alternative, more optimistic and positive view of the personal aspects of change adopts McGregor's Theory Y view of humans (see Chapter 3). Indeed much of the business literature regards it as an essential feature of successful organizations that they attend to the employee's needs as well as to customers' needs – the internal and external markets respectively.

The need to develop and utilize the creativity of participants finds expression in the notion of intrapreneurialism and intrapreneurship (Brown and Weiner, 1984; Pinchott, 1985). The spirit of intrapreneurship is the individual equivalent of the perhaps aggressive notion of 'superteams' (discussed in Chapter 7); the idea of the intrapreneur is of a high risk-taking, deeply committed, creative, dynamic, goal-seeking, free-thinking innovator who is able to pursue innovation and creativity with energy, verve and style and who, in business, is rewarded in plenty financially.

A likely innovator (Amabile, 1983) has the ability to: 1) break the existing practices and mind-set (existing ways of looking at organizations and practices); 2) identify possibilities and hold open options for enough time to give them considerable examination (usually a long time so they can be revisited); 3) suspend his or her judgement (echoing the comments from Chapter 2 that it is dangerous to plunge into premature judgement before all aspects of an innovation have been considered and that it is desirable to pause for some time on the consideration stage – see also Arroba and James, 1987: 43–4); 4) draw on an excellent memory; 5) block out distractions and see to the heart of an issue and stick with the core

A primary school teacher returns from a prolonged absence through illness to find that 'her class' of 6-year-olds has now been placed with another teacher permanently, and she has been placed with a class of 11-year-olds. No consultation had taken place about this. She tries to discuss this with the headteacher but the headteacher refuses to discuss the matter, simply saying that he has the right to place teachers wherever he wishes in the school and that the move was for the good of the children. After repeated attempts to discuss the matter and repeated refusals the teacher takes out a grievance procedure against the headteacher as a device for forcing him to discuss the matter. At the grievance hearing the teacher raises the following issues:

- she has been taken out of her age group of expertise;
- there was no consultation over the decision;
- the headteacher has refused to discuss the matter;
- the teacher has a right to return to the job that she held before her illness;
- the good of the children has not been served because her former class has been deprived of an experienced teacher and her new class is working with an inexperienced teacher;
- no reason has been given for the change;
- she has suffered unnecessary emotional and professional stress;
- there has been favouritism in the headteacher's actions because he has placed another teacher – at that teacher's request – into the formerly absent teacher's class;
- the other teachers in the school condemn the headteacher's behaviour as shabby in the extreme;
- unjustified advantage has been taken of her illness to make changes against which the headteacher knew she would be strongly and vocally opposed;
- she has been subject to what, in effect, is bullying by the headteacher.

For his part the headteacher makes the following points:

- he has the right to make decisions;
- the teacher could not be consulted because she was absent through illness;
- the school is developing a policy of moving teachers around age groups;
- he does not need to consult if he does not wish to;
- he has the backing of the governors;
- the formerly absent teacher is putting her own interests before those of the school.

Some might regard the headteacher's actions as decisive and perfectly legitimate – simply the exercise of authority, for which he was appointed. Others might regard the actions as autocratic, overbearing, unreasonable, illegitimate, inadvisable and simply wrong-headed. Whichever of these two interpretations one wishes to adopt, clearly this is an example of an inept piece of management of a change. The headteacher has violated nearly every principle of effective management of conflict: he has not listened; he has refused discussion, consultation and negotiation; he has not faced up to problems and disagreements as they have arisen; he has tried to side-step a necessary problem-solving approach; he has avoided communication; he has failed to address the 'people' issue in the change – people's concerns, expertise and emotions; he has taken a unilateral decision and is managing by diktat; he is unconcerned that others are suffering because of his decision; he has failed to give reasons for his initial decisions; his actions are ill-timed and damaging.

Figure 5.4 Conflict management in a primary school

features of it; 6) break out of existing ways of doing things and existing roles; 7) use his or her high intelligence and creativity.[16] The intrapreneur has to possess the ability to galvanize colleagues and to demonstrate a high degree of tenacity of purpose (see also Pinchott's (1985) 'ten commandments' for intrapreneurs).

Intrapreneurs might be uncomfortable people to have in an organization, not simply because they might be seen as the 'awkward squad' – not fitting into the company routines and practices – but because they ask the unsettling questions and throw in the explosive ideas. They are prepared to countenance the unthinkable! Creativity is unsettling, it is unreasonable, but, as Bernard Shaw commented, we need unreasonable people to bring us out of stagnation.

Adopting a perhaps less individualistic stance than that advocated in the notion of intrapreneurship, it is possible to support and empower the development of creativity and personal autonomy in an organization. This can happen in a variety of ways (Peters, 1987; Clarke, 1994; Carnall, 1995). For example:

- the delegation of power;
- the enlargement of the role of middle managers;
- reduction of reliance on 'rational' controls, e.g. monitoring and measuring of performance;
- increasing the emphasis on satisfying intrinsic motivation;
- placing emphasis on trust;
- giving, tolerating and incorporating criticism and feedback;
- practising empathy;
- engaging in action research projects with devolved responsibility from senior management.

In education this suggests the advisability for senior managers to: give a leadership role to as many members of staff as possible (allied to flatter management structures and extended teamwork); encourage and support educationally defensible initiatives taken by staff wherever possible; be open to suggestion, discussion and 'running with an idea' – listening seriously and providing feedback; disseminate developments and ideas throughout the school; support in-school initiatives with in-service development.

Carnall (1995) sets out several negative actions that can discourage creativity, for example: 1) interrupting, criticizing, disagreeing, arguing, challenging and reacting negatively; 2) being competitive; 3) making fun of people; 4) being pessimistic and exposing flaws; 5) not listening and being inattentive; 6) responding with silence, lack of feedback or anger; insisting on facts; 7) standing on position or being distant. Regardless of the specific strategy adopted, the message of this chapter is that change needs to takes seriously the concerns of all participants, and that these concerns are not simply those couched in austere rationality but are emotional, emotive and passionate.

Summary of educational implications of individual motivations for and against change

The personal dimension of change is vast. It was mentioned in Chapter 2 (the work of Hall and Hord (1987) on the Stages of Concern project in education) that people will be concerned about different aspects of a change, e.g. informational, personal, management, consequential, collaborational and refocusing, and that these factors are crucial issues to be engaged in the planning and management of change. Further, it is important for educationists to identify facilitating and inhibiting factors at the key stages of innovation (Fullan, 1991) – see Table 5.2.

Table 5.2   Identifying inhibiting and facilitating factors at the stages of change

Change stage	Inhibiting factors	Facilitating factors
1) Initiation	Meaning of change is unclear at the start; process is unclear; change is imposed; unrealistic proposal for change; lack of support; limited resources; senior leaders are obstructive; the change is not an improvement	Clear and well structured approach to change; voluntary participation; common values and concerns; availability of resources; active initiation and advocacy; ownership of change; change seen as improvement; contributes to continuous improvement
2) Implementation	Power conflicts; lack of vision; absence of early rewards; lack of trust; poor communication; inertia; lack of monitoring; opposition from senior staff	Early success; meets felt needs; open communication; presence of incentives; peer interaction and support; successful use of levers of change; integration of top-down and bottom-up strategies; external support
3) Continuation	Lack of interest/support/ funds; limited capacity for sustained continuous improvement; unsustained change in behaviour and values; no ownership of change; departure of leaders and staff	Change is institutionalized; change in the organizational culture; interest shown in fundamental change; ownership; availability of resources; clear direction of change; support of local facilitators and trainers; elimination of competing or contradicting practices

Source: Adapted from Lung, 1998.

This chapter has suggested that it is important to locate people on a continuum of reactions to change (e.g. rejection to commitment) and to identify facilitating and inhibiting factors. It has suggested the need to identify personal motives/incentives/resistances/emotions/motivations in the change, and how to work on and with these, to identify the reasons for support and resistance.

With regard to facilitating factors this chapter has suggested the need to

- support change on the personal front;
- empower and involve those affected by the change and build in ownership;
- ensure the sustained support of senior management;
- foster security;
- envisage and promote positive new relationships;
- be both proactive and reactive in the personal dimension of change;
- mark and support the break with the past (e.g. rites of passage) and transitions to the new situation;
- 'sell' the attractions of the new situation;
- improve communication and information flow;
- generate empathy and mutual support;
- promote a positive social, intellectual, emotional and physical environment;
- develop people's autonomy and enable them to become self-actualizing;
- meet individual needs;
- foster career development through the change;
- build in, and on, the need for trust;
- identify expectations and contingencies;
- create the humanistic workplace;
- balance concern for relationships and results;
- create a collaborative and supportive problem-solving environment;
- foster and develop creativity and desired intrapreneurship.

With regard to inhibiting factors this chapter has suggested the need to

- identify types of resistance/resistors/support/supporters;
- define and overcome barriers to change;
- mobilize support and minimize the effected of resistance and resistors;
- provide workplace counselling ('upstream' and 'downstream');
- avoid being seen as manipulative and operating a thinly disguised instrumentalism;
- reduce the need for compulsion;
- cope with reactions to change;
- overcome perceived loss of status and control;
- overcome fear of the unknown;
- overcome lack of clarity of purpose;
- overcome uncertainty and ambiguity;
- overcome feelings of vulnerability;
- overcome lack of clarity on the benefits of the change;
- overcome reluctance to let go of the present;
- overcome threats to expertise and established skills;

- overcome the feeling of having surprises sprung on them;
- overcome fear of failure and threats to self-esteem;
- handle the admission that the present situation is unsatisfactory;
- address concern about ability to cope;
- overcome fear of loss of control;
- handle stress;
- manage increased workload;
- avoid blame;
- address the micropolitics of the organization and negotiate power;
- identify and work with the possible exchanges sought in a micropolitical reading of the change;
- cope with change as loss;
- overcome defensiveness;
- manage dysfunctional emotions (personally and well as organizationally dysfunctional);
- handle conflict and disagreement.

To ignore the personal dimension of change is to court danger. It was mentioned in Chapter 2 that just as change changes people, so people change change, and that the best laid plans stand or fall on the people involved. This chapter underlines the significance of that statement and how it can be addressed in practice. Human resource management involves working in the whole gamut of factors in humans – affective, social, physical as well as rational and narrowly intellectual.

Notes

1. Harvey-Jones (1988: 96) suggests that people will resist change because it challenges their comfortable position in a fool's paradise.

2. Kanji and Asher (1993) argue that complacency, cynicism ('it's just another bandwagon or flavour of the month') as well as fear can contribute to rejection or resistance.

3. This is the 'sell' style of management from Tannenbaum and Schmidt (1958).

4. The promise of an incremental pay rise may be insufficiently alluring to compensate for the increased workload and stress that a change inevitably brings.

5. Hampden-Turner (1994: 113), in an analysis of British Airways, concludes that one major determinant of the success of the company was the cultural change it wrought. Passengers were treated with extreme care and this corresponded with the way in which the employees themselves were treated by the company.

6. Wickens (1995), like Deming before him, inveighs against the use of simplistic performance-related pay incentives, arguing that all they succeed in achieving is short-term compliance rather than the necessary long-term attitudinal and behavioural changes, and they are often at the cost of the disaffection of those who do not receive the extra pay.

7. Robertson *et al.* (1992) summarize criticisms of Herzberg's theory, suggesting that: a) it is unrealistic; b) it is the result of flawed research

methodology (in which it was inevitable that the intrinsic and extrinsic categorization would be found); c) it focuses on outcomes rather than processes (a failure of operationalization of the research); and d) it neglects behavioural factors (e.g. absenteeism, performance, staff turnover), i.e. a failure to include both satisfaction and behaviour in a theory of motivation. Further, Adair (1983: 131–2) and Cowling and James (1994: 57) suggest that the issue of motivation is much more complex than the either/or mentality of Herzberg's research and that the consigning of certain factors to hygiene matters (e.g. money and supervision) is misplaced.

8.   Clarke (1994: 37) suggests that a company will need to look carefully at its reward systems and career development systems if it to address the issue of motivation. With regard to reward systems he suggests that: a) an emphasis should be laid on team performance as well as individual performance; b) there should be rewards (and no blame) for risk-taking if innovation is to occur; c) rewards should be attached to people development as well as product and operations development and productivity, cost effectiveness, sales and profit; d) crossfunctional developments should be rewarded; e) individuals should be able to avail themselves of a 'cafeteria' approach to benefits and rewards, selecting the package of options for development and their associated rewards.

9.   Bessler (1995), discussing the Toyota Motor Manufacturing Company in Kentucky, indicates that expectancy theory suggests that a person's motivation for involvement in change is a function of his or her effort-to-performance expectations, his or her performance-to-outcome expectations and the perceived attractiveness of the outcomes.

10.   An adjunct of expectancy theory is the self-fulfilling prophecy, linking to the discussion of the management of perception. Just as employees act on the basis of their expectations, so will employers, often producing a self-fulfilling prophecy (Bowman and Asch, 1987). For example, an employer's expectation that employees will resist change may lead him or her to behave negatively towards the employees which, in turn, evokes a negative response from employees; the negative cycle spirals downwards into hostility, suspicion and resistance. In turn the employer feels compelled to used a power-coercive strategy, that in turn furthers resistance, even sabotage and subversion. It is a classic win/lose situation that leads inexorably to a lose/lose situation. Everyone loses.

11.   Carnall (1982: 26) argues that the higher the degree of trust the less specific, more diffuse will be the obligation, and the lower the degree of trust the more specific and concrete will be the obligation. Individuals and subgroups, often informal structures rather than formal structures and alliances, join to resist or support change.

12.   Deal (1990: 129) reports an example where, during a talk he was giving to two hundred managers of the Bell Telephone Operating Company, in which he spoke of the impact of the closure of the American Telephone and Telegraph Company, he was surprised to find the audience both hushed and in tears because of their sense of loss.

13.   See the comments on absence and illness by O'Leary (1993) and Cartwright and Cooper (1994).

14.   Beer *et al.* (1990) argue that the old view that one changes attitudes

and values before behaviour is anachronistic and entirely the wrong way round; if one wishes to affect change, particularly organizational change, then it is behaviour that must change first, and attitudes and values will follow (perhaps the adage 'drag them by the hair and their hearts and minds will follow' – see Chapter 2 – is relevant here!). They suggest that the most effective way to change people is to place them in a new organizational context, thereby requiring them to take on new responsibilities, relationships and roles, and that, by so doing, new changes are forced on to people and they accommodate them.

15. Senge (1990: 243) suggests that it is essential for all participants in a change to be prepared to: a) suspend their assumptions and judgements so that they can be examined; b) regard each other as colleagues rather than as adversaries; c) maintain the context of dialogue, maybe through a facilitator.

16. These features resonate with Belbin's (1981) work on teams (see Chapter 7). He suggests that it is essential to include a 'plant' in a team, a creative innovator who can identify and explore new ideas, raise questions and grasp the essentials of a situation.

6

Organizational factors and change

Introduction

There are certain features of institutions and organizations that have to be addressed if change is to be successful. Egan (1994) has referred to the 'shadow side' of organizations – the dynamics at work in them – and has stressed the importance of ensuring that they are working effectively to promote and facilitate change.[1] If companies are to survive they need to become more flexible, responsive, adaptive, and engaged in continuous development and change (Coulson-Thomas, 1991). Work will need to be delegated to multifunctional teams, and project managers will replace hierarchical management structures, i.e. management structures will become flatter, extensive networking will take place and change will be facilitated through experts and expertise.

Champy and Nohria (1996a: xv) suggest that the new business organization is characterized as being information based and staffed with a diversity of knowledge workers with powerful information links through technology; decentralized and collaborative; able to adapt creatively, rapidly and with agility to new developments; team based; self-controlling and based on trust; defined by clear and shared operating principles. Such operating principles, they suggest (*ibid.*: xx) de-emphasize a hierarchical centre and emphasize co-ordinated action at local levels – flat management.[2] Everyone in the organization will have specialisms that complement each other, information is everybody's responsibility. Drucker (1996: 8) suggests that employees will have to answer the questions 'On whom do I depend for information?' and 'Who depends on me for information?' This translates directly into education, where schools (maybe through their appointing strategies) should ensure that all teachers are able to contribute something particular to the organization, so that they can take a leadership role by dint of their expertise and experience and so that unnecessary duplication of expertise is avoided.

How, then, can we begin to understand organizations and organizational change? Pugh (1993) suggests that 1) organizations are akin to organisms; 2) organizations are political systems as well as occupational systems; 3) everyone in the organization operates in three systems

148

simultaneously – the occupational system, the political system and the rational (planned, operational) system.[3]

Walton (1997) argues that change is a political matter and the micropolitics of organizations are significant features in managing change. Change can occur at several levels (Goodstein and Burke, 1993), e.g. the individual level (e.g. attitudes, values, behaviour, skills); structures and systems (e.g. the organization of work, incentives and rewards); organizational climate and interpersonal style (e.g. styles of decision-making and management of conflict). It is the structures, systems and organizational climate – the culture of the organization – that this chapter addresses.

If schools are to be 'culturally effective', then they will need to address a range of questions. For example, to what extent

- have multifunction teams replaced hierarchical management?
- is there a 'flat' management structure in the organization?
- is change facilitated through expertise rather than positional power?
- can the organization respond rapidly to demands for change?
- are teams autonomous?
- are relationships of trust practised?
- is staff expertise complementary?
- are staff able to give and receive information?
- is change planned, supported and rational?
- has attention been paid to the individual, personal and interpersonal aspects of change?
- has attention been paid to motivation, incentives and rewards?
- are decisions the outcome of genuine consultation and collegiality?
- is the recent history of the organization conducive to change?
- is the organization's vision being realized in practice?

Cultures in schools are developed and maintained through carefully managed communication, they focus and depend on people for their effectiveness (Bennett, 1993: 28).

Perspectives on organizations and organizational culture

The concept of an organization is at best fuzzy. For example, Nadler (1993: 87) argues that an organization comprises tasks (what it does), the individuals in it, the formal and informal structures and organizational arrangements. Burnes (1996: 151) suggests that the components of an organization include structure, politics, culture and managerial style. Organizational change here comprises three elements (*ibid.*: 323): the process of choice (how decisions are taken in the organization), the trajectory process (where the organization is coming from and where it is going to – its history/biography and vision) and the change process (how the vision will be realized in practice).

In many ways the concept of an organization is a function of the lenses that are used to examine it. For example, the human relations approach (linking to McGregor's Theory X and Theory Y) rejects the classical organization theory as being too rationalistic, mechanistic, coercive and simplistic, for regarding people simply as economic beings who are motivated only by financial gain, for separating conception from execution and establishing hierarchies and highly prescriptive work practices (e.g. in Taylorism) and for adopting McGregor's Theory X. Instead, the human relations approach emphasizes the humanitarian and emotional side of people and organizations, arguing for flexibility, for McGregor's Theory Y, for networking, for the need for motivation and for the move away from rigid rules.

Paine (1994) argues that one should replace a strategy of compliance with a strategy of integrity. A strategy of compliance regards people as being guided by material self-interest and having to conform to externally imposed norms, practices and standards. Paine suggests that this should be replaced by a strategy of integrity, which regards people as guided by self-interest to some extent but also by values, ideals and indeed their peers, and they will respond positively to the opportunity for self-governance in accordance with self-chosen standards.

The human relations approach, contrasted with the classical organization theory approach, suggests several questions that will need to be addressed in schools (see also Rodger and Richardson, 1985):

- How coercive is the style of management in the school?
- How are staff motivated other than by financial reward?
  How detailed are job specifications, and how conducive to change is this level of detail?
- How much control do participants have over both conception and execution of tasks and projects?
- How flexible are the staff, how flexibly do they work, how flexibly are they used?
- How much does the management of change address humanitarian and personal needs in managing change?
- How far is a strategy of compliance replaced with a strategy of integrity?
- How unnecessarily constraining are rules and procedures?
- To what extent are people's views, values, ideals, standards taken account of in managing change?
- How autonomous are individuals?
- How successfully do staff work with and relate to each other?
- How often do staff mix together informally?
- Do staff enjoy working in the school?
- Is morale high?
- How welcoming, stimulating and attractive is the school?

Davis and Kanter (1995), however, argue that both classical theory and the human relations theory suffer from adopting the 'one best method' approach. Because organizations are diverse social structures that evolve over time, they argue that it is misplaced to adopt a single 'best method' approach to understanding and explaining organizations and behaviour in them. Rather, they advocate the *contingency theory* (see Chapter 2), arguing for a much more pragmatic, evolutionary, sensitive attention to the contingencies within the organization at any particular moment.

The contingency approach echoes the work of Peters and Waterman (1982) (the culture-excellence approach – Burnes, 1996) in their study of leading successful industries and companies.[4] They argue for the eight properties that were set out in Chapter 4. Their bias for action argues for the establishment of voluntary groups with a limited life span (3–6 months) whose objectives are limited, focused and whose documentation is kept to a minimum. They advocate extensive and intensive formal and informal communication that is supported by appropriate systems development and resourcing. The culture of the organization, they argue, should identify its priority purposes, keep them simple, adhere to them strictly and develop people as partners in the realization of those purposes. Success, for them, lies in the ability of the organization to manage the internal culture and system so that it serves the priorities outlined by the organization, in short so that the organization meets its identified contingencies and situation. The culture-excellence approach of Peters and Waterman is premised on flat management structures and the dismantling of hierarchical organizations. Employees are partners in development rather than its victims or recipients.

Contingency theory echoes Kanter's (1983; 1989) advocacy of the need to find synergies in organizations through opening boundaries in order to form new alliances and encouraging innovativeness, entrepreneurship and intrapreneurship. Synergy, she suggests, is where the whole is greater than the sum of the constituent parts – the football team is more than eleven isolated players or, as Handy (1994) puts it, one plus one equals three! One identifies the subsystems that, together, create synergy, for example: 1) values, objectives and goals; 2) technical systems; 3) psychological and social systems; 4) managerial systems. If these are aligned then they pull together in combination to achieve success.

The culture-excellence and contingency theory approaches suggest several questions schools can address:

- To what extent does the organization and groups within it demonstrate a bias for action?
- How effectively and clearly are the school's priorities established?
- How straightforward, concrete and realizable are the school's priorities?
- To what extent are professional partnerships within the school developed and utilized?
- To what extent are staff partners in, rather than victims of, developments?
- How open is the system to suggestion, criticism, change, development and structural change to meet contingencies?
- To what extent does the organization develop and build on the creativity of staff in all spheres of its operations?
- How task orientated is the school?
- How purposeful an atmosphere is there in the school?
- How permeable are boundaries in the school (however defined, e.g. by curriculum teams, management teams, subject teams, informal teams)?
- To what extent does the school foster and promote new alliances and synergies?
- How innovative is the school and each of its staff?
- How does the school support innovativeness, entrepreneurship and creativity?

Contingency theory, whilst it adopts a greater sensitivity and pragmatic stance towards organizations, nevertheless has attracted one of the same criticisms as human relations theory and classical organization theory (Burnes, 1996), viz. that it can still support a hierarchical, prescriptive organization and that it neglects the significance of power and politics in organizations. This issue is addressed in the cultural perspective. Deal and Kennedy (1983a) suggest that organizational culture, rather than its structure and strategies, is the principal factor at work in organizations, as behaviour is affected by shared values, beliefs about the organization, how it does, and should, operate, and how people behave in it. Change should embrace the organizational culture as well as the substantive project. Cultural change can be wrought by changing recruitment and selection, by redeployment and redundancies, by reorganizing the organization so that staff who display the 'right' (desired) qualities occupy influential positions, by extensive communication of the new cultural ethos and values, and by changing structures and systems for incentives, monitoring and reward.[5]

The culture of the organization comprises its values (Schein, 1985), operational norms, attitudes to and care for its employees, rites and ceremonies, celebrations of achievement, formal and informal networks and systems of communication, the ideology that the organization espouses (Mintzberg, 1973), perceptions, expressions of need and interest (Martin, 1985), patterns of expectation (Schwartz and Davis, 1981) and general orientations. The term 'culture' is being used here in the same sense as anthropologists would use it, for example as knowledge, beliefs, morals, customs, attitudes, habitual behaviour patterns (e.g. Tylor, 1871; Linton, 1940). In the educational sphere Lawton (1983; 1989) suggests that a cultural analysis will address nine systems: social, economic, communication, rationality, technology, morality, belief, aesthetic, maturation. Though he uses these systems to analyse macrosocieties, none the less they can also be used to analyse school cultures.

Harrison (1994) describes four types of organizational culture – a role culture, a power culture, an achievement culture and a support culture.[6] Clearly schools are not of a single type, and indeed it would be desirable for all four types to be present and in alignment (pulling in the same direction) in schools, as this would indicate that key components of the formal, informal, micropolitical, personal and interpersonal aspects of the organization were being addressed. It would be a salutary exercise for a school to consider to which type it most strongly corresponds, what are the reasons for this and the desirability of this. For example, a school that was strong on roles, power and achievement but weak on support might be a relentless, soulless place in which to work; a school that was strong on a supportive and role culture but weak on an achievement culture might be stagnating; a school that was largely a power culture might be riven with factions, cliques and tensions – clearly undermining its potential for student achievement and being an unpleasant environment in which to work.

It would be a useful exercise for schools to identify the *components* and *indicators* of the four cultures, perhaps by completing the indicators in Table 6.1.

Table 6.1 Four cultures of an organization

Culture	Components	Indicators
Role culture	Bureaucratic; line management; hierarchical decision-making; clear division and demarcation of labour and strata of decision-making and responsibility; formal and inflexible operational procedures; detailed job specifications; close monitoring of performance; concern for task achievement; propensity for stagnation; limited adaptability to change	
Power culture	Centralized control; significance of leaders; limited collegiality; high significance of micropolitics; fluid, negotiated power; competitive; frequent low morale amongst non-leaders; blame culture for failure; strong and flexible	
Achievement culture	Emphasis on results, standards, outcomes; collaborative and collegial; task focused with task groups and teams; much autonomy of teams; using power to co-ordinate tasks in order to achieve results; extended and flexible use of expertise; significance of project leaders; high capability to change	
Support culture	Person centred; formal and informal support services; consensus based; positional power replaced by the authority of expertise; individual concerns over-ride organizational concerns; personal empowerment; limited constraints on staff; resource rich	

With regard to change theory a culture which effectively balances all four major elements is the most conducive to change. The cultural perspective is useful in identifying sources of resistance and facilitation in organizations. Burnes (1996: 119–20) suggests that too shared a culture can lead to stagnation, can stifle individuality and can be so powerful as to resist change. In short, culture might not be able to be managed – a feature that is striking about 'failing' schools. The development of the culture of the organization is a key component of managing successful change and has to be addressed as a long-term and ongoing feature. Indeed Pfeffer (1981) argues that an organization's culture and structure must support each other if the organization is to operate effectively and efficiently.

Though the cultural perspective identifies some key dynamics of an organization it is the power-political perspective that catches the importance of its micropolitics. This was discussed in the previous chapter and was rooted in exchange theory. This perspective argues that it is essential to recognize that interests, diversity, conflict, power, negotiation and struggle are probably more important to an organization than bland uniformity or naive consensus (e.g. Burnes, 1996),[7] indeed that a culture might not be able to be managed at all (Legge, 1995). The power-political perspective suggests several questions schools can address:

• To what extent are the micropolitics of the organization aligned with the formal structures of the organization to facilitate change (i.e. where idiographic and nomothetic dimensions are mutually supportive)?
• How supportive of change are the informal groups and informal leaders?
• How are consultation, negotiation, conflict and dissensus managed?
• How is a spread of opinions and attitudes towards an innovation managed?
• How is power used, negotiated, renegotiated, circulated, resisted and invoked to facilitate and inhibit change?
• Whose interests usually prevail in decision-making?
• To what extent is the institution marked by conformity, compliance, creative conflict, opposition, warfare, silence, silencing, cliques, factions, dissensus, bargaining?
• How are decisions taken and who takes them?
• How powerful are the micropolitics of the organization?
• How powerful and effective are the senior managers (and how is effectiveness defined)?

Contingency theory and the power-political theory of organizations link to the theory of emergence. In this view (introduced in Chapter 1) organizations are open and constantly restructuring, adapting, evolving, autocatalytic and changing in a process of continuous feed-forward and feedback.[8] Dawson (1994) argues that the emergent approach regards change as processual (see also Pettigrew, 1985), often a bottom-up process; organizations, in this view, learn new things and adapt themselves to the new things they have learned, i.e. continuously improve.

Beer *et al.* (1990) argue that the emergent approach is most suited to the turbulent, unpredictable and dynamical systems and times in which we find ourselves. In this view organizations are constantly scanning the world and their environment in order to be able to change themselves to fit into it most effectively and proactively. Hence information gathering, the notion of the learning organization and extensive communication are fundamental tenets of this approach.

Theories of emergence and complexity, and processual approaches, suggest several questions schools can address:

• How capable and used is the school of restructuring itself to meet new circumstances and contingencies?
• How adaptive and 'autocatalytic' is the school in facing change?
• How capable and used is the school of using continuous feedback and feed-forward to anticipate, meet and respond to change?

- How effectively does the school integrate bottom-up, top-down, externally and internally generated change?
- To what extent is the school itself a learning organization (see below)?
- How desirably stable, unstable, equilibrium seeking, deliberately equilibrium disturbing is the school?
- How capable is the school of transforming itself? What needs to be done to improve this capability?
- How alert to changes in the outside environment (however defined) is the school, and how does it address these?
- How does the school gather, use and communicate information to inform itself of internally necessary changes to meet, anticipate and respond to changes outside the school?
- How used and capable is the school of adopting problem-posing, problem-analysis and problem-solving strategies to cope with change?
- Does the school take risks and experiment?

Organizations, then, can be examined through several lenses, those of classical theory, human relations theory, contingency theory, culture-excellence theory, exchange theory, the cultural perspective, the power-political perspective, theories of emergence and processual approaches. The truth of effective organizations and their dynamics probably lies in the combination of all of these. It is very clear that successful organizations have moved away from being mechanistic and hierarchical towards being organic and democratic. All aspects of the culture of the organization need scrutiny so that the organization has the ability to change. Indeed it is frequently the culture of the organization that needs to be improved rather than having the organization simply take on a specific innovation.

Carnall (1995: 38) argues that the old culture of organizations (hierarchical, bureaucratic, with clear boundaries and demarcations, paternalistic and an emphasis on control and risk avoidance – McGregor's Theory X applied to organizations) must be replaced by the new culture of teamwork and connection, empowerment and trust, risk-taking and innovativeness, and support for action (McGregor's Theory Y applied to organizations). Indeed, one of the strengths of the concept of a culture is the significance it places on shared norms, assumptions, values, beliefs and practices.

Mechanical, bureaucratic, organic and collegial organizations

The advocacy of organic organizations is by no means new in the business literature. For example Burns and Stalker (1961) and Bennis (1969) contrasted mechanical and organic systems. Mechanical systems, they suggest, are characterized by

- an emphasis on individuals;
- a relationship of obedience to authority and the status of hierarchy;
- rigid adherence to divided and delegated responsibility and division of labour;
- centralized decision-making;
- the management of conflict through control, suppression, formal mechanisms (e.g. arbitration) and power;

- rigid job specifications and standardization of practices;
- formal channels of communication;
- loyalty to the company.

On the other hand, organic systems are characterized by

- an emphasis on relationships;
- mutual trust and confidence;
- shared responsibility and interdependence;
- membership of several, often crossfunctional teams and groups;
- power-sharing, and sharing of responsibility;
- the management of conflict through problem-solving approaches;
- few specific job specifications;
- formal and informal channels of communication as appropriate;
- loyalty to the team and the group.

The business literature articulates the importance of the moves away from mechanical, bureaucratic methods of organization and management and towards organic, collegial principles and practices. Indeed Argyris (1990) identifies characteristics of failing companies: 1) they had inflexible procedures and rules; 2) managers were not committed to, or expert in, managing change; 3) there were problems within and between groups; 4) there was inadequate and ineffective communication; 5) there was insufficient strategic thinking; 6) senior managers were only concerned with the short term; 7) levels of trust were low. Argyris is describing here several features of the mechanical system.[9]

Clarke (1994) cites the example of BP as an organization which transformed itself in order to cope with change, moving from a committee-obsessed, hierarchical, control and direct mentality which fostered second-guessing, mistrust and fear to an organization characterized by a flatter structure, teamworking and networking, empowerment of employees, openness, trust and support for risk-taking. The 'revamped' BP, he suggests (*ibid.*: 104), provides three important messages for change, viz. the need to build on a 'tripod' of appropriate structure, culture and processes.

Similarly Pfeffer (1993: 210–11) suggests that there are several problems with trying to use the authority of hierarchy to achieve tasks: it is undemocratic and unpopular, and we usually need the co-operation of others who are outside our immediate line of command. Further, hierarchies assume that the judgement of the person in power is correct – which may be mistaken.[10]

More recently, however, voices have been heard to support more hierarchical systems. For example, the Aston Group (Burnes, 1996: 67) reports the larger the organization is the more likely it is to need and to use a bureaucratic, mechanistic structure, and the smaller the organization is the more likely it is to need and to be able to adopt a flexible and organic structure. The research is important, for it is arguing that bureaucracies and hierarchies need not be dysfunctional.[11]

In an influential paper, Jaques (1990) argues that properly structured and administered hierarchies are able to: 1) harness and develop the creativity and energy of participants; 2) rationalize productivity; 3) make account-ability clearer; 4) ensure that people are not promoted beyond their capability or are responsible for doing tasks for which they are unsuitable. He argues that tasks are more and less complex and that they require different types of mental activity and cognitive capacity.[12] Jaques suggests that it is necessary to recognize people's limitations and motivations as well as their strengths, and that a hierarchical situation enables this to be undertaken efficiently so that productivity is maximized.

This latter point echoes Judson's (1991) suggestion that hierarchies (indeed an authoritarian style of management) have several important features:

- the hierarchy is clear to all and is well planned and structured;
- responsibilities are clearly divided and resources can be targeted appropriately, both of these avoiding inefficiencies;
- conflicts are resolved through appeal to a higher level (i.e. there is a clear mechanism for conflict management);
- status is earned and deserved and reflected by one's rank within the hierarchy;
- communication within and between each level is clear.

Hierarchical models might achieve more immediate action and can overcome the problem of reluctance or resistance by the use of positional power. The bureaucratic model captures the hierarchical view of manage-ment and differentials of power, thereby enabling innovations to be driven in within short time frames. This model cuts through lengthy discussions, regards collective ownership of an innovation as unnecessary (echoing the comment earlier about dragging people by the hair into an innovation), reinforces the right of managers to manage (though this is to direct rather than to manage, perhaps), sets agendas and goals, and clarifies employees' rights, freedoms and powers, thereby minimizing the effects of disagree-ment and micropolitics, relieving workers of the need to be involved in extensive discussions and decision-making, and 'keeping workers in their place' – 'a place for everything and everything in its place'.[13]

Organic institutions possess an adaptive style of management (*ibid.*) in which the organization's objectives are widely disseminated and under-stood throughout the organization, with shared responsibility for their realization. Organic models are akin to collegial models. Collegiality in educational terms has been described by Bush (1993):

- participatory approaches to decision-making;
- democratic and consensual decision-making;
- shared values, beliefs and goals;
- equal right of participation in discussion;
- equal rights to determine policy;
- equal voting rights on decisions;
- the deployment of subgroups who are answerable to the whole group;
- shared responsibility and open accountability;
- an extended view of expertise;
- judgements and decisions based on the power of the argument rather

than the positional power of the advocates;
- shared ownership of decisions and practices.[14]

Bush (1993; 1995) argues that the collegial model is strongly normative, recognizes the authority of expertise, assumes a consensus in decision-making and a common set of values, and possesses several characteristics. However, he suggests that

- advocacy of collegiality is based on prescription rather than description;
- for groups to be effective they need to be small enough for every voice to be heard;
- group cohesion develops slowly so collegiality takes time to become operational;
- the senior manager's role is crucial in determining the extent, nature and boundaries of collegiality;
- collegiality involves a whole-institution approach; the relationship between the whole institution and individual autonomy is complex but the two are not mutually exclusive;
- collegiality may require subgroups to be arranged before the whole institution meets;
- careful staff selection is important;
- both independent and interdependent modes of working are included;
- collegiality raises the profile of the micropolitics of an institution.

This is not to say that collegial models are unproblematic. For example, the negative aspects of collegial models include the view that

- they are cumbersome and time-consuming;
- they generate excessive paperwork;
- they enable factions and interest groups to exert disproportionate influence;
- they fail to account for, or to address and seek resolution of, real conflict and justifiable differences of opinion;
- they sit uncomfortably with the promotional ladder and hierarchical model of accountability (often enshrined in law) in many institutions;
- they depend on the senior manager's (e.g. headteachers') willingness and ability to devolve power;
- they operate best in small rather than large institutions (e.g. primary rather than secondary schools);
- they involve whole-institution levels of an organization;
- they assume that consensus and involvement/engagement are possible – which does not fit with the realities of unwilling teachers;
- they require much commitment and energy from already overworked staff (Riches, 1993a).

Indeed in the paper by Jaques (1990) cited above, he argues it is nonsensical to advocate collegial and group models. He suggests that it is individuals rather than groups who are held accountable, that it is individuals rather than groups who are promoted or fired, and that group authority and practice without group accountability are dysfunctional.

For schools, one can suggest that hierarchical models might be useful if

- short-term change is required;
- rapid change is required;
- discussion, consultation, possible disagreement, opposition, conflict and negative short-term micropolitical issues want/need to be minimized;
- the weight of positional power is needed to drive in change;
- the institution is so large as to require a bureaucratic organization;
- people need to be coerced, controlled and directed;
- formal structures are to be kept clear;
- career development up a hierarchy is to be fostered;
- staff turnover is high.

For schools, one can suggest that collegial models, on the other hand, might be useful if:

- longer-term and sustainable change are required (because the culture of the school changes to become open to, and used to handling, change);
- slower change – of an organizational culture – is seen to be as important as single innovations or projects;
- consultation, collegiality, collaboration, participation, flexibility, complimentary expertise and creativity are to be utilized fully;
- democracy is to be practised;
- staff are prepared for the investment of time to make collegiality work effectively;
- mutual trust, accountability and responsibility are to be developed;
- problem-solving, problem-owning and problem-sharing are to be the main strategies for handling change;
- a learning organization is to be developed (discussed below);
- the organization is to develop is adaptability and capability for change;
- communication (formal and informal) is to be maximized;
- everyone is to adopt some leadership role in the organization;
- disagreements and debates on values are to be exposed and faced;
- the organization believes that it is important to have the micropolitics 'surfaced' and addressed openly;
- the institution is small enough to be able to work effectively in a collegial style;
- staff are capable of working collegially (and maybe are happy to do so).

Though collegial models have attracted some criticism, nevertheless the overwhelming message from the industrial literature is in their favour.

Organizational structures

The culture of the collegial organization has to be matched and supported by the structures within the collegial organization. Organizational structure refers to the deliberate, formal systems and processes of authority, power, decision-making and relationships in the organization through which the organization's work is done (Charan, 1996: 19). It comprises procedures for organization, administration, resourcing, monitoring, co-ordinating, accountability, division of labour, documentation, positions and seniority of authority, roles and tasks (O'Neill, 1994: 112–13).

Indeed, Bolman and Deal (1984) suggest that a major task for an effective structure is the balancing of the demands for differentiation (division and specialization of work) with the demands for integration (co-ordination and integration of roles to develop interdependence).

Organizational structures can be regarded as networks. Networks integrate the formal and social architecture of the organization. In a networked structure work is shared rather than divided and there is an emphasis on teamwork and crossfunctional teams (Champy and Nohria, 1996a: xviii). That renders the role of the middle manager changed, if not redundant (*ibid.*). Whereas their tasks had included the passing of information and decisions up and down the organization, the flatter, delayered organization that teams and networks of specialists imply require less formal supervision and more informal feedback and accountability. Hence authority in the organization is a function of expertise rather than position in a hierarchy. This, Champy and Nohria suggest, enables an agile organization to be developed that is capable of responding rapidly to pressures for change and its development of individual employees. Echoing the theories of complex organizations as adaptive dynamical systems from complexity theory in Chapter 1, individuals here are self-controlling and creative, responsive to the environment and generative of new environments.

In the field of education, O'Neill (1994: 112–14) uses the language of complexity theory in his reference to 'adaptive structures' so that schools are sufficiently flexible to cope with turbulence and uncertainty. He suggests that bureaucratic structures are required to cope with account-ability demands but that flexible structures are required to be able to cope with change, particularly with multiple innovation (see also Wallace, 1991).

Networks are characterized by open dialogue and by the constructive development and use of initiative. Information in a network is direct, immediate and open. As Charan (1996: 29) suggests, when information is available simultaneously to all members of the network the nature of informed decision-making is changed and improved – an interesting interpretation of the just-in-time and synchronous systems discussed in Chapter 3. Because membership of the network is seldom linked to seniority or position in a hierarchy the social architecture of the network is fluid. Those senior managers whose behaviour is dysfunctional to the smooth operations of the network are exposed, and those informal leaders who have not had space to demonstrate their talents are freed from the strictures of hierarchical constraint. Much of the discussion and significance of networks are echoed in typifications of organizational structures. Carnall (1995: 17–32) identifies six types of structure and outlines their strengths and weaknesses.[15]

The entrepreneurial structure is characterized by the absence of structure! Here much depends on the owner of the company who is often the entrepreneur, who takes the decisions which other workers simply act on as directed. This is an *ad hoc* and often flexible type of organization that depends very much on the quality of the leader and his or her ability to galvanize and inspire others. This is not a particularly applicable model for schools as it is too uncertain; further, it tends to characterize small groups and organizations rather than larger organizations such as schools.

In the functional structure there are clear departments (e.g. finance, marketing, personnel) that are co-ordinated by the executive board. This structure is one in which differentiation and specialization can occur and which builds on the expertise of participants and enables them to develop them along specific career paths. On the other hand it can risk stagnation and become unresponsive to new demands and the development of new initiatives (products). For schools this allies itself to the hierarchical model outlined earlier – with both its strengths and weaknesses.

In the product structure the product drives the organization, creating groups and tasks around specific products and services, thereby fostering involvement, commitment and specialization, and able to keep close to the customer. On the other hand it is perhaps difficult to see how *changes* in product and product demand might be met in this model, particularly if a product or service is in decline.[16] For schools this is the task-orientated and project/specific innovation model, where teams come together to undertake specific projects or activities, typically in development of curricular, assessment, monitoring and recording practices.

The divisional structure subdivides the organization into comparatively autonomous units that serve a particular product or market. The attractions of the devolved budget resonate here with the notion of local management of schools. Accountability here is 'pushed down the line' in the organization. Clearly there is some similarity between the divisional structure and the product structure, though the former is larger. For schools this implies subbudgets (e.g. by department or faculty), faculty and departmental planning, and phase-specific planning. It is a major arrangement for schools.

The matrix structure is designed to be able to develop and co-ordinate projects, products and services that have multiple specialities, necessitating structures for managing projects, accountability and various functions. This structure has the attraction of developing teams of specialists whose specialisms will be used in several ways whilst enabling specialist career development to be addressed. There is in this structure a tension between the need for flexibility and the need for careful project control and co-ordination. This is a common pattern for schools, for typically all staff will be members of different teams, for example a curriculum team, and age-phase team, a cross-school team (e.g. assessment, behaviour, pastoral, record-keeping, work experience), a management team, etc. Typically, also, this structure places great demands on people's time, as they have multiple team membership – a common feature of schools.

The federal structure represents the further decentralization of the divisional structure outlined earlier, maintaining clear accountability at the level of each unit and enabling groups to respond to changes in the market – to develop or limit growth. It is exemplified in the notion of a split-site campus for some secondary schools; more recently this is a model that is beginning to find its way into larger schools where activities become diversified. For example the school might be used as a community resource, necessitating the employment of a site manager; it might have 'units', e.g. for open and adult learning, for students with hearing or behaviour difficulties, a technology suite for service to the public, sports facilities, language centres, meeting rooms that are available for hire, restaurants for the public (where students following catering courses are able to learn in a supervised and 'real' atmosphere with the public), theatres and music rooms to host public performances, broadcasting and recording suites, citizens advice centres, information centres (e.g. producing materials in several languages). In this structure each unit has autonomy but contributes to the overall mission and direction of the (parent) institution.

Clearly the types of organization that are being discussed here might not always match exactly with educational organizations, in terms of size, function, location (and dispersal). Nevertheless the message from an analysis of Carnall's work for education is that organizational structures need to be designed to enable the organization to realize its mission most effectively and efficiently, to be able to respond proactively as well as reactively to ongoing change, to address issues of co-ordination and consistency, and to build in the opportunities for personal and professional development in participants, thereby building on their motivation. The message here echoes that discussed in Chapter 4 on quality, that 'fitness for purpose' is an important criterion.

One can tease out from an analysis of mechanical, hierarchical, flexible, organic and variously structured institutions a series of dilemmas for organizational management. Carnall (1995: 23) sets these out as

- centralization versus decentralization;
- efficiency versus effectiveness;
- professional management versus line management;
- using control versus developing commitment;
- managing change versus managing stability.

Child (1984) suggests that centralization is useful because it: 1) identifies the locus of decision-making and power; 2) enables senior managers to maintain an up-to-date overview of activities; 3) enables several strands of the organization to be co-ordinated; 4) avoids duplication and eliminates waste; 5) ensures that top managers have earned their seniority. On the other hand decentralization can claim several advantages, as it: 1) reduces the stress and overload on senior management; 2) increases employees' motivation through the development of their autonomy and empowerment; 3) ensures that necessary delegation is achieved in a complex organization; 4) enables flexibility of response to matters arising; 5) enables accountability to be identified in subunits.

In charting the tension between efficiency and effectiveness Carnall (1995) suggests that the decision here is whether to adopt an internal focus (on efficiency for stated goals) or external focus (effectiveness in terms of externally determined criteria and future goals, e.g. responsiveness to customers, ability to cope with change). To address efficiency and effectiveness Carnall suggests the need for job rotation, careful recruitment, improved communication, support for risk-taking, greater participation and involvement, problem-solving groups and the identification of new products and services.

The tension between professionals and line management signals the difficulty in having job demarcations and the need for specialist advice in changing circumstances. Line managers might become redundant as specialism grows. The task, therefore (and one which is pertinent to educational institutions – see West-Burnham, 1994: 18) is the effective management of professionals, and the advice from Carnall echoes the tenor of many of the preceding discussions: 1) emphasize decentralization; 2) reduce the need for unnecessary monitoring and 'rational controls'; 3) emphasize and develop personal – intrinsic – motivation; 4) emphasize and develop teamwork; 5) develop the art of conflict management; 6) use matrix structures and product structures (discussed above); 7) practise trust; 8) reinforce the importance of values, beliefs, mission and ethics.

The tension between control and commitment has already been rehearsed in the discussions of Theory X and Theory Y; indeed the move from control to commitment is advocated at length throughout this book as it builds in ownership and the ability of the organization to adapt and change.

Finally the tension between stability and change points to the need, recognized in school development planning (Hargreaves and Hopkins, 1991), to balance the best of the present with the needs of the future and the changes they will bring. This is a function not only of their mission but also of the resourcing available (and decisions about their targeting).

The agenda for schools that are seeking to develop their organizational structures to support change, then, might be set in response to several questions:

- What is the relationship between the school's structures and its culture (how do they influence each other) in preparing for and supporting change?
- In what ways does the school balance the demands for integration and differentiation?
- How are networks developed and used in the organization?
- What are the tasks of middle managers in facilitating change within a flatter organization?
- What steps is the school taking to be adaptive, dynamical, self-controlling in its management of change?
- How is the balance struck in the school between meeting bureaucratic demands and the flexibility required for the exercise of creativity and entrepreneurship within collaborative approaches?
- What networks are there in the school and how are they used to facilitate or impede change?
- How can the school integrate the hierarchical structures required for career development and incentives that might impede change and inure the school to change with the flatter management practices required for flexibility and the ability to promote change?
- How is the school promoting and managing task and project-orientated teams?
- What are the divisions in the school; how co-ordinated and aligned are

they to the overall vision and direction of the school? How capable are they of promoting and sustaining change?

- Where is the accountability in the divisional structure?
- How is the tension balanced between flexibility and co-ordinated innovations?
- How are the pressures of time managed for staff who are members of several teams simultaneously?
- How is the school managing and supporting the diverse, and diversification of, activities in a federated structure?
- How do diverse 'federal states' contribute to, and draw from, the main direction of the school?
- How autonomous are the 'federal states'? To whom are they accountable?
- How is the school balancing the differing demands of centralization and decentralization, efficiency and effectiveness, professionalism and line management, control and commitment, change and stability?

These are summary questions only; clearly they need to be fleshed out with reference to concrete practices in the schools themselves.

The organization as a learning organization

Carnall's (and Handy's – see note 15) work is important, for it signals the importance of regarding the organization as a learning organization, constantly evolving and developing, echoing the notions of emergence from Chapter 1 and the commitment to *kaizen* in Japanese companies from Chapter 3.[17] The move in the west to regard companies as learning organizations was signalled by Argyris and Schön in 1978, and is premised on participatory philosophies, learning from collective experience and an acceptance that learning cannot simply be left to chance – it has to be planned. For Senge (1990; 1993) and Otala (1995) the learning organization is one which is continually expanding its horizons and capabilities through the development of its employees, both individually and collectively, in order to achieve individual and organizational goals.

For Bennett and O'Brien (1994) the learning organization in industry is not only an organization that is changing but also an organization that is developing and enhancing its *capacity* to change, i.e. an organization that is focusing on the processes and contents of change and the capacities to sustain them. For Garvin (1993) the learning organization is one which is skilled in creating, acquiring and transferring knowledge, and in adapting its behaviour in light of the new knowledge gained.[18] Senge (1990) argues that the learning organization is built on five disciplines:

1) systems thinking (*ibid.*: 73), e.g. seeing relationships to the whole, patterns and inter-relationships rather than simple cause-and-effects chains;
2) personal mastery (*ibid.*: 141, 149), realized through support rather than coercion and premised on the view of one's life as a creative process;
3) mental models (*ibid.*: 176), our constructs of the world, that, if the organization is to learn, will need to be exposed and shared in the organization, so that new insights will be gained;

4) building a shared vision (*ibid.:* 206) that has the genuine commitment of participants rather than being imposed from above (which brings merely compliance);
5) team learning (*ibid.:* 234) fostering dialogue and maximizing energy, outcomes and abilities, and ensuring commitment to an aligned vision.

In his view leaders become designers and teachers (*ibid.:* 340) and teams have to practise dialogue and discussion (*ibid.:* 237). Senge suggests (*ibid.:* 272) that the learning organization will need to be able to: 1) transcend internal politics and internecine conflicts; 2) create time for learning; 3) balance delegation, control and co-ordination; 4) develop the facility for personal mastery to be practised in the workplace; 5) ensure that people can learn from experience by living with the consequences of their actions. Senge's fifth discipline (the title of his book) is systems thinking, the ability to manage the dynamic inter-relationship of all the disciplines.

How does an organization learn? Garvin (1993: 81) argues that the learning organization will need to utilize several modes of learning. For example:

- problem-solving (discussed in Chapters 2 and 4);
- experimentation with new ideas and approaches;
- learning from experience (that of the organization itself and from other companies – see the comments in Chapter 4 about benchmarking).

This requires effective and rapid communication, attentive listening, openness to criticism and the breaking down of boundaries in order to facilitate the exchange of ideas.

Miller (1996) echoes Garvin and identifies six modes of learning in and for organizations. Analytical learning is rational, systematic, linear, formal and often deductive, focusing on optimizing the goals of the organization. Synthetic learning is more emergent and holistic, combining knowledge in new ways. It emphasizes discovery, induction, interpretation, systems thinking (echoing Senge) and synergy. Experimental learning is incremental, exploratory, generative and concerns information seeking and the testing of ideas in practice. It is strongly focused on innovation, experimentation and adaptation. Interactive learning in organizations is adaptive, participative and *ad hoc*, emphasizing experiential learning, negotiation and inductive thinking (and echoing the advocacy of 'adhocracies' by Burns and Stalker (1961) and Mintzberg (1994)). It is focused on 'satisficing' the needs of participants and the organization (finding the minimal – sufficient – solutions that satisfy all the parties). Structural learning is cybernetic, bureaucratic and emphasizes change through established channels and learning through routines. Its thrust is towards reliability. Institutional learning is vision building, symbolic, concerned with values, ideologies, values and beliefs. Its emphasis is on coherence in the organization. Miller argues that a learning organization will need to address learning on all these fronts.

One can detect in the work of Garvin and Miller the matching of individual with organizational learning; individuals use particular strategies for learning and these can be used at an organizational level to explain how organizations can plan learning. Individual reactions to change match organizational reactions to change. For example, Chapter 5 sets out a continuum of individual responses to change – from rejection to commitment. The same is true of companies and organizations.[19] The implications, therefore, are highly significant. Organizational learning might be individual learning writ large.[20]

Senge (1990) argues that schools, as they currently operate, are not learning organizations, because they are bound by too many rules and teachers feeling obliged to adhere to them, because they deal in received knowledge, because staff are unused to working collaboratively, and because there is no adherence to a clear and unifying vision – rather activities are fragmented and compartmentalized. What collegiality there is concerns the implementation of mandates rather than genuine entrepreneurialism and vision creation.

The concept of the learning organization is not without its problems, however. For example Kuchinke (1995) suggests that it is simply another management fad that is under-researched (see also West, 1994; Jacobs, 1995) and unfairly seen as the great panacea for a range of problems organizations face. West (1994) suggests that advocacy of the notion of the learning organization overstates the need for companies to be constantly transforming themselves in order to cope with the change that surrounds them. Kerka (1995) suggests that the concept has exhortatory appeal but is too fuzzy to be of real service.

Despite these reservations it is clear that the notion of the learning organization is entirely consistent with the notions of continuous improvement, participation, flexibility, autonomy and expertise, ownership and problem-solving that have been advocated throughout this book. A school seeking to become a learning organization, then, may face an agenda (Kline and Saunders, 1993) in the fields of assessment, promoting the positive, safe thinking, taking risks, regarding people as valuable resources, learning potential and ability, mapping and modelling the vision, systems thinking, inaugurating action (see Figure 6.1).

Organizational health and climate

Miles (1965) introduced a useful metaphor for understanding organizations, arguing that an organization has to be healthy if it is to be able to cope with change. He suggested that there were three elements against which an organization could be evaluated as being healthy – task needs, maintenance needs, and growth and development needs.

His task needs include: 1) goal focus (clarity, acceptability, realistic, consistency with demands); 2) communication adequacy (communication that is as free from distortion as possible, is open and used, is widespread); 3) optimal power equalization (power is negotiated and can travel in vertical and horizontal directions – the practice of collegiality). His maintenance needs include: 1) resource utilization (personnel in particular, avoiding overloading individuals or keeping them idle, and ensuring that individual goals harmonize with organizational goals); 2) cohesiveness (collaboration and a sense of belonging – and wishing to

- Do people speak their minds honestly?
- Are different views encouraged?
- Is there time for reflection?
- Do people learn from their mistakes?
- Do people learn from each other?
- Do people learn from the unexpected?
- Are there opportunities for people to review lessons learned?
- Is there crossfunctional learning?
- Are mistakes seen as opportunities for learning or cause for blame?
- Can people see better ways of doing things?
- Are people willing to try new ideas and to experiment?
- Are different learning styles used and respected?
- Are learners self-directed?
- Are there adequate resources for learning?
- Are people keen to improve?
- Are staff enabled to improve?
- Is life at work getting better?
- Do staff expect improvement?
- Are obsolete practices being replaced?
- Is learning structured?
- Does learning take place at all levels of the organization?
- Do people learn outside their speciality?
- Is improvement real or just rhetoric?
- Is training provided for everyone and actually undertaken?
- Does training lead to learning?
- Do middle managers play an important role?
- Are middle managers prepared for their roles?
- Do managers cope well with change?
- Do managers take risks?
- Are there team rewards?
- Are systems flexible?
- Is stress made manageable?
- Are people overloaded?

Figure 6.1 An agenda for a school as a learning organization

belong); 3) morale (morale and group satisfaction are high). His growth and development needs include: 1) innovativeness (where the organization creates new structures, procedures, goals over time); 2) autonomy (where it is not driven exclusively by the external environment and pressures); 3) adaptation (where the organization is able to correct its internal problems and to develop); 4) problem-solving adequacy (where the usedness of the organization to problem-solving is high and where minimal energy is needed to solve problems), echoing the discussions of planning change and planning for quality development in earlier chapters.

It is notable that the attention Miles devotes to achieving a balance of maintenance and development needs is echoed in the work of Hargreaves and Hopkins (1991) on school development planning, in which they also add the need for careful target-setting and task focus. The need for deliberate and practical task focus is taken up in the business literature. For example, Beer *et al.* (1990: 159) suggest that effective change is the outcome of a focus on the realities of tasks and activities rather than on the vacuous advocacy of abstractions like 'culture' and 'participation' – doing things rather than talking about them.[21]

In their support for action rather than words, the business writers cited above echo the comments earlier that behavioural change precedes attitudinal change, and that 'task alignment', therefore, should focus on individual behaviour, roles and responsibilities of group members, and relationships. This is 'sticking to the knitting', 'a bias for action' and the avoidance of 'paralysis through analysis' (Peters and Waterman, 1982) *par excellence*.

Hoyle (1969) suggests that the health of an organization must be robust if change is to be effective, making the point that unless this is so then 'tissue rejection' is likely to occur. One can liken this to organ transplantation. For example, not only would one use a defective heart in a heart transplant operation but one would also transplant the donor heart into a body that had not been prepared to receive it.

Miles's work on organizational health is useful for its suggestion that diagnosis precedes action and that it is actually possible to improve an organization. The elements of his analysis suggest what might be the focuses of this improvement. Indeed he suggests some interventions that might be addressed in promoting the organizational health of the institution, for example: team training, survey feedback, role workshops, target-setting, organizational diagnosis and organizational experimentation. On the other hand one has to exercise caution in adopting Miles's view, for it appears to minimize the significance of conflict, adopting, rather, a functionalist and consensualist perspective, and it focuses on structures and systems rather than people. This is not to undermine Miles's work, it is simply to suggest that it might be an incomplete account. Nevertheless the metaphor of organizational health is powerful and memorable. An exercise to examine the organizational health of a school that could be used at an in-service session is outlined in Figure 6.2.[22]

In an analogous metaphor, the literature on analysing companies and organizations uses the concept of organizational climate. Gilmer (1966), Litwin and Stringer (1968) and Tagiuri (1968) suggest that organizational climate refers to the particular characteristics of an organization, its social systems and structures, its working practices, its defining qualities, its distinguishing features (from other organizations), the perceptions that employees have of the organization, all of which combine to impact on work and achievement.

Halpin (1966), writing on the administration of organizations, uses the concept of organizational climate to identify those types of organization where change is more or less likely to occur. He suggests that if the climate is not propitious for change then it is unlikely to be successful. He sets out six climates on a continuum from openness to closure, arguing that the more open is the climate the more conducive it is to change. The climate that is most conducive to change is the open climate. Here the

Task: One purpose of the task is to generate a range of significant and/or critical factors within an organizational culture/structure/system that are conducive to change. A second purpose is to introduce how these factors might be operationalized in examining the organizational health/climate of the institution.

Step 1: Brainstorm all the points/factors that contribute to a positive organizational culture, i.e. a culture that promotes, stimulates, supports and sustains change.

Step 2: Review the list of factors and arrange them into clusters of grouped items, under headings. It may be necessary to include one factor in more than one group.

Step 3: Evaluate the subitems in each group, taking out the less practicable or less important suggestions, leaving only key factors. For each main item, generate two questions/statements to which responses can be arranged on a rating (Likert) scale of either:

1 = 'not at all'; 2 = 'very little'; 3 = 'a little'; 4 = 'quite a lot'; 5 = 'a very great deal'

or

1 = 'not at all true of the institution'; 2 = 'scarcely true of the institution'; 3 = 'a little true of the institution'; 4 = 'moderately true of the institution'; 5 = 'very true of the institution'.

Examples of the first set of rating scales might be:

Question: How seriously are the views of senior managers taken by the headteacher?

Statement: Accurate and informed needs assessment usually forms the basis of the school development plan.

Examples of the second set of rating scales might be:

Question: How successful is the curriculum development that is undertaken by the individual curriculum co-ordinators?

Statement: Communication in our school is open.

The former tend to focus on *personal* views, opinions and attitudes whereas the latter might be seeking an *institutional* perspective (even though, of course, this will be attitudinal/perspectival).

Step 4: Prepare a list of the headings that you have used to present at a plenary session.

Time allowed: one hour.

Figure 6.2 Identifying key factors of a school's organizational health

distinguishing features are high morale, openness, co-operation, the minimum of bureaucracy and records, high job satisfaction and motivation, mutual respect for all employees and a feeling of genuineness. The leader is a model of appropriate behaviour and runs a loose–tight organization. Collegiality abounds. Indeed social relationships extend outside the organization.

Slightly less conducive to change is the autonomous climate. Here the distinguishing features are a very high level of autonomy that is accorded to employees, often to the neglect of co-ordination or alignment with the organization. The satisfaction of social needs often overtakes the achievement of the task. The leader adopts a 'hands-off' approach, being impersonal and sometimes aloof, and guidelines for procedures replace 'the personal touch'.

Less conducive still to change is the controlled climate, in which the thrust is towards task achievement at all costs, with a highly directive, dominating and often authoritarian leader, and inflexibility and lack of autonomy in work practices. That this might cause resentment and be counterproductive is noted by Senge (1990) and Wickens (1995).

Halpin suggests that a climate that is yet more closed to change is the familiar climate. This is distinguished by the emphasis on the 'big happy family', with morale and job satisfaction being average, with everybody trying to tell each other how things ought to be done, where social interaction is extensive and involvement is high. This climate embodies both the best and worst of family life and it is a truism to acknowledge that many families are dysfunctional and damaging. Many families have multiple goals or maybe do not know where they are going (simply having to survive!), both of which, as has been argued in preceding chapters, do not enable change to thrive.

Concomitant with the familiar climate is the paternalistic climate, of which attempts (often vain) by the leader to control the organization and the people are the hallmarks. The organization is characterized by low morale, it is riven with factions and the leader is highly intrusive, thereby causing overt resistance. Because it is a divided institution it does not augur well for sustained change; the micropolitics of the organization undermine attempts at change.

Finally Halpin's closed climate is the least conducive to change. Everything stagnates. There is low morale, little incentive for change, little sense (or indeed practice) of involvement. Workers simply 'go through the motions' of work with minimum commitment, with the leader giving generalized exhortations to work, without setting a good example. Inflexibility and a divisive organization in which participants are apathetic, controlled and intolerant are the hallmarks of this type of organization.

Halpin's work is useful in providing heuristic tools for analysis. One has to be cautious, perhaps, in adopting any typifications of organizations because they are just that – typifications rather than actualities – and are possibly over-reductionist and simplistic. Nevertheless, Halpin's identification of degrees of openness and closure to change at an organizational level is helpful, and indeed his placement of the familiar and paternalistic climates at the closed end of the continuum is perhaps salutary.

Hoy *et al.* (1991) apply Halpin's work to the educational context and identify four climates in education that are conducive to change. They, too, set these out on a continuum of openness to closure, and identify the open, engaged, disengaged and closed climates along this continuum from openness to closure to change respectively, the features of which are strikingly similar to the work of Halpin (which they acknowledge).

One can detect in the literature on organizational climate the same feature that was observed above in connection with the work of Garvin (1993), Wickens (1995) and Miller (1996), that organizations and organizational learning resemble individuals and individual learning writ large. Indeed Hoy *et al.* (1991: 4) suggest that the climate of the organization can be conceived as its 'personality'.

An example of the need for the organizational health and climate of the school to improve is given in Figure 6.3 (Morrison and Carroll, 1986).

Innovations were launched in two primary schools and evaluations were undertaken of their success. In both schools part of the evaluation used the DION questionnaire (see note 22) to chart the organizational health of the schools in terms of: environment; staff selection; structure and roles; leadership; creativity and innovation; resources; problem-solving capacity; teamwork; motivation; aims; staff development. The responses from the leaders of the innovations in the two schools were recorded separately from the other receiving staff in the innovation.

In school A the innovation was successful, there was considerable agreement between the leader and the recipients of the innovation about the organizational health/climate of the schools. The organizational health in the school was scored to be strong though it was not excellent in all elements, but both parties (leaders and recipients) identified the same strengths and weaknesses in the organizational health/climate (though the recipients were slightly stronger in their analysis of weaknesses). In school A there were shared perceptions and the health/climate was generally robust. Innovator and recipients agreed on needs.

In school B the innovation failed. There was considerable disagreement on the health/climate of the school between the innovator and the recipients, the recipients painting a much more pessimistic view than the innovator. Overall, the health/climate of the school was scored to be very poor. It was as though the innovator was blind (deliberately or subliminally) to the poor organizational health/climate of the school and to the perceptions of the staff. Innovator and recipients disagreed on needs.

Whilst it is dangerous to attribute causality when there is only association (one cannot say that the organizational health/climate was the cause of the success and failure of the two schools respectively – a strong hypothesis), nevertheless it is perhaps more than coincidence. A weaker hypothesis would be to suggest that if the climate is not propitious in the school then innovations may have little chance of success and that a positive climate is far more conducive to sustaining and institutionalizing change. Given the preceding discussions about the importance of interpersonal relations and the management of perception the weaker hypothesis is perhaps unsurprising.

Figure 6.3 The significance of organizational health and climate

Planning for organizational development

The discussion so far has stressed that organizational development needs to be an integral part of the change process and that the organization should be developing towards an organic and collegial structure. Drawing together the strands of this chapter Kanter *et al.* (1992) identify eight elements in the planning of change that an organization will have to face. These are germinal to developing the organizational culture that supports change:

1) a change will need to clarify its supporters;
2) symbols, signals and rewards must be public in marking the change;
3) standards, measures and feedback from these must be in place;
4) participation is essential;
5) communication must be widespread;
6) appropriate education and training must be assured;
7) there must be a guidance structure and process in the organization;
8) a shared vision is essential.

Beckhard (1992: 97–9) suggests that ten prerequisites are necessary if transformational change is to occur in an organization. He presents these in order of priority:

1) the top leaders must be committed to the change;
2) there must be a written description of how the changed organization will function;
3) the present situation must show that change is an improvement to the status quo for employees;
4) a critical mass of support must be present (see Wickens's (1995) view that this is roughly the square root of the total workforce);
5) long-term and medium-term perspectives must be used;
6) resistance must be recognized and addressed;
7) education must be provided;
8) there must be an acceptance that the change should be tried;
9) resource support for change must be secure;
10) communication and information flow must be free and widespread.

Peters (1987: 27–36) suggests that the development of an organizational culture that is conducive to change can benefit from an examination of successful companies (benchmarking), for they are: 1) flatter in their structure; 2) organized into autonomous units; 3) orientated towards differentiated, niche markets; 4) very conscious of quality; 5) obsessively conscious of service (to consumers and employees) and responsive to these demands; 6) rapid in their handling of innovation; 7) able to utilize highly trained, adaptable and flexible staff as the main means of adding value to the product, service and organization. Peters is arguing that successful companies are 8) highly proactive; 9) constantly innovating in all sections; 10) able to operate through partnerships (a win/win situation); 11) led by people who relish change and who can inspire others with their vision; (12) able to exert minimal controls.

Peters' message is important, for it argues for the need for human resource development (beyond initial – entry – training) and development of people's abilities to identify and solve problems. Development, he argues (*ibid*.: 322), should attach itself to each rung of the promotional ladder – each time people are advanced they receive training. Training in middle management might involve re-educating the middle manager for a new role – away from being the expert and line manager and towards being the facilitator and breaker of boundaries, i.e. a model of non-bureaucratic behaviour (*ibid*.: 380).

Kotter (1996) sets out eight steps for transforming an organization:

Step One: Establishing a sense of urgency, identifying pressures, crises and opportunities.

Step Two: Forming a powerful coalition of people who, as a team, will have sufficient power to effect change.

Step Three: Creating a vision to steer the change, together with strategies for realizing that vision.

Step Four: Communicating the vision as widely as possible and in as many ways as possible (including by example).

Step Five: Empowering everybody to realize that vision, overcoming barriers to change through personal, structural, systemic support mechanisms.

Step Six: Planning for and creating short-term achievable gains and improvements, coupled with rewarding for those improvements.

Step Seven: Consolidating those improvements and generating further changes through the development of everybody's capabilities, motivations and contributions, and through the injection of new projects.

Step Eight: Ensuring that new approaches are institutionalized, clarifying the links between the changes and improved performance. Developing leaders.

The development of an organizational culture that is conducive to change is a long-term matter (see the discussions earlier of collegiality). For example Harvey-Jones (1988: 114) puts an initial time frame of five years. Clarke (1994) argues that developing a culture is not a 'quick fix' but a much more gradualist matter, including, for example:

• testing ideas, opinions and attitudes;
• identifying resistances and their sources;
• providing training and education;
• making the familiar strange to those who are immersed in the company so that they can see it with fresh eyes;
• scanning the external environment and customers in order to make change proactive and in order to identify the pressures for change;
• developing employees' self-image as entrepreneurs;
• making communication effective;[23]
• developing a shared vision (a vision that illuminates rather than a vision that blinds – Fullan, 1991);
• making clear what the requirements will be of the change – from the short term to the long term;
• identifying responsibilities and accountability;
• collective identification of problems;
• development of a genuinely humanistic organization;
• ensuring that changes are sustained and that regression is avoided.

One can see the importance that is placed on the personal aspects of the change. This can extend to the micropolitics of the organization. For example Wickens (1995: 304) argues that it is essential to have a critical mass of people in an organization and stakeholders who are committed to the change (the flywheel effect – Goss *et al.*, 1996: 132). Here the informal networks and messages of the organization must be addressed.[24] The process as well as the content of change is manifestly important.

Organizations need the ability to withstand the vulnerability to disaster that change brings. Obeng (1990) suggests that organizations can take action to reduce their vulnerability. Highly vulnerable organizations are characterized by rapid strategic change with an emphasis on rapid results; unclear goals; a significant commitment of resources; uninterested, unsupportive and unrealistic senior managers; unrealistic expectations; lack of clarity about how to change or how to resource the changes; lack of clarity on responsibilities; extended reliance on overcomplex interdependencies (including dependence on third parties); many 'knock-on' effects of the change; conflicting perceptions and values; multipurpose changes.

On the other organizations that demonstrate low vulnerability to the potential dangers that change brings are characterized by operational rather than strategic changes (first order rather than second-order changes – Cuban, 1990); slower change with results taking a long time to appear; limited additional resources; realistic and supportive senior managers; realistic expectations of the change; clear ownership and responsibility; clarity on how the change will occur; limited reliance on interdependencies; limited 'knock-on' effects of the change; shared perceptions and values; limited-purpose changes.

The marginalization of resistance and the incorporation of facilitating factors are a key factor in managing organizational change. From the discussions so far one can suggest that these latter might include:

- positive interpersonal relations;
- external pressure and realization of the needs for change;
- a climate of problem identification and problem-solving in the organization;
- a willingness to try out new ideas;
- creativity and innovativeness;
- clear objectives and communication structures;
- a tradition of change in the organization;
- problem-posing, problem-analysing and problem-solving capability;
- the existence of a positive organizational climate and a healthy organization;
- adequate support structures and staff development;
- acceptance of current difficulties in the organization;
- grassroots involvement in the organization in order to generate ownership;
- the ability to build on existing staff expertise;
- staff support for the proposed change;
- incentives, motivations and resources to undertake the change;
- a tradition and practice of teamwork and collegiality in the institution;
- delegated and clear responsibilities;
- a critical mass of support;
- a view of the organization as organic rather than mechanistic;
- an identification of the most appropriate modes of learning in the

organization;
- the consonance of the proposed change with perceived requirements;
- the practicability and manageability of the organization;
- anticipation of necessary support for the change (e.g. reskilling);
- the support and commitment of the senior managers;
- the possibility of divisibility and triallability of the innovation;
- the perceived relative advantage of the change;
- the opportunities for promotion that the change might bring.

In planning for successful change one can identify several steps that can be taken at an organizational level to ensure success (Beer *et al.*, 1990):

- the mobilization of commitment to the change by collective diagnosis of the business problems;
- the development of a shared vision of what is needed and how the organization can meet these needs and vision;
- the fostering of consensus about the new vision;
- the development and deployment of abilities required to implement the new vision;
- the collective will and cohesion to ensure the vision is realized;
- the energizing of all departments without mandate from 'on high' and through policies, systems and structures in the organization;
- the monitoring of the change and ability to make adjustments where appropriate.

Kotter (1995) echoes this, suggesting the need to

- establish a sense of urgency for change;
- establish a powerful coalition to steer the change;
- create the vision;
- communicate this vision extensively;
- ensure that everyone is empowered to act on the vision;
- ensure that short-term advantages and rewards can be secured;
- consolidate changes and build on these in further changes;
- ensure that changes are institutionalized.

One can see the links here between Kotter's recommendations and the stages of change that were outlined in Chapter 2.[25] An example of Kotter's work in educational terms is given in Figure 6.4.

The significance of developing the appropriate organizational culture is stressed by Thomas and Ely (1996), with an emphasis on an expectation of high standards and achievement that is matched by opportunities to stimulate personal development. The culture of the organization must be non-bureaucratic and relatively egalitarian, with a commitment to openness and a valuing of everybody in the organization.[26]

Kanter (1994) acknowledges the advantages of collaboration and constructive alliances in organizations as they lead to a win/win situation. She sets out 'eight Is' that, she suggests, will create successful 'wes'!: individual excellence, the importance of partnerships, interdependence and integration; the significance of investment and information; and the need for institutionalization and integrity. The management of change,

A secondary school has a strong academic tradition in which it is highly successful. There is minimal staff turnover; for many staff this has been their first and only school and there is little 'new blood'. Departmental and individual autonomy are very high. The teaching is formal and traditionalist, representing the former grammar school status it possessed. The school has not encountered structural changes and has only been concerned to maintain the certainty of a steady state that is untouched by novelty and innovation ('why fix something if it is not broken'!). The school commenced appraisal, led by the new internally promoted deputy headteacher. However, upon her retirement the project foundered for several reasons:

- it had not become institutionalized in the school;
- it was still heavily dependent on one person who retired;
- the staff in the school saw no relevance in it to their everyday duties of teaching;
- it was seen as a managerial, cosmetic exercise with no impact;
- the links between appraisal, personal and professional development and their contribution to the overall aims of the school were not made;
- the innovation was seen as 'bolt-on' and marginal;
- the other senior staff lent little weight or support to the project;
- staff saw it as 'inspection by the back door';
- the links between appraisal and effective teaching were not made.

It was not that people were hostile to it; rather it was simply that they regarded it as entirely unnecessary and a bureaucratic encumbrance. It had neither value nor significance for them. It is no surprise that the innovation failed here. Any innovation would, because the organization was not used to change. Here, introducing appraisal was secondary to developing the school's organizational climate and culture so that it was conducive to change. How could this be done?

A far more assertive and demanding stance from the whole senior management team could be the impetus to change, stemming from a careful diagnosis of the needs of the organization for cultural change. Extensive communication of the principles, purposes, methods, uses and outcomes of appraisal is necessary, so that staff are persuaded or compelled (e.g. by evidence, requirement, argument, reason, force) to give appraisal a much higher profile than it had. Further, though it had been desirable, perhaps, to introduce it on a gradualist and non-threatening basis with only a few staff involved, it is now necessary to disseminate it far more widely and involve far greater numbers of people. The links between appraisal, personal and professional development and their contribution to the overall aims of the school need to be made more clearly, as do the links between appraisal and effective, improved classroom practice and student achievement. In short, the innovation needs to be 'managed' much more centrally so that its impact on the staff and their practice is inescapable. On a slightly longer-term basis, the contribution of appraisal to improving standards and working practices needs to be evidenced.

Figure 6.5 Planning for change at an organizational level

then, is based on fundamental principles of human interaction.

Summary of educational implications of organizational factors for change

At the heart of this chapter has been the centrality of understanding, working with and developing the organizational dynamics of the institution, the interpersonal relationships in managing change. Whilst attempting to avoid sloganizing, the message of this chapter is for the need to empower all participants in the organization. This argues for a flatter management style, the development and practice of collegiality and networking, and the practice of continuous improvement. The development of the organization as a flexible, responsive, quality-conscious and adaptive, dynamical system, is premised on the development of the culture of the organization.

The culture of the organization can be developed by addressing the formal and informal networks and arrangements, the development of partnerships and shared responsibilities, participation and attention to attitudes, skills, expertise, behaviour, values and beliefs of the participants in the organization. An appropriate culture for change in the organization emphasizes openness, synergy and widespread communication, building in and on feedback. In principle the organic and flexible structure and organization are more conducive to change than mechanistic and rigid bureaucracies and hierarchies respectively.

If organizational development for substantive change is to be managed effectively then the organization needs to examine the contingencies it faces, the micropolitics of the organization, the possibilities for developing synergy and how it will develop the culture-excellence model. The organization will need to examine how it can eliminate blame, promote teamwork (e.g. through project groups) and flexibility (DFE, 1993b: 98), reduce narrow job specifications, encourage extended responsibilities, and plan within realistic time frames.[27]

The structure of the organization will need to be examined in order to maximize its potential for change. This will include an evaluation of what is an acceptable level of bureaucracy, how promotion will be managed within the bureaucracy, and what are the strengths and weaknesses of bureaucratic and collegial structures for facilitating (and impeding) change. The type of organizational structure will have to be envisioned (e.g. federal, product, functional) and the strengths and weaknesses of different types of organization for the promotion of change and added value will need to be examined for the institution in mind. In turn this will necessitate the institution examining the strengths and weaknesses of 1) centralisation; 2) the drive for efficiency versus the drive for effectiveness; 3) devolved use of professional rather than line managers; 4) balancing control and commitment; 5) balancing stability and change.

The ability of the organization to become a learning organization will need to be examined, entailing, for example, an evaluation and development of its problem-solving capability, its ability to experiment, its ability to identify how it will learn as an organization (what it should do and how it should do it). The organization will need to examine its resources and resource use, undertake development of a shared vision and promote its innovativeness.

The organization, then, needs to foster a climate of openness to promote change and the development and sustenance of strong organizational health. To do this involves serious self-evaluation of the elements of task needs, maintenance and development needs, so that 'tissue rejection' will not occur. Indeed the organization will need to examine what might cause tissue rejection and what needs to be done to prevent this, how far consensus is desirable and achievable, and what must be a critical mass of support for change to be successful. Further, the role of leadership and leadership style are important in this organization for change, as is the necessity for the ongoing support for change by the leader and the support by senior management for risk-taking.

It has been argued, that, properly managed, organizational change both lays a solid foundation for change and itself promotes change. The notion that organizational change needs to be planned is certainly not new, and indeed many educational institutions have been taking this issue seriously for years. Sustainable change requires continuous improvements and support and the organization's cultural development.

Notes

1.   The development of a corporate strategy (Johnson and Scholes, 1993) necessitates examining the full scope of the organization and its activities because these impact significantly on the productivity of the organization, its operations, management, long-term goals and direction.

2.   Drucker (1996) suggests that businesses typically will be knowledge based and operated by knowledgeable, self-disciplining specialists who provide feedback to each other (*ibid*.: 3). Because organizations will become information based there will be a premium on information specialists. For Hammer (1996) the rise of information technology affords the opportunity to break out of existing organizational paradigms. He suggests that information technology should be used not to automate existing operations but to enable new processes and thinking in organizations to be developed (*ibid*.: 112), to enable organizations to undergo re-engineering.

3.   Kanter *et al.* (1992) suggest that there are three forms of change in an organization: identity changes (changes with regard to the external world), co-ordination changes (changes with regard to the internal workings of the organization) and changes of control (the political structures and dynamics in the institution).

4.   Peters and Waterman (1982) suggest that the rational approach of classical theory is flawed for its misconception of organizations, being overly simplistic and wrong in the faith it places in the single right answer.

5.   The concept of organizational culture can be traced back to the work of Barnard (1938), Mayo (1945), Selznick (1957) and Ouchi's (1981) Theory Z, discussed in Chapter 3. These emphasize the importance of understanding and developing the norms, types of interaction and value systems

within the organization. Indeed Selznick suggests that it is preferable to view organizations as 'institutions' as this connotes something additional to the operation of rationalistic systems; institutions have values that transcend the technical.

6. Harrison's work links closely with Handy's (1976) four cultures of an organization – the power or club culture, the role culture, the task culture and the person or existential culture.

7. Burnes adds the salutary comment (*ibid.*: 122) that those who are in power positions in an organization are less likely than those who are not in such positions to see their actions as political; the management of perception is also a matter of the education of perception, perhaps! Indeed Pfeffer (1981) argues that one of the defining characteristics of political behaviour is its attempt to conceal itself and its true motives.

8. This echoes the comments in earlier chapters about the need for incremental changes that are often small scale in nature.

9. Price and Murphy (1993: 158–9) comment on the elements of organizational culture that had been giving British Telecom cause for concern, including: minimal identification with the aims of the business; a punitive style of management which encouraged employees not to open the Pandora's box; widespread apportioning of blame; the alienation of the junior management. See also Beckhard's (1992) analysis of Pilkington's glass plant.

10. Fromm (1944) suggests that hierarchies bring dull uniformity, destructiveness and authoritarianism, minimizing effective change!

11. By way of contrast, Carnall (1995) identifies the successful company International Engineering as demonstrating certain characteristics of the organic system, for example: 1) excellent systems of support; 2) developing people and retaining them in the organization; 3) effective management development.

12. Jaques establishes seven layers of a hierarchy (the same number as advocated by Drucker (1988), but two more than those advocated by Peters (1987)). He argues that people's ability to occupy these layers is a function of the degree of responsibility required, the timespan of the project or task, the complexity of the task and the cognitive capacity required for the task.

13. Preedy and Wallace (1993) argue, however, that this view of management confuses leadership with management.

14. Within collegial models the exercise of control can still be practised (Simons, 1995), through the identification and utilization of four 'levers of control': belief systems (the core values of the organization); boundary systems (identification of the risks that need to be avoided); diagnostic control systems (identification of the critical factors for effective performance); interactive control systems (identification of 'strategic uncertainties' – those elements that await planning).

15. Carnall's (1995) six structures of organizations echo Handy's (1989) three types of organization – the shamrock organization, the federal organization and the Triple I organization (using information, ideas and intelligence). Handy emphasizes that the most effective way to run an organization of intelligent people is by consent and partnership rather than control and coercion (echoing McGregor), and that collegial cultures are important.

16. Buchanan and Boddy (1992: 72) suggest that projects might founder for several reasons, for example: inefficient support/commitment from senior managers; unclear objectives; insufficient involvement of line managers; insufficiently clearly defined or assigned responsibilities; reluctance to face up to problems until it is too late; corrective actions not implemented; inadequate and irregular monitoring; the failure of the project team to work together; insufficient investment of time and effort; critical players left out of operations and discussions; sectional interests over-riding organizational interests; an inappropriate mix of interpersonal, business and specialist expertise in project leaders.

17. Nonaka (1991) suggests that Japanese companies are founded on the principle that an organization, a company, is an organism rather than a machine, and that an organism, using its self-knowledge, identifies what it wants, where it is going and what it needs to do to reach its goals and targets.

18. Peters (1987) argues that both individuals and organizations must learn to welcome change and innovation rather than to resist it, echoed by Pettigrew (1985) in his processual and contextual views of change.

19. Wickens (1995: 74–6) argues that there is a range of organizational types, from the apathetic, through the alienated, autocratic, authoritative, amiable, ardent and anarchistic to the ascendant. The implications are that one can identify organizational reactions to change that are made up of the experiences of individuals, and that if one wishes to effect organizational change and learning it is possible to arrive at the most effective ways of achieving these through the identification of effective strategies for individual learning.

20. Brown and Weiner (1984) argue that the learning organization must combine individual development with organizational development. They emphasize the need for the organization to construct an environment which will motivate people to learn for themselves.

21. Beer *et al.* (*ibid.*) suggest (echoing Deming, 1982) that 'buzz words' simply obstruct analysis and implementation. Mintzberg (1996) also suggests that buzz words are part of the problem of change rather than the solution.

22. There are several examples of commercially produced questionnaires for examining the organizational climate of the school, e.g.: a) the popular Diagnosis of Individual and Organizational Needs for Staff Development and In-service Training in Schools (DION) questionnaire by Elliott-Kemp and Williams (1979); b) the research techniques from the Mapping Change in Schools project at Cambridge (Ainscow *et al.*, 1994); c) the Sigma project on managing change (Elliott-Kemp and Elliott-Kemp, 1992); d) West-Burnham (1997). These need to be taken with caution because they are perhaps simplistic, generalized and only crude indicators, they allow for little differentiation of intensity of response, and they tend to adopt a 'systems' rather than a person-centred view. Nevertheless they can be useful in setting agendas and raising awareness of the current state of a school's organizational health. On the other hand they can be 'dynamite', hardening up differences and animosity between staff; they work best, perhaps, in a supportive, problem-solving rather than a blaming climate.

23. Clarke (*ibid.*: 40) notes the importance of communicating the culture to the outside world, citing the example of the Body Shop's environmentally friendliness and Sony's synonymity with quality. The importance of marketing is a feature that many schools are facing.

24. IBM took pains to disseminate its message that: a) it was committed to continuous improvement from the senior management onward to everyone in the organization; b) management would be very visible; c) customers were the main priorities in the organization; d) goals and targets would be set annually; e) there would be support for staff development; f) there would be recognition and rewarding of achievement; g) communication would be constant.

25. The thrust towards sustainability of the change in Kotter's later recommendations is reinforced by Weller (1996: 25), who identifies common elements in successful sustained change, including: a) having enough resources ('external conditions'); b) having the sustained commitment of senior managers ('external conditions'); c) willingness of everyone to change ('internal conditions'); d) pressures to change – both internally and externally ('triggering events') – that are brought about by dissatisfaction with the present; e) careful planning of the process of change (the 'change strategy') which includes the involvement of powerful 'players' at all levels of the organization.

26. Leaders, Thomas and Ely (1996) maintain, must recognize, accept and work with the several different perceptions of work within the organization, and recognize that these different perspectives can be used as opportunities for learning and productive challenge for the organization, for example in the development of its mission. These views are reinforced by Mintzberg (1996) who suggests that organizations are more akin to a circle rather than having tops and bottoms, and that, concomitantly, once great organizations have been created they do not require great leaders.

27. The Department for Education (1993b: 97) noted that many schools were suffering from innovation overload as too much was being required too rapidly, occasioning stress.

7

Teamwork

Introduction

The argument has been made throughout the book so far that teamwork is a powerful contributor to the success of a company, and indeed the chapter on Japanese business practices placed teamwork as one of its cornerstones. Katzenbach and Smith (1993b: 211) and Wickens (1995: 64–5) suggests that teamwork breaks the former Taylorist mentality by rejoining conception and execution (thinking and doing) and, thereby, bringing the ownership that control over productivity brings (see also Peters, 1987: 164–5). Peters (*ibid.*: 296) also suggests that it is the medium-sized and largely semi-autonomous and self-managing team that should constitute the main building block of the successful organization.[1]

Katzenbach and Smith (1993b) advocate teamwork for successful companies and performance, with opportunities for teamwork existing everywhere in organizations. Indeed, they suggest that teams are natural ways of integrating performance and learning. In teams individual accountability is complemented by mutual accountability and mutual support; everybody is expected to use their brains as well as their bodies; people are expected to take on multiple roles and tasks interchangeably so that they can work together rather than simply perform a narrow range of tasks expertly; line management control is replaced by joint responsibility for operations. They suggest that an appropriate degree of challenge will motivate a team, frequently coupled with strong performance standards that are promoted by the organization's leaders. Indeed they argue that hierarchies and teams are by no means mutually exclusive. Teams can recommend things, make things, do things, run things, solve problems and promote the organizational health of the institution. Much is claimed, therefore, for them! This chapter will examine some of these claims.

Defining a team

A team is a group of people with a common objective, whose members possess different areas of expertise, skills, personalities and abilities that complement one another, and who are committed to working together co-operatively on a common, shared task and a common purpose (e.g. Deming, 1982: 64; Adair, 1987: 138; Woodcock, 1989; Katzenbach and Smith, 1993a: 112). A team is aware that it is a team and individuals work towards team cohesiveness and positive interpersonal relations, i.e. the team has a dynamic of its own as well as being focused on a substantive task.[2] An effective team maximizes all these properties and an ineffective team minimizes them. Teams grow and develop rather than remain static, they are a learning organization in microcosm. In an effective team people demonstrate concern for each other, there is a spirit of openness and honesty (in feelings as well as in application to the task), conflict management is practised skilfully and positively, trust is high, members are committed to the team and decisions are taken consensually. Hence effective team membership is a function of expertise, personality, social skills of individuals and their willingness to be involved in and to contribute to the team.[3]

The advantages and disadvantages of teamwork

Many claims have been made for teamwork. Clearly their greatest claim is the appeal to synergy: a team is able to achieve something that each individual working on his or her own might not. There are several claimed attractions to teamwork. For example:[4]

- the team can tackle a greater range, a greater number and a greater difficulty of problems than the capabilities of an individual person or department ('two heads are better than one');
- the comprehensiveness and quality of the solutions to problems are improved;
- commitment to work, projects and activities is increased (resulting in lower absenteeism and staff turnover);
- problems are identified by the people who are the closest to them;
- commitment to implementation of solutions to problems will be high if the team has had responsibility for suggesting the solutions;
- crossfunctional and crossdepartmental boundaries are broken for the good of the organization and enterprise;
- a greater range of expertise and skills is available and used;
- teams extend the range of expertise of individuals, enhancing their 'promotability' (vertically and horizontally) and flexibility;
- communication is improved and is immediate and accurate;
- people enjoy being members of teams and working in teams, i.e. the quality of the workplace is improved;
- peer pressure is considerable;
- teams develop the social aspects of work and this improves performance;
- everyone is united in working together for the good of the organization or enterprise;
- the burden is shared rather than removed;
- teamwork is a strategy for controlling employees;
- teamwork empowers all participants and improves morale;
- growth is facilitated through collaboration;

- collaboration, co-operation and partnership replace competition – a necessary ingredient for the successful companies of the future;
- teamwork changes roles, i.e. they are devices for organizational change, for example middle managers cease to become line managers and become coaches and facilitators;
- teamwork can put concerted pressure on people;
- teamwork fosters mutual respect and awareness;
- teamwork is useful if insufficient time is available for individuals to undertake a task.

In educational terms, these can be turned into 20 questions to evaluate the desirability of teams, i.e. to decide whether the teamworking approach is desirable (Figure 7.1).

---

1) Will the team be able to tackle more – and more difficult problems – than an individual?
2) How will teamwork improve the quality of solutions to problems?
3) Will team membership improve commitment to work, to the proposed solution to problems and to activities in this instance?
4) Will teamwork enable problems to be voiced by those closest to them?
5) Will teamwork break down barriers between working structures and groups?
6) Will teamwork enable different types of expertise to be brought to bear on a problem?
7) Will teamwork improve or impede communication?
8) How will teamwork improve morale?
9) How desirable is the degree of peer pressure that teamwork will bring?
10) How will teamwork enable everyone to participate positively?
11) How desirable are the social inter-relations that teamwork will bring?
12) Will teamwork bring people together positively?
13) Will teamwork improve or exacerbate differences between people and their perceived contributions to a situation?
14) Will the additional effort required for teamwork be worth it?
15) How will teamwork ensure equity of workloads?
16) How will teamwork increase collaboration and minimize competition?
17) How will teamwork promote or inhibit change?
18) How will roles change in teams?
19) Will teamwork improve awareness and mutual respect?
20) Will teamwork save time and individual work (through a division of labour)?

Figure 7.1　Evaluating the desirability of teamworking in education

This is not to say that teamwork is an unqualified good; it has its critics. Very many of the drawbacks that were cited against collegiality in Chapter 6 apply here also,[5] viz. that it

- is clumsy, cumbersome, slow and creates vast amounts of paperwork;
- can enable a group to exert disproportionate influence on the organization;

- over-rides the advantages of hierarchical approaches;
- is unrealistic in the demands that it makes of members;
- understates the power or problems of conflict and consensus;
- can run into dangers of 'group-think', for example: an inability to examine alternative goals and practices; a neglect of examination of risks; incomplete searches of information (being too selective in line with the group's preferences);
- can produce high stress levels;
- relies on compliance;
- is regarded as a thinly veiled strategy for controlling workers, i.e. the agenda is not 'up for debate', only the means of achieving it;
- can reduce output in the drive for involvement;
- can suffer from too great a cohesiveness, e.g.: making the induction of new members difficult; debarring the generation and serious consideration of new ideas; being resistant to new practices; creating dull conformity, territorialism, intergroup rivalry and ill-feeling that leads to awkwardness, hostility and mistrust between groups;
- can create role conflict, role overload (with people having to fulfil too many roles simultaneously) and role ambiguity (uncertainty on what roles actually are);
- can create disproportionate ill-feeling towards perceived 'slackers';
- requires extensive co-ordination that in turn puts pressure on time for this to occur.

Teamwork can be a mixed blessing. This is an important feature, for it argues against blind advocacy of teamwork and replaces this with an awareness that teamwork brings with it its own difficulties. The notion here, perhaps, as with the views of quality discussed in Chapter 4, is that of fitness for purpose. The decision to adopt a teamwork approach should fulfil specified purposes.

Within the field of education a major consideration in the adoption of teamwork, then, is to decide its fitness for purpose and to weigh up its relative advantages and disadvantages. For example, it is important to ask whether a team is actually necessary (Adair, 1987: 137) or whether it obstructs the effective working of an individual who might be the only person who possesses the required area of expertise. Adair (*ibid.*: 140) argues that there are vast tracts of work where teamwork is unnecessary, even though there are small areas where it is vital in regard to a manager's work.

Types of team

The business literature identifies (and advocates) several different types of team, particularly the crossfunctional team and the project team. Within a hierarchical setting Woodcock (1989: 4–5) suggests the management team (providing leadership, setting goals and strategies, controlling others' work and allocating resources), the operator team (those who do the work), the technical team (those who set the standards and ensure standardization) and support teams (to ensure the smooth operation of the work). Drucker

(1995) identifies three types of team: 1) the baseball team (fixed positions and no communication); 2) the football team (fixed positions but flexible working and clear leadership); 3) the tennis doubles team (constant adjustment to the partner's play and the demands of the game). However a more wide-ranging typology of teams can be addressed. These are discussed in turn.

The crossfunctional team

The predominant type of team that emerges in the business literature[6] is the crossfunctional team, a characteristic type of team in the 'ascendant organization' (Wickens, 1995). A crossfunctional perspective can best be served by a crossfunctional team (Hammer, 1996). This type of team is able to harness the benefits of synergy that break down departmental boundaries and enable all relevant parties to come together to focus on the multifaceted nature of problems. For example the Rover group developed crossfunctional teamwork as a deliberate strategy to put people first (Burnes, 1996: 246) and to enable conflicts and disagreements to be aired and reduced in the spirit of collaborative problem-solving. The crossfunctional team brings together all the key members of the organization to focus on a problem, issue, product development, etc., echoing the practice from Japanese companies that the experts are the people who are closest to the job and that if something is worth saying it is worth saying face to face (Wickens, 1995). This type of team is also ultimately time saving as it reduces several meetings between different members of the organization – it brings them together simultaneously to 'get on with the job'. Figure 7.2 gives an example of a crossfunctional team in education.

A secondary school is working on a school improvement project of raising standards of literacy. The team comprises: 1) the deputy headteacher with responsibility for curriculum; 2) the head of special educational needs within the school; 3) the head of the faculty of languages; 4) the library and resources manager; 5) the head of the English department; 6) a science teacher in the school. It operationalizes its tasks as: 1) identifying trouble spots of underachievement; 2) setting targets for improvement; 3) identifying specific actions that need to be taken and who will have to take them; 4) identifying specific implications and time frames for all teaching staff, not just the language teachers.

It can be seen here: 1) that those with particular expertise, experience, influence are brought together to discuss the project; 2) those close to working with the problem are included; 3) the team is small (therefore manageable and manoeuvrable); 4) the tasks and roles are specific, time-framed and concrete; 5) one of those teachers who will be implicated but who might not see it as a main priority (the science teacher) is included, to represent other teachers in that position 6) a member of the senior management team is included. What is being argued for here is careful team membership – sampling – to ensure full representation, expertise and manageability.

Figure 7.2 A crossfunctional team in education

Iles and Auluck (1993: 176-7) suggest that the multifunction team can cross several levels or types of function, for example: disciplines, structures, interests, membership, power and status, rules for procedures and operations. Putting the function as a high priority enables boundaries – however defined – to be crossed. Peters (1987: 210) is unequivocal in suggesting that multifunction teams are essential for all development activities, bringing the advantages of synergy.

The project team

This team, which may have a comparatively short lifespan, is useful as a 'taskforce' for creating, initiating and stimulating change (McKaskey, 1988). Its task is carefully bounded (whatever the project is) and it has very clear brief, clearly defined purposes and tasks, and is intended to focus on producing concrete outcomes. This is not to suggest that it is merely a lower or middle-level operational team; indeed the experience of the automobile industry (e.g. Burnes, 1996) suggests that this team requires the presence of the senior managers as policy decision-makers, and is concerned with the ways in which the project will fit into the overall strategy and mission of the organization. In this respect it shares some properties of the multi-functional team, where several functions are brought together to focus on a particular task; it thus combines specialization, individualism and team membership (Peters, 1992: 154). An example of a project team is given in Figure 7.3.

In education an example of this might be a team that is established in a secondary school to develop schools/industry partnerships (e.g. Morrison, 1997b). Its tasks are: 1) to establish programmes that integrate work placement and school curricula, that develop core and transferable skills in literacy, numeracy and IT; 2) to bring together representatives of industry and the school to plan programmes, monitoring, assessment and accreditation; 3) to appoint a co-ordinator within the school and an 'action team'; 4) to liaise with local employers and careers services to enable programmes to be planned that will lead to post-school employment; 5) to plan effective work experience programmes that build into each student's portfolio for employability (action planning). To this end the team comprises: the director of careers programmes in the school; two local employers (from a small and a large-sized company); the head of year-10 and year-11 programmes; the head of the school sixth form; a representative from the local careers service.

Figure 7.3 A project team in education

Superteams

Hastings *et al.* (1986) identify the interesting phenomenon of the 'superteam', a group that possesses several distinguishing characteristics. For example (*ibid.*: 10–12), superteams

- are persistent and obsessive in the pursuit of their goals, but creatively flexible in their strategies for getting there. They are continuously returning to the question 'What are we trying to achieve?'
- confront people or situations which lie in their path. They are tenacious and inventive in their efforts to remove all obstacles;
- are committed to quality in performance and all aspects of teamworking. They have very high expectations of themselves and others;
- display significant understanding of the strategy and philosophy of their present organization or that part of it which is important to their success;
- are inspired by a vision of what they are trying to achieve. This provides a strong sense of purpose and direction. They also have a realistic strategy for turning the vision into reality;
- actively build formal and informal networks which include people who matter to them and who can help them;
- make themselves visible and accessible to others. They communicate strongly what they stand for, but they welcome advice and comments from outside;
- are driven by success. They exude the energy, excitement and commitment that being successful releases. They also thrive on the recognition that success brings;
- are action orientated. They respond quickly and positively to problems and opportunities and are optimistic even when the going gets tough. But above all they don't wait for things to happen to them. They go out and make things happen; things happen;
- are committed to the success of their parent organization. They thrive in an open culture where responsibility and authority are delegated to them to produce agreed results;
- have a significant influence on the parent organization. The power to influence is not based on formal authority but on the team's credibility. Team and organization feed off and learn from each other;
- work best with principles and guidelines as procedures rather than rules. In this way they preserve one of their key qualities – flexibility;
- distinguish the important from the urgent, and while valuing change and flexibility will make routine those activities which can be dealt with most effectively in that way;
- value leaders who maintain the team's direction, energy and commitment. They expect the leader, with their help, to fight for support and resources from key figures within the parent organization;
- are able to sustain communication and momentum as well when they are working apart as when they are working together;
- pride themselves on being creative and innovative and as being prepared to take legitimate risks in order to achieve significant gains;
- understand why they are successful but are never satisfied with that. They are constantly looking for ways to 'do things better';
- value people for their knowledge, competence and contributions rather than for status and position;
- will always try to work *with* others rather than working for or against others;
- sometimes seem arrogant – this can be the cause of their downfall!

Clearly this is an aggressively entrepreneurial, hard-working, target and achievement-orientated, maybe manipulative and highly committed group which is given massive autonomy, high status and high rewards. It is the think-tank that is also combined with a commitment to action and delight in being 'where the action is'. The risk of arrogance this brings has been alluded to by Hastings *et al.* (*ibid.*); this may be an important team in the organization but its members may not be particularly likeable. This is a clear example of the dangers of intragroup cohesiveness being potentially deleterious to intergroup relations. One would not wish to have, or perhaps be able to tolerate, more than one superteam in the organization or indeed to have even one. This is the team that has ideas and creativity.[7]

Although elements of superteams can be found routinely in schools (e.g. commitment, hard work, creativity, collaboration, action orientation, valuing people), it is perhaps hard to envisage this happening completely in education for several reasons. First, most teachers do not have the luxury of time to work as the superteam; secondly, many teachers have multiple and divided tasks and responsibilities; thirdly, teachers have to work within a high degree of prescription, delivering a given curriculum, the creativity lies in the delivery system; fourthly, teachers do not have the luxury of the freedoms (freedom from constraint and overload, freedom to be autonomous) that superteams typically display, they have duties; fifthly, most teachers are struggling to keep up with the burden of existing stress and teaching. This is not to say that teachers cannot form superteams; indeed many teams in schools are truly superhuman in their achievements. Rather, it is being argued here that the singularity of purpose and operations that characterizes superteams is tempered by other demands on teachers in schools. Nevertheless one can identify several characteristics of superteams in schools (Figure 7.4).

Teams that:

- constantly ask themselves what they are trying to achieve;
- are not put off by interruptions and obstacles, i.e. that demonstrate dogged persistence;
- set themselves high but achievable targets and expectations;
- utilize effective strategies to achieve their goals;
- demonstrate a singularity of purpose;
- are personally highly committed to the team and to the task;
- network and communicate extensively in pursuit of their goals;
- work very hard and enjoy hard work and success;
- are highly and assertively proactive;
- are able to prioritize and keep to their priorities;
- are constantly, but positively, dissatisfied;
- bring others into their work to ensure the task is completed.

Figure 7.4 Elements of superteams in schools

Transition management teams

This is a team that comes into being at moments of change, addressing the process of change and its management rather than its substance. Duck (1993) suggests that this type of team has eight tasks. To

1) set a context for change and innovation and to provide advice and guidance on it;
2) stimulate discussions about the change;
3) manage the provision and organization of appropriate resources;
4) undertake a co-ordination role, ensuring that projects are co-ordinated and that they are aligned to the overall mission of the organization;
5) ensure harmonization of the policies, tasks, behaviour and purposes of the change;
6) ensure the provision of opportunities for joint projects;
7) anticipate and address people-focused problems that might occur;
8) identify and work with the critical mass of participants.

One can detect here a concern for the proactive preparation for change and the human side of change. Underlying this is the significance of the overall mission and vision of the organization, so that projects can fulfil the mission.[8] This type of team was used with great success at the Rover group, where the change management team was able to plan a step-by-step approach to change. In educational terms this kind of team will probably be the senior management team, who will co-opt members and act consultatively as far as possible. Indeed the numbered points above set an agenda for the management of change with regard to the responsibilities of the senior managers.

Roles and makeup of teams

Recognizing that people matter and figure in planned change – they influence and shape change plans – argues for the need to build on the people involved in change, the participants and stakeholders. This view reinforces the need for teams, teaming, team development and the promotion of the effective team. Belbin (1981: 20–30) conceptualizes teams on two continua of introversion/extroversion and anxiety/stability. He argues that 'stable extrovert' teams pull together well, enjoy group work, are versatile and make good use of resources, though they can become euphoric and lazy. 'Anxious extrovert' teams are dynamic, entrepreneurial, good at seizing opportunities, prone to discussion, debate and argument, and are easily distracted; they function well in times of rapid change but their performance at other times is unreliable. 'Stable introvert' teams plan well, function well in an organization but are slow moving, prone to indifference and liable to neglect novelty. 'Anxious introvert' teams can produce good ideas but they tend to be preoccupied and lacking in team cohesion. Indeed Belbin argues against 'pure' teams, suggesting that a 'mixed team' is the most successful. The successful team, then, has to attend to the personalities and personal concerns of each member. This is echoed by Riches (1993a) who argues that individuals join teams for a range of reasons:

- affiliation needs (opportunities for socializing);
- security needs (emotional support);
- esteem needs (promote an individuals' self-respect through positive feedback);
- self-fulfilment needs (supporting individuals' attempts to achieve their potential);
- reduction of tension (though mutual support);
- increase job satisfaction (through a sense of belonging and receipt of positive feedback on contributions).

A 'mixed team' is defined not only in terms of personality attributes but also in terms of role membership. Belbin (1981: 65–78) sets out a variety of roles that people might adopt in a team: company worker, chair, shaper, plant (creative thinker and innovator), resource investigator, monitor-evaluator, team worker and completer-finisher. He subsequently added a 'part-time' member – the specialist consultant – who would join the team when required (see also Mottram, 1982). Belbin (1981: 93–111) argues that a successful company and team depend on having

- a successful Chair (a patient but commanding figure who generates trust and looks for and uses ability, who possesses an ability to take a back seat and to take critical decisions when appropriate);
- an effective Plant (a creative and highly intelligent thinker);
- a spread of personal attributes in the team members (a range of roles and personalities in the team members);
- the careful matching of members' responsibilities with their interests and attributes (with some pairing of attributes in members in order to avoid over-reliance on a single member);
- an adjustment to the realization of imbalance (of roles, attributes, personalities, abilities);
- a spread of mental abilities in the team (with above-average intelligence in the Chair and the Plant and perhaps slightly below-average intelligence in other members).[9]

Belbin's work is useful in indicating the significance of personality types and roles within a team. Indeed he argues that it is positively counter-productive to have more than one Plant in a team, or to have an intrusive Chair, or too many dominant personalities or leaders (which might lead to conflict or 'paralysis through analysis' – Peters and Waterman, 1982).

The approach that Belbin adopts is not, however, without its critics and problems (e.g. Adair, 1987; West-Burnham, 1997). For example, one could argue that the behaviour of individuals is highly context specific. We behave differently according to the group in which we are placed, according to the task we have to undertake, according to our perceptions of others, according to our commitment and motivation, according to the presence of others, and according to which areas of our expertise we are being asked to use. Indeed Adair signals the dangers of stereotyping and categorizing people and the problems of the self-fulfilling prophecy that ensues. West-Burnham (1997) draws attention to the possible inapplicability of Belbin's work to education and to the biased (sympathetic) sampling that gave rise to his findings. Nevertheless Belbin's work represents an empirical attempt to understand successful teams and his conclusions should not be dismissed lightly.[10]

An alternative to Belbin is provided by Plant (1987), who argues that role effectiveness comprises ten elements:

1) centrality (whether a person feels his or her role is central or peripheral);
2) integration (whether a person can utilize and integrate his or her specific skills and expertise in the tasks and roles he or she performs);
3) proactivity (whether a person can behave proactively rather than responsively);
4) creativity (whether this is encouraged and utilized);
5) connections (whether a person's roles – plural – connect with each other);
6) giving and receiving help (whether a person has the opportunity to give and receive help);
7) wider organizational value (whether a person feels his or her contribution is valuable to the whole organization);
8) influence (whether a person can exercise influence in his or her role);
9) personal growth (whether the role affords a person the opportunity for personal growth);
10) confronting problems (whether people face problems squarely or refuse to own their problems).

In examining team effectiveness, then, the major implication for education is the need to match role with person, role with ability, role with personality, role with preferred ways of working.

One can suggest that a 'mixed team' will comprise members with multiple roles, multiple personalities, multiple intelligences and multiple abilities. This enables strength-through-diversity to be exercised (Gardner, 1993). Though the mixed team is the most successful, Belbin (1981) argues that runners-up (in order) are the team of co-operative stable extroverts, the team with the charismatic leadership and drive of a 'superstar' (the Chair having overwhelming superiority in intellectual or creative abilities) and the 'Apollo' team (a team that hoards its ample resources and talents of mental abilities to deal with complex problems, even though it is lacking in knowledge of how to use these).

Adair (1987: 157–8) extends the notion of multiplicity, suggesting that effective teams will comprise members with a range of *skills*, for example: analysis, reasoning, synthesis, thinking holistically, valuing others' contributions, creativity, intuitive thinking, the possession of an excellent memory, and high numeracy and literacy skills. One can see clearly, here, that there is a strong link between these skills and the ability to adopt problem-solving approaches to development.

The literature on teams is replete with delineations of the roles team members perform (e.g. Adair, 1987: 41–3; Everard and Morris, 1990: 264). These include, for example: initiator, information seeker, facilitator, dynamizer, contributor, co-ordinator, consultant, process facilitator, orienter, reminder, information giver, elaborator, pace-maker, resource-investigator, evaluator, norm-establisher, harmonizer, catalyst, discussion-leader, compromiser, smoother, recorder, observer, exemplar, challenger, standard-setter, regulator, controller, synthesizer, completer and critic. The lists is as long as there are types of human behaviour! Hence Belbin's (1981) work is useful in identifying key roles in the makeup of the team. Chaudhry-Lawton *et al.* (1992) suggest that an effective team comprises an appropriate combination of expertise and skills, personalities that are compatible with each other and effective styles of working. Figure 7.5 gives an example of a balanced team in education.

In a secondary school a suitable curriculum development team might comprise: 1) the headteacher (as chair and information provider, e.g. on resources) who should be enthusiastic, extrovert and an effective communicator – see the discussions of leadership in Chapter 8); 2) the deputy headteacher with responsibility for curriculum matters (as both creative, unorthodox problem-poser and problem-solver and yet as a reliable and methodical manager who can work out the implications of ideas for practice and ensure they happen); 3) a senior teacher (working with the deputy headteacher to attend to the fine-grain details of implementation, ensuring that smooth operations take place and that problems are anticipated and solved meticulously); 4) a senior member of staff who is co-operative, unruffled, a good listener, able to calm disputes and arguments, to provide support and to smooth difficulties; 5) faculty and/or department heads; 6) volunteers who want to join the team. There is a risk that this team might become too large and, therefore, unwieldy, leading to inaction. There is a powerful case for a small executive. On the other hand a major team like this of no more than ten staff might be small enough to prevent inertia and large enough to ensure healthy debate and full examination of matters.

Figure 7.5 A curriculum development team in education

Team leadership

It is clear that the effectiveness of a team is partly a function of its leadership. Adair (1987) and Katzenbach and Smith (1993b) identify several tasks of the team leader. For example, to

- ensure that every individual is both supported and giving his or her best;
- ensure that tasks are distributed equitably;
- manage meetings and development;
- focus the team on the shared goals and to ensure they are meaningful;
- ensure the team works together effectively to achieve the shared goals.

Gibb and Gibb (1955) suggest that the tasks of team leaders fall into five categories: initiating; providing information (communication); supporting; regulating; evaluating (together with providing feedback). This resonates with Adair (1987), who suggests that an effective leader should be able to plan, control and support people and developments.

Adair (*ibid*.: 117–19) and Katzenbach and Smith (1993b) identify several characteristics of the effective team leader. For example:

- an ability to enthuse team members;
- an ability to set directions and goals;
- an ability to lead by example – actually 'doing' things;
- integrity;
- the ability to develop and build on the commitment and the confidence of team members;
- facility in interpersonal relations;
- an ability to develop the leadership potential of others in the team;
- a high degree of self-awareness and awareness of the needs of everyone in the team;
- an ability to establish and communicate trust;
- expertise in representing the team within and outside the organization;
- a personal commitment to the team;
- an ability to set the direction of the team;
- ability to maximize resources;
- an ability to create opportunities for everybody's development;
- a willingness to be exposed (i.e. to be out-in-front);
- flexibility of style of leadership;
- effectiveness in team-building (discussed below);
- an ability to set and achieve high standards both personally and for the members of the team.

In the education field, using the practice of 'triadic elicitation' (Kelly, 1955; Nash, 1973) one can undertake a straightforward task to identify characteristics of effective team leaders (see Figure 7.6).

In Figure 7.6, if one replaces the focus on team leadership with a focus on effective and ineffective teams, then the same exercise can be used to identify characteristics and constructions of effective and ineffective teams. The question of leadership is taken up much more fully in Chapter 8.

---

1) on your own think of three effective team leaders with whom you have worked;
2) on your own identify and note down characteristics/constructs that render any two of them similar to each other but different from the third;
3) on your own repeat this until you have exhausted the constructs, until you can no longer think of any more;
4) share these constructs with others in a group activity;
5) organize these constructs into categories with category headings;
6) compare the category headings from your groups with those from other groups.

This exercise is useful in applying construct theory to identify key dimensions of leadership, i.e. ways in which effective leadership is being construed in participants' terms, echoing the comments in previous chapters on the importance of working with people's perceptions and constructions of a situation.

Figure 7.6   An exercise to identify characteristics of effective team leaders

Characteristics of effective and ineffective teams

It has been suggested that one abiding characteristic of effective teams is the notion of 'fitness for purpose'. Until one knows the purposes for which the team has been established it is invidious to evaluate the success or otherwise of the team. That said, it is possible nevertheless, from the discussions so far, to identify some common properties of effective teams.[11] These can be grouped into the component elements of action, team qualities, leadership and communication.

Action

- Their existence is appropriate for the task;
- responsibilities and roles are clear and shared;
- there is an emphasis on real action as well as on discussion;
- the tasks of the team are clear and concrete;
- methods and practices are appropriate for the purpose;
- the activities of the team are subject to review and formative feedback;
- the team is disciplined and linked to performance standards;
- they are quick to produce decisions that are effective and appropriate;
- they make few errors;
- they are committed to continuous improvement and achieve this;
- they are decisive and able to meet specified targets within specified time frames;
- they can accommodate change that is externally generated;
- they are able to manage pressure and stress by attempting to distribute it amongst the team;
- the team takes decisions collectively and collaboratively.

Team qualities

- Members are proud to be in the team;
- the team is marked by honesty, mutual trust, truthfulness and openness;
- individual development takes places within overall group development;
- a high premium is placed on effective interpersonal relationships;
- a concern is demonstrated for the individuals in the group;
- conflict and disagreement are anticipated and are viewed constructively as opportunities;
- values are explicit and shared;
- there is a shared (owned) vision and purpose.

Leadership

- Team leaders are genuine members of the team rather than outside figures;
- leadership is based on need, function, skills and expertise rather than on position within a hierarchy.

Communication

- Communication throughout the team is widespread and effective;
- communication beyond the team (e.g. to other teams) is effective.

Evenden and Anderson (1992: 180) suggest that effective teams are also a product of the possession of key characteristics of the individuals in them. They suggest that effective team members should be goal directed, enthusiastic, assertive, competent, open, flexible, supportive, constructive and be able to take on leadership roles. In the field of education West-Burnham (1997: 138–40) summarizes literature to show that effective teams possess nine principal characteristics:

1) explicit and shared values;
2) situational leadership (the team's leader's responsiveness to the situation, e.g. preparedness to stand back as the occasion demands, enabling others to take a lead);
3) pride in the team (bringing high morale, commitment and involvement);
4) an emphasis on action (with participants being clear on their tasks and contributions);
5) collaborative decision-making and decision-reaching;
6) clear tasks (concrete, specified, realistic, time bound, suitably resourced, clear achievement criteria);
7) lateral communication (open, within and crossteam communication);
8) feedback and review (information sharing and team self-review);
9) openness and candour (absence of hidden agendas), honesty without blame.

Hargreaves (1994) argues for genuine collaborative cultures to be developed in educational institutions rather than 'contrived' collegiality (which is administratively regulated, compulsory, implementation orientated, fixed in time and space, and predictable – (*ibid.*: 195–6). Contrived collegiality occurs where more spontaneous and unpredictable (and hence possible uncontrollable) collaboration is discouraged or where administrators strive to contain collegiality through formal operational mechanisms and procedures (*ibid.*: 80). Genuinely collaborative cultures, he suggests (*ibid.*: 192–3), are spontaneous (emerging from teachers themselves), voluntary, development orientated, pervasive across time and space, and unpredictable. They provide the informal and ongoing lubricant to the organization. The question this provokes is the extent to which people need to be compelled to be part of a team against their will.

One can identify those roles and behaviours that appear to be counterproductive to effective teamwork. Adair (1987: 43) suggests that people might be dysfunctional to the team if they are aggressive, awkward or out simply to block proposals, if they are seeking largely only personal recognition and gain, not serious about the activity in hand, overdominant, concerned for sectional interests and always requiring help. To complement the negative attributes of individuals in teams Weller (1995) identifies several types of dysfunctional teams as a whole. For example:

1) *The warring factions team*, which is characterized by a lack of cohesion. Therefore, he suggests, differences have to be aired openly if this team is to be effective.
2) *The Kalamazoo team*, in which there is a false consensus, or a misreading of silence as giving consent, often because of an overdominant leader. In this situation, Weller suggests, it might be necessary to elect a leader or to rotate leaders so that the team can move forwards.
3) *The leaderless team*, which is marked by a lack of clarity about goals and targets, in which, therefore, there is low morale and no decisions are taken. To overcome this problem, Weller suggests, requires the team to set goals, to define roles and tasks, to offer feedback and to provide training in problem-solving approaches.
4) *The bus-rider team*, in which there are indifference, fear of commitment or lack of real exchange of ideas (the term derives from the human tendency to confide more freely in strangers, as on buses). To overcome this problem, Weller suggests, requires the development of trust and consistent behaviour that is matched by effective communication.
5) *The party team*, in which socializing and joke telling is more important than the work. To address this, Weller suggests, it is important to find out what excites and motivates people about the team's work, to find out what members find challenging and to address these features in subsequent operations.
6) *The ground-zero team*, in which there is open hostility, with members being destructive, dogmatic, jealous and argumentative, and in which there are serious personality clashes. If this is to be addressed without disbanding the team or removing some of its members, Weller suggests it is necessary to identify some common denominators in the team on which they are united, and to ensure that differences are resolved in private – but nevertheless are resolved (i.e. to move from a win/lose situation to a win/win situation).

Katzenbach and Smith (1993b: 151) identify characteristics of 'stuck' teams, including a loss of enthusiasm and energy, a feeling of helplessness, a lack of identity and purpose, a lack of openness and honesty, a lack of concern and constructive contributions, cynicism and suspicion, *ad hominem* attacks on members, an unwillingness to own responsibility (rather, blaming senior managers and the 'rest of the organization') and a lack of outcome of meetings. To address these features, they suggest, will require the team to revisit its brief, to strive for small rewards and 'wins', to inject new approaches, to provide new information, to use the services of a team facilitator and training support, even to change the membership of the team (including the leader). It is clear that they are arguing that drastic, radical problems require drastic, radical solutions.

Teams will be ineffective, then, for personal and interpersonal reasons. They may also be ineffective because the organization's demands on the team are unrealistic or unattractive. It might be, for example, that insufficient resources are available, that unrealistic time frames are set, that the teams are too large or too small, that people outside the team become too intrusive, that the team is not given the degree of autonomy it needs, that the team is used exploitatively by senior management, that the team is physically too remote or too scattered, that the organization does not provide adequate incentives for the commitment required.[12] In the field of education Coleman and Bush (1994) suggest that teams might be ineffective if they: 1) focus too heavily on tasks rather than on processes; 2) try to address issues over which they exert little control; 3) behave too reactively rather than proactively; 4) pay too little regard to the personal and interpersonal aspects of their members; 5) neglect team development.

Developing teams

It is clear that teams don't just succeed overnight. Team development and effectiveness have to be worked at and planned. Hence part of the responsibility of senior managers is to create the environment and circumstances which will enable teamwork to flourish (e.g. Senge, 1990: 95; Wickens, 1995: 35).

That teams need to learn how to develop as teams is a critical factor – they are part of the learning organization. Tuckman (1965) makes the much-rehearsed observation that teams go through four stages: forming (initiating the aims, purposes, activities and membership of the team), storming (conflict and its management), norming (setting its norms) and performing (implementing its plans). Senge (1990: 236–7) suggests that teams need to learn how to think about complex issues, how to co-ordinate innovative action, how members will manage their membership of several teams, how effective discussion and dialogue can be developed and how negative forces can be overcome. He suggests that team members will need to learn how to suspend their assumptions and judgements and examine issues coolly; they must learn how to facilitate one another and how to be facilitated, and they must learn the value of conflict as opportunity.

In the field of education Bell (1992: 53) suggests that the development of teams hinges on four features:

1) clarity of objectives;
2) shared decision-making procedures;
3) clarity of tasks, roles, responsibilities, organization, time frames;
4) regular review to spring forward into team development.

Further, Bowring-Carr and West-Burnham (1994: 112–13) suggest that effective and efficient teamwork can be developed through the acronym of the POWER approach: Purpose, Ownership, Winning, Empathy and Review. In similar vein Clarke (1994: 138–9) reports the acronym RATIO being used in the Glaxo organization, where Role clarity, Acceptance of change, Teamwork, Innovation and Output orientation were key elements in the management of change.[13]

Wickens (1995: 123–5) suggests that the process of making an effective team reaches right back to the appointment process, where teams are established with attention to abilities, expertise, competence, skills, personalities and remit of the task.[14] He argues that people need to be placed in a team in which they can really benefit from membership and that the team itself should set its own goals and monitor its own progress.

He argues that teams must participate in developing their own culture and that this will evolve over time. Teams must have autonomy in deciding their own best methods of working and must participate extensively in setting their own goals within the general direction of the organization.

Peters (1987: 215–17) suggests that team development is conditional upon several factors, for example: multifunctional team development; full-time involvement in the team; group rewards as well as individual rewards; rewards being given not only for products but also for process (e.g. co-operativeness);[15] co-location (with teams being able to 'live' together well); effective communication; the setting aside of specified space for the team; the effective involvement of outsiders to the team.

Katzenbach and Smith (1993b: 119–27) identify a set of principles and activities for effective team development that translate directly into education:

- establish a sense of urgency;
- clarify the direction in which the organization is moving;
- select team membership on the basis of skill and expertise rather than personality;
- ensure that the first meetings of the team are highly organized and productive;
- ensure that each meeting produces action;
- establish clear roles of procedure and behaviour;
- identify some short-term tasks and goals that will produce immediate results/rewards and returns;
- ensure the group is challenged regularly with the provision of new information;
- ensure the groups spends a lot of time together as a group;
- use positive feedback, give public recognition and rewards.

This list of factors stresses the harnessing and development of motivation for change. Stevens and Campion (1994) complement this, identifying knowledge, skills and ability (KSA) required for effective teamwork. They organize these into interpersonal KSAs and self-management KSAs. In interpersonal KSAs they include:

- conflict resolution (the ability to promote desirable conflict and the ability to reduce undesirable conflict; the ability to identify the type and the source of the conflict and to suggest how it might be reduced; the ability to resolve conflict with a win/win rather than win/lose outcome);
- collaborative problem-solving (the ability to identify those situations where collaborative problem-solving might be useful and the ability to implement it effectively; the ability to identify and overcome impediments to problem-solving);
- communication (the ability to understand and utilize networks; the ability to communicate openly and in a supportive fashion, e.g. to communicate messages that are focused on behaviour or an activity and that will be able to be owned by recipients).

In self-management KSAs they include:

- goal-setting and performance management (the ability to set concrete, challenging but achievable tasks the group accepts; the ability to monitor and provide feedback on individual performance and contribution to the group's performance);
- planning and task co-ordination (the ability to co-ordinate information, roles and activities of team members; the ability to set appropriate demands of team members and to ensure that tasks and responsibilities are distributed equitably).

Adair (1987: 196–9) sets out a very clear agenda for team development that is premised on task development, team development and individual development. For task development to be effective a high degree of clarity is required about several aspects of the task: purpose, objectives, targets, responsibilities, the programme of events, working conditions, resources, the line of authority and accountability, training, priorities, monitoring progress and supervision. For team development a high degree of clarity and appropriateness needs to be achieved on objectives, performance standards, safety standards, team size, team membership, team spirit, team discipline, grievances procedures (formal and informal), genuine consultation, regular briefing, representation to other groups, support from the team leader. Finally, for individual development to be effective, he suggests that the following items need to be addressed: targets, induction procedures, achievement (how an individual contributes to the group's achievements), responsibilities, authority, training, recognition, growth, performance, rewards and incentives, fitness for the task, personality factors, time available, security of membership and employment, monitoring and appraisal. Adair also sets a very clear agenda for team development.

Many of the features discussed so far in this chapter can become principles for team development in education,[16] and it is possible, therefore, to make suggestions for how to enable a team to gel:

- provide team-building time;
- ensure that the team knows and agrees to how it will work;
- ensure a common brief;
- ensure that the team knows what its purpose is – what it is trying to do;
- ensure equal status of members, avoid hierarchies;
- ensure that all ideas have equal and fair consideration;
- provide opportunities for people to speak freely;
- provide opportunities for members to work together on a common focus;
- ensure effective communication – within and between teams;
- develop a climate of trust;
- ensure the necessary continuing professional development;
- involve everybody in an identifiable task and role;
- ensure that members know each other's tasks and roles;
- ensure that everybody has the opportunity to contribute;
- provide opportunities for members to experience success and to develop their enthusiasm;
- increase members' personal input and their access to a broad range of people;

- avoid stifling creative individualism;
- avoid assessing/evaluating/judging people/projects/tasks too soon;
- clarify and agree how decisions will be reached;
- keep to agreed time frames;
- ensure that the emphasis is on the solution of problems rather than on individual personalities and agendas;
- develop a climate of support;
- be prepared to change structures and practices through agreed strategies.

This summary list provides a set of guidelines for effective practice. Clearly team development abides by the same principles as those for the development of collegiality that have been discussed in preceding chapters.

Summary of implications for education

With regard to education, this chapter has advocated very many advantages and possibilities for teamwork for managing change. Many types of team can be identified and established, with multiple membership of teams facilitating empowerment, communication and effectiveness. Clearly educational institutions will need to identify the purposes of setting up teams as well as their type, constitution, activities and remit. It was suggested that an organization will thrive on a diversity of different types of team. With this is mind the criterion of 'fitness for purpose' was seen to be important in deciding what types of team to establish and what their purposes and tasks will be. Concomitant with this has been the need for team-building and development. The need for ongoing training for members echoes the messages of continuous improvement and support that were outlined in Japanese companies in Chapter 3. Individual development within team development, and team development *per se* are both essential ingredients for the effective team.

A team has a commitment to a culture of teamwork; hence it was argued that support and training for the development of that culture were an essential ingredient of utilizing teams for promoting change. An identification of the factors that make for team coherence and commitment is necessary so that they can be maximized and countervailing factors minimized. How team spirit can be fostered is a significant factor in managing teamwork; clearly it has implications for resource allocation.

It has been suggested that participation in teams will require attention to incentives (individual and group), rewards and motivation. Concomitant with this is the setting of performance standards for teams, and the monitoring and evaluation of their achievement. Further, it was suggested that mutual responsibility and accountability were key features of teams; how these are to be developed is an important factor in the planning of change in education through teamwork.

In planning for teamwork it was suggested that a major question to be faced was the extent to which teamwork was necessary, appropriate, desirable, unnecessary or undesirable. Given that problems with teamwork might be encountered, it is important, perhaps, to see whether the longer-term benefits that can accrue from teamwork are worth the short and long-term costs.

The constitution of a team was seen to be important, and emphasis was laid on the adoption of an extended view of complementarity, which would include skills, abilities, expertise, personality, roles, intelligence, attributes, motives and motivations in the makeup of the team. It was argued that if its constitution were inappropriate then the team would be dysfunctional. In many respects this echoes the comments in the previous chapter about the need for the organizational health and climate to be robust and fair respectively. Effective teamwork moves beyond simply performing a set of tasks well with complementary skills, and includes considerable attention to the individual, personal, social and interpersonal aspects of the team and its activities.

It was argued that communication, an essential feature of effective teams (both within and outside the team), was premised on openness and honesty. That this would bring conflict into the open was seen as an unavoidable, and perhaps desirable, byproduct of this process. Conflict management (discussed in Chapter 6) was seen to be an important factor in the effective team, leading to the win/win situation through a problem-solving approach. Conflict becomes an opportunity and a possibility rather than a dampener on creativity and synergy.

The discussion of superteams suggested that it might be advantageous to have some teams in the organization who are the powerhouse of developments and creativity and that it might be desirable to 'give them a clear head'. Whether this is empty rhetoric might be a function of staffing in schools, though it must be observed that teams for developing new initiatives are springing up in higher education.

If teams are to be effective then their management and leadership need to be effective. This chapter has summarized some of the characteristics of effective leadership, though these will be discussed in more detail in the next chapter. The argument was made for a view of leadership as extending beyond that of leadership by senior managers only to embrace leadership at all levels of an organization. Indeed it was suggested that one of the characteristics of effective leaders was their ability to develop the leadership potential of others. Leadership was seen to be based on competence and expertise rather that status or position in a hierarchy.

One of the principal features of effective teams was a high degree of clarity about tasks, purposes, responsibilities, roles, targets, authority, standards, objectives, individual tasks, incentives and motivations, and the need for careful selection, induction and the development of team spirit. How collective team decision-making can be realized is a major feature for educational institutions.

It is striking to note that industry has moved massively towards teamwork and the satisfaction of social as well as financial needs of employees and that, together, these have contributed significantly towards the productivity and output of the organization. At a time when a return to whole-class teaching is commanding media attention, and where the experience of the overwhelming number of teachers is of an isolated delivery of a curriculum in the 'egg crate' organization of many schools, one wonders whether the short-term benefits of isolation might sacrifice the longer-term benefits of more collaborative approaches to education.

Teamwork has a huge amount to offer education. It has been happening for years in the planning of curricula; it is happening more with the development of whole-school and through-school policies and practices. Is it happening in pedagogical principles and practices to the same degree? Perhaps not enough!

Notes

1. So great is the advocacy of teamwork in industry that a National Society for Quality Through Teamwork exists (Mortiboys and Oakland, 1991).
2. That this can present a danger has been alluded to by Wickens (1995: 120) where he comments that the most effective team at Ford's in Dagenham comprised the group of very militant shop stewards!
3. In the business and company sense a team is different from a work group. In a work group there is a common task and the group exists for a very specific task under an identified leader. Work groups tend to be temporary, with clearly defined membership and a clear brief or purpose. Their operational procedures are clearly defined and their shared purpose, which is explicit, is in close alignment with the organization's mission. There is individual accountability and individual work products. Meetings are efficient and discussion leads to decisions and delegated tasks. In some senses this contrasts with teams where leadership might be shared, where there is both individual, mutual and whole-group accountability, where a sole collective product is produced, where open-ended meetings and discussions adopt a problem-solving approach and where collaborative decision-making leads to collaborative work (Katzenbach and Smith, 1993a). Wickens (1995: 119) argues that teamworking is a culture whereas a work group is a structure.
4. Adair, 1987; Peters, 1987; Harvey-Jones, 1988; Judson, 1991; Mortiboys and Oakland, 1991; Bell, 1992; Murgatroyd and Morgan, 1993; Bowring-Carr and West-Burnham, 1994; Clarke, 1994; Wickens, 1995.
5. Adair, 1987: Jaques, 1990; Bush, 1993; Murgatroyd and Morgan, 1993; Beale, 1994; Wickens, 1995.
6. Peters, 1987; Adair, 1987; Buchanan and Boddy, 1992; Katzenbach and Smith, 1993a; 1993b; Wickens, 1995; Champy and Nohria, 1996c.
7. Related to the superteam is the notion of the 'hot group' (Leavitt and Lipman-Blumen, 1995). The hot group – only a handful of people – is a group that is motivated by achievement, is highly dedicated and relishes challenges. Hot groups live to work. They are completely preoccupied with their work and value the intellectual stimulus of the other members of the group as well as of the task itself. There is a powerful emotional bond and emotional intensity within the group that generates a mutually supportive spirit and a corporate sense that they are the keepers of the flame of creativity. They have no rules and procedures, generating these if and when necessary. They are characterized by openness and flexibility within

the group coupled with independence and autonomy from other groups. Membership of a hot group can lead to premature burn-out and isolation from other parts of the organization. The notion of the hot group might be exciting and energizing, but it is difficult to see how membership can be sustained. It is a transient gadfly rather than a reliable cart-horse!

8.   Wickens (1995: 120) argues that it is essential that the team keeps sight of its overall direction and purpose rather than becoming introverted and bound up with its internal politics and management.

9.   Belbin (1981) is clear that it is very uncommon to find both highly successful teams and an exact makeup of 'types' of members in a team (see also Katzenbach and Smith, 1993b).

10.   Margerison and McCann (1990) echo Belbin, particularly in their notion of the significance of the linker, who advises, explores, co-ordinates, organizes and controls the running of the team. The view of multiple abilities and differentials of intelligence within a team resonates with Gardner's (1993) notion of 'multiple intelligences': linguistic (exemplified at its best in poets); logical-mathematical (including scientific); spatial (ability to form a mental model of a spatial world, exemplified at its best in sailors, engineers, sculptors, surgeons and painters); musical (exemplified in the great musicians); bodily-kinesthetic (ability to solve problems and make products using one's whole body or part of the body, exemplified in dancers, athletes, surgeons, craftspeople); interpersonal intelligence (the ability to understand people and how to work with them, exemplified in successful salespeople, politicians, teachers, clinicians, religious leaders); intrapersonal intelligence (an ability to form an accurate 'veridical' model of oneself and to be able to use this effectively).

11.   Harvey-Jones (1988: 51); West-Burnham (1992: 121), Katzenbach and Smith (1993b: 12–14); Murgatroyd and Morgan (1993: 143–6), Bowring-Carr and West-Burnham (1994: 105); Arcaro (1995b: 14).

12.   Ineffective teams are characterized not only by the absence of the characteristics of effective teams but also by the presence of additional characteristics that appear to impede their effectiveness. That said, it is noticeable in the literature cited that ineffective practice, in principle, is remediable. Whether that is overoptimistic is an empirical matter.

13.   At Glaxo, this was coupled with a careful identification of individual training needs, the need to provide training and support for increased communication and co-operation right across the organization, and a review of working practices in the organization.

14.   Garvin (1996: 169) suggests that the selection process needs to focus not only on knowledge and cognitive expertise but also on the 'soft skills', including communication and the ability to act as a member of a team.

15.   Garvin (1996: 165) suggests that team development will need to examine the reward systems that support team behaviour, arguing that traditional reward systems – that are exemplary of hierarchical organizations – can disempower crossfunctional teams.

16.   See also Bowring-Carr and West-Burnham, 1994; West-Burnham, 1997.

8

Leadership, senior management and the expertise of the change agent

Introduction

In the current drive towards school improvement and school effectiveness, effective leadership is seen as a critical element (e.g. Reynolds, 1994; DfEE, 1997). Here strong leadership involves setting the mission, standards and culture of the school. It was suggested in the previous chapter that leadership is not the exclusive property of senior managers but that it can be exercised at all levels of an organization. Leadership is less about status and position in a hierarchy than the possession of essential competencies, skills and expertise. As such leaders and potential leaders can be found everywhere in an organization. It would be a salutary lesson for many headteachers to ask how each member of staff has exercised leadership in a single week! Indeed Brandon (1992: 32) suggests that a company cannot afford not to recognize that its leaders of change can be found everywhere in the organization.[1]

The linking of leadership and expertise argues against a bureaucratic approach and for the use of leaders within a collegial structure. This is not to deny the importance of senior managers being effective leaders; rather it is to suggest that one can look beyond the senior managers of an organization to find leaders. It follows that people can be prepared for leadership from an early point in their career, rather than waiting for promotion to a senior position before leadership development is undertaken.

Overlaps between leadership and management

Leadership and management are both similar and different. As West-Burnham (1992: 102) argues, leadership concerns vision, strategy, creating direction and transformation of the organization, whereas managing concerns the effective implementation of the vision, ways of ensuring the vision happens in practice, organizational and operational matters, creating the systems and means of ensuring the organization is run most effectively and efficiently to achieve its purposes and strategies. That said, management and leadership are not an either/or – either one is a leader or one is a manager. The roles of the leader include the roles of manager and, often, *vice versa*; leadership and management constitute a Venn diagram rather than existing as polar opposites. The overlap is particularly true in the case of senior managers of an organization, where they have considerable input into policy and strategy formation.

Mintzberg (1973), in a seminal work on management, indicates the overlap, suggesting that managers need to fulfil: 1) interpersonal roles (being leaders, figureheads and liaising between several parties); 2) informational roles (monitoring and disseminating, and acting as spokesperson); 3) decisional roles (being an entrepreneur, a negotiator, a handler of disturbance and conflict, an allocater of resources).[2]

Mintzberg suggests that management is concerned with practical action whereas leadership is concerned with visioning, setting the tone and direction, establishing long-term objectives, generating an appropriate ethos in the organization, i.e. with long-term strategy rather than day-to-day affairs and operations. This echoes Kotter's (1990: 104) view that, whereas management is concerned with coping with complexity, leadership is concerned with coping with change. For Kotter, managers are involved in planning, budgeting, organization, staffing, managing people and problem-solving whereas leaders are concerned with setting direction and bringing people into alignment with that direction, with motivating rather than controlling and organizing people.

Zaleznik (1992) suggests that managers need a dogged persistence in achieving tasks, coupled with sheer hard work, tough-mindedness and a degree of resilience (see also Harvey-Jones, 1988: 87). They need neither to be heroes not geniuses, but to be capable of careful analysis, tolerance and effective interpersonal relations. They are concerned with the present; leaders with the future (Wickens, 1995: 102).[3] Leaders need to have vision and to be visionary themselves. In this field the 'hero-leader' is identified by Clarke (1994) as having several characteristics. The abilities to

- identify and maintain the special character of the company;
- symbolize clearly to the outside world exactly what the company is and what it stands for;
- set challenging but manageable standards of performance (echoing Harvey-Jones's view (1988: 60) that heavy demands should be made on people consistently in order to 'stretch' them, making the most of people);
- motivate all employees;
- be a positive role model.

Though in principle there may be a separation of leadership and management (e.g. the former setting agendas and the latter enacting them), that separation is less likely to be the case with regard to senior management. Much of the literature on business organizations regards senior managers as the bearers of a leadership role.[4]

Burnes (1996: 152) suggests that leaders and senior managers overlap considerably and that the difference between them is largely a matter of management style. A convergent management style is focused on generating a stable state with an emphasis on predictability and an ability to optimize resources to implement policy, whereas a divergent style is more unpredictable, open and pragmatic, creating new visions and challenging rather than accepting the status quo – moving beyond the stable state (Schön, 1971). For Burnes (1996: 231), senior managers must have a clear vision of the future and the personal strength to challenge existing practices and norms. They must be able to win over the critical mass of the workforce and, indeed, other managers. Indeed Harvey-Jones (1988: 87) suggests that leaders are very concerned with the how of processes, and are heavily involved in planning, co-ordination and oversight of the processes.

The tasks and roles of the leader/senior manager

The business literature treats the notion of leadership in two easily recognized ways. First, it regards as essential the view (set out above) that the senior managers of the organization must exercise leadership for change and direction of the organization, i.e. they must set the direction of changes and developments. Secondly, by dint of their seniority in the organization, senior managers must support changes that have been initiated in other quarters of the organization, to lend the weight of status to an initiative.

Echoing the notions of chaos theory and complexity theory from Chapter 1, McDaniel (1997) suggests several major tasks of leadership, for example: 1) making sense of situations and making connections (between situations and people); 2) planning for diversity; 3) promoting self-organization; 4) making oneself complicated (in order to reflect the complexity of the outside world); 5) increasing the emphasis on co-operation and interdependence. In this view planning is a defence against stress and anxiety, whilst control is an attempt to stabilize inherently dynamical, unstable systems. Indeed Heifetz and Lawrie (1997) argue that one important task of leaders is to regulate stress – turning up the heat whilst, at the same time, enabling steam to escape!

More conventional views of leadership in the business literature include directing, protecting, orientating, managing conflict, setting goals and norms. Adair (1984) suggests that the tasks of leaders involve selection, decision-making, problem-solving, creative thinking, communicating (including effective speaking, listening and writing), managing meetings and deciding action programmes. The business literature highlights many tasks of leaders.[5]

Overview and vision

- Having an overview of the organization and the outside world;
- assessing the internal and external environment (discussed below);
- identifying the challenges to which the organization must adapt itself;
- creating a shared vision that focuses on critical factors in the organization;
- reviewing management structures and practices to achieve the vision.

Direction, alignment, aims and objectives

- Setting the direction and strategy of the organization;
- establishing the identity, initiative and integrity of the organization;
- focusing attention in the organization on the achievement of a common goal;
- identifying core values, beliefs, goals and objectives and documenting and communicating these;
- promoting coherence in the organization;
- creating commitment to the objectives and their achievement;
- aligning activities and people to the direction of the organization;
- involving everybody in reaching the organization's goals;
- disseminating the main messages of the organization.

Change and strategic thinking to achieve aims

- Leading change;
- linking operational change with the overall strategic changes desired;
- developing clear strategies to achieve aims and objectives;
- identifying the critical tasks and processes necessary to achieve aims and objectives;
- promoting initiatives;
- managing transitions;
- managing the politics and micropolitics of organizational change;
- creating momentum in the organization;
- resource allocation;
- ensuring appropriate training for employees;
- self-protection and protecting other individuals from the undesirable pressure from groups.

People, organizational culture and teamwork

- Managing the task, the individuals and the groups involved in change;
- effective human resource management;
- recruitment and selection;
- developing the culture of an organization;
- giving people enough 'headroom' to work autonomously – without being crushed by layers of management;
- promoting teamwork (all leaders can be team-builders);
- enable groups to achieve their purposes and tasks;
- promoting organizational health and a positive organizational climate;
- delegating responsibility and autonomy;
- developing and empowering employees;
- bringing out the best in employees;
- developing employee participation.

Quality

- Monitoring progress and recognizing achievements;

- ensuring high standards of performance;
- ensuring quality improvement and how to achieve it with – and through – people.

They are echoed in the field of education by West-Burnham (1997), who suggests there are four major elements of effective leadership:

1) vision (e.g. hopes, aspirations, direction, purposes, principles, rationale, identity, meeting clients' needs, overcoming problems, strategy formation, core purposes, morality, planning for the future);
2) creativity (e.g. handling complexity and abstractions, using problem-solving approaches, synthesis and application, honesty and accepting criticism, seeing all round an issue, self-analysis, challenging, lateral thinking, imagining alternative scenarios, evaluation);
3) sensitivity (effective interpersonal relationships, consistency, listening and empathizing, personal behaviour, giving and receiving feedback, negotiating and managing conflict, networking);
4) subsidiarity (empowering others, developing and utilizing self-managing and autonomous teams, 'letting go' (see Handy's comments on the 'federal structure' in Chapter 6), genuine delegation (devolution of power)).

Riches (1993b: 12) summarizes five main tasks of leaders in education: 1) setting clear goals; 2) leading by example; 3) supporting and respecting colleagues; 4) developing and sustaining the culture of the school; 5) setting and translating a mission and vision into action.

Leadership can be applied at all levels of an organization. Champy and Nohria (1996a: xxvi–xix) argue that leaders have to move beyond simply visioning, aligning and motivating to establishing the identity, initiative and integrity of the organization. Identity enables the organization to take with it into the future those best aspects of the past ('sticking to the knitting'). Initiative involves tapping into the creative capacity of employees (they state that currently less than 10 per cent of employees' productive capacity is harnessed – *ibid.*: xxviii). The enemies of initiative are orthodoxy and dogma; therefore, they suggest, new management structures and styles (away from the command-and-control mentality and towards the empowerment of all employees) are required. Integrity, they suggest, requires open, honest, authentic and full communication, including the exemplification of the key values and principles of the organization.[6] Pettigrew and Whipp (1993) set an explicit agenda for the leadership of change. They identify five key factors for effective leadership of change:

1) *Effective assessment of the environment* (e.g. availability of key people; the internal character of the organization; environmental pressures; the role of planning and marketing; the construction of networks with stakeholders; the use of specialist taskforces).
2) *Leading change* (e.g. fostering a context and culture that is conducive to change; legitimating change; creating the organization's and individuals' capabilities for change; setting the content and direction of change; operationalizing the change agenda; creating the critical mass for change within senior management; communicating the need for

change and detailing the requirements for the change to be managed effectively; achieving and reinforcing success; balancing continuity and change – maintenance and development – and sustaining coherence in the organization).

3) *Linking operational change with the overall strategic changes required* (e.g. justifying the need for change; building the capacity for appropriate action to be possible; generating a shared vision; setting the values and direction of the business; translating the strategy into manageable activities; appointing managers of the change; setting up necessary structures and systems; setting challenging targets and negotiating ways of achieving them; reviewing communications; activating and utilizing systems for incentives and rewards; making the vision realistic in light of situational contingencies (see the discussions in previous chapters of contingency theory)).

4) *Human resource development* (human resource management and development).

5) *Ensuring coherence in the organization of the change* (e.g. consonance; relative advantage of the change; ensuring consistency of purpose and practice; feasibility of the change; effective leadership; maintaining the integrity of the senior management team; harmonizing objectives and activities; developing expertise and necessary competencies; ensuring coherence between different areas of the organization; managing interrelated changes).

An example of this can be seen in Figure 8.1.

Quinn (1993: 65–6) suggests that leaders and senior managers need to be proactive and deliberate in their planning of change in order to: 1) improve the quality of information for use in decision-making; 2) cope with different lead-times and their effects on different elements of the change; 3) handle resistance and the micropolitics of the organization; 4) develop organizational awareness of and commitment to change in employees; 5) minimize uncertainty through effective communication; 6) involve all necessary participants and experts in informing strategic decision-making; 7) allow sufficient time for the effective fermentation of ideas and their implications.

In relation to education, what is being argued here is the case for 'transformational leadership' (Stewart, V., 1990; Caldwell and Spinks, 1992; Sergiovanni, 1990; 1992; Senge, 1993; Coleman, 1994) in which leaders are able to effect vision-driven, values-based, structural, cultural and systemic changes in the school with regard to their internal and external environments, through commitment, example, empowerment, being proactive, developing ownership, communicating widely, enthusing others, hard work and energy, both in themselves and in others.[7]

It is important for leaders to be able to identify their key roles, tasks and developmental needs in relation to the possibilities outlined above. It is possible to summarize the key roles of leaders in the business literature (see note 5) that enable us to cut a swathe through the list of tasks, though, as with the discussion of team roles, the list of roles could become unmanageably long: initiator, diagnoser, protector, orientator, manager

A secondary school modern languages department has recently appointed a new head of department with a remit to develop the school as a language specialist school.

With regard to effective assessment of the environment, the new appointee has established links with outside potential funding sources and community organizations to identify the main languages that should be offered (international and community languages), staffing needs (full-time, part-time, permanent, temporary staff), resourcing and outsourcing needs, targeted client groups within and outside the school (using the school as a community resource) and channels of dissemination.

With regard to leading change, at a series of departmental meetings she has agreed the overall aims and objectives of the innovation, its rationale, mission and vision. Three teams to work on the developments have been established: a modern languages team; a community languages team; a team to further the teaching of English as a second language. These teams have established team leaders who regularly meet with the head of department in order to keep each other informed of progress and to discuss issues arising that effect the work of the department as a whole. A time frame of two terms has been set for each team to bring back to the whole department its development plans, action plans and needs assessments, priorities, main issues to be faced, so that subsequent departmental planning can be co-ordinated.

With regard to linking operational change with overall strategic change, the four leaders (head of department and three team leaders) meet regularly with the senior management team to discuss progress, funding, budgeting, direction, strategy, links with other developments in the school, whole-school issues (e.g. qualifications, work experience, community liaison, assessment) and to identify problems and their solution. The senior managers are actively pursuing external funding for the project, including capital expenditure, advertising, materials and equipment, staffing.

With regard to human resource development the staff have identified their own development needs (e.g. skills in adult teaching and learning, IT skills) and in-service money has been allocated to meet these. The senior management has allocated substantial in-service funding to buy in cover in order to free staff to plan developments together on four days in the two terms.

With regard to ensuring coherence in the organization of the change, the head of department meets on a weekly basis (or more if the occasion demands) with the team leaders to facilitate communication and to discuss common matters, problems and issues, and to ensure that appropriate matching and co-ordination of activities takes place between teams, so that the overall aims of the department are being addressed by each of the three teams. Coherence is managed by widespread discussion and agreement on developments.

Figure 8.1 Pettigrew's and Whipp's leadership tasks in education

of conflict, setter of goals and norms, mentor, innovator, broker, producer, director, monitor and evaluator, regulator, co-ordinator, information provider and communicator, facilitator and supporter. To combine these roles effectively is clearly a difficult task as many of them might exist in tension with each other. Hence the need for leadership training presents itself clearly.[8]

Leaders, power and empowerment

Leaders implement their tasks and roles through the exercise of power. The argument throughout this book has suggested that it is essential to move away from a coercive, blaming and bullying style of leadership and replace it with an empowering view of leadership at all levels. Peters (1987: 253–5) suggests that a manager can support innovation in a variety of empowering ways, for example: 1) being very aware of one's every actions; 2) behaving with 'purposeful impatience' and being very responsive to requests for innovations; 3) finding the innovators in the organization, celebrating and rewarding them and all those contributing to the innovation; 4) rewarding small as well as large innovations.

The issue here, in part, is that the leader can use his or her positional authority to give weight, legitimacy and recognition to an innovation. However, leadership is more subtle than this, for the argument is that leadership from senior managers is concerned with promoting leadership at all levels in the organization – it empowers everybody (The National Economic Development Office, 1991; Wickens, 1987; 1995;). This restates the benefits of flatter styles of management (e.g. Clarke, 1994: 43). Leading by empowering people is a key principle, with the leader listening attentively, acknowledging that the experts are the 'front-line' workers, that delegation is important and that bureaucracy ought to be removed (Peters, 1987: 380–90, 434–51). Everyone can contribute to the developing vision, everyone can lead by example, everyone can take on a leadership role.

Kanter (1996: 190) suggests that the effective leader is one who is sensitive to the politics of the organization and who is able to develop synergies and strategic alliances. She recognizes the move from vertical to horizontal relationships of influence (*ibid.*: 185) and that the distinction between the managers and the managed is evaporating in networks. Effective leaders, she suggests, are acutely aware of the micropolitics of the organization, and recognize that they have to bargain, negotiate and sell ideas instead of commanding practices by unilateral fiat (*ibid.*: 190).

Leadership at all levels of an organization maps easily on to supporting middle and junior managers in schools. Here a middle manager, maybe a co-ordinator (Morrison, 1986; West, 1995: 12–22), may have responsibility for

- the subject and pedagogy of the subject through the school;
- advice, documentation and support for staff (from policy formation to planning, developing schemes of work, and consultation);
- resource management (needs analysis, resourcing, networking);
- assessment and record-keeping;
- communication and public relations (sharing and developing good practice, communication within and outside the school);
- review and evaluation (undertaking monitoring, audits, reviews, evaluations and taking subsequent action);
- identifying staff development needs;
- reviewing job descriptions and practice;
- identifying key tasks with teams and individuals;
- balancing maintenance with development tasks.

An example of this is presented in Figure 8.2.

The mathematics co-ordinator has undertaken an audit of the mathematics teaching and achievement in the school, and is commencing a programme of development for the staff. This, she suggests, involves

- developing the mathematics policy with the staff (to include: rationale; aims and objectives; curriculum planning – long term to short term – structure and organization; teaching and learning; resources; development; equal opportunities; assessment, recording and reporting; review, evaluation and audit; quality assurance; continuing professional development);
- harmonizing the policy with other school policies (e.g. on: teaching and learning; assessment; quality assurance; equal opportunities; curriculum leadership; differentiation and matching; marking; early years; later years; overall school aims, objectives and mission statement) to ensure an 'aligned' organization;
- monitoring and developing quality and quality assurance indicators and systems;
- facilitating curriculum planning (schemes of work, guidelines, practical suggestions, review of National Curriculum documentation; developing subject and pedagogical expertise);
- developing and implementing school and staff development plans for mathematics within the context of the whole-school development plan and priorities;
- developing a portfolio of assessed work from students to facilitate assessment, moderation and consistency;
- liaising with staff in developing practice (practical advice, consultation and feedback, active listening, classroom observation and shared teaching);
- contributing to the senior management team's overall strategic planning and management through discussions, provision of information and data, consultation;
- networking with outside parties and agencies (e.g. local authority, curriculum groups, governors, parents, in-service providers, an institution of higher education);
- managing change and development through teamwork (identifying team members, roles and tasks, communication and decision-making, action research projects and problem-solving approaches);
- preparing for inspection, within a given time frame.

She ensures that everybody has a range of tasks, roles and responsibilities in the mathematics work, and that time frames for the development and implementation of projects (through project teams – see Chapter 7) are set. In this example, not only does the middle manager have considerable responsibility, but this responsibility is also multidirectional – to senior managers, to other teachers, to outside parties. Moreover, this responsibility is also accompanied by the development of strategies that will necessarily involve other teachers. It is a picture of a person fulfilling a multifunctional role with a multifunctional team.

Figure 8.2 A middle manager in a primary school

The notion of an empowering leadership engages the central issue of power in effecting change in organizations. In a hierarchical organization the locus of power is clear and fixed, whereas in a flatter structure power is much more fluid and constantly being negotiated. This is not to say that differentials of power are not present, for clearly they are in most organizations. Adair (1983: 16) suggests that authority in an organization derives from position (in the hierarchy and its concomitant status), personality and knowledge (expertise). Carnall (1995: 135) suggests that there are five social bases of power in organizations: legitimate power (one's position in a hierarchy); expert power (the power that is brought by the possession of knowledge, expertise and experience); referent power (how people relate to each other and to those who can summon power); reward power (the power one has to control rewards); coercive power (the power one has to sanction behaviour). French and Raven (1959) and Riches (1993b: 15–16) add to this charismatic power (e.g. personality and magnetism); connection power (the leader's connection to sources of power and influence inside and outside the school); communication power (control of information – knowledge is power!). This suggests that if power is to be used effectively for change it needs to be addressed on many fronts, empowering leaders at all levels within the organization. An example of the use of different types of power is provided in Figure 8.3.

Kotter (1978) suggests that it is important to understand the types of power and methods of influencing people, to utilize different types of power as appropriate, to seek out those leadership roles that enable one to utilize the types of power with which one feels most comfortable, to be able to use power to create more power, and to temper the use of power with mature self-control, recognizing that use and abuse of power impact immediately and directly on others.

What is being argued here is that power is inescapable and that those in positions of power and leadership should adopt a subtle and sensitive approach to its exercise. There is no doubt that the use of power can be an effective way of overcoming resistance. For example, Judson (1991: 100) suggests that there are only two fundamental ways in which resistance to change can be overcome. One method is to reduce the pressures from and causes of resistance. This echoes Harvey-Jones's (1988: 16) view that it is very hard to teach adults but comparatively easy to create the conditions under which they teach themselves and Senge's comment that one should remove the obstacles to growth rather than pushing growth (Senge, 1990: 95). The other method is to increase the pressures to over-ride resistance, perhaps through compulsion, threats and coercion. The deleterious effects of the latter approaches have already been rehearsed in the discussions earlier of McGregor's Theory X.

Kanter (1983) identifies a range of 'power skills' which can be used by leaders and change agents. These, she argues, can be used to block out interference and resistance and include: waiting out the interferers and resisters (give them time and they will simply go away); wearing down the interferers and resisters (persistent attrition and abrasion through argument and pressure will eventually be successful); appealing to a higher authority (e.g. senior managers or the examples of 'best practice' – the moral argument that only the best practice should be allowed); inviting involvement (co-option into the 'club'); sending an emissary to persuade (the emissary chosen being a friend of the interferer or resister); public display of support for your proposals (e.g. ensuring that people who are on your side are visible and vocal at meetings); reducing the stakes and

A secondary school headteacher has recently been appointed to try to 'turn round' a failing school. He has a commitment to students' high achievement that overrides his concern for upsetting the many long-serving staff in the school. With regard to legitimate power, he insists that staff set targets for achievement for students, that planning, assessment and review are undertaken in great detail, that departmental and faculty heads review the planning, assessment and record-keeping policies and practices of all staff and that this be done within half a term. Though this meets fierce opposition he persists and engages several very difficult meetings – individually and with groups. He has the backing of the governors of the school and is not afraid to suggest to entrenched staff that if they are not prepared to work in his way then they should leave. On the other hand, several newer members of staff welcome the moves, and he lends his positional support to suggestions they make for improving quality assurance measures, whole-school issues (e.g. behaviour, assessment, parental involvement). His positional power is used to support and drive in change, even in the face of opposition.

With regard to expert power, as a former science specialist he focuses in some detail on the science department as an example for the rest of the school to follow. Further, as a specialist in management (the school is his third headship) he knows where to push, where to step back, where to insist, where to concede. His somewhat autocratic style, coupled with his extensive understanding of current practices, projects, development and research into curricula, pedagogy, and assessment mean that he is formidable in steering through changes, in argument, in persuasion through evidence, and this creates a sense of certainty and security amongst the staff – they feel they know the leader of the institution is up to date.

With regard to referent power he quickly analyses the micropolitics of the school and cultivates alliances within it, engaging the interest groups and informal groupings, and making clear those matters over which 'bargaining' is not an option. He ties the cultivation of support with the use of reward power in a newly established faculty structure, appointing heads of faculties from within and outside the school to these senior, highly paid but very demanding jobs. Further, with the agreement of the governors, he makes one-year additional responsibility payments for staff to undertake development activities in the school. He couples this with the requirement that all departmental heads will ensure that development tasks are shared throughout departments, with clearly identified tasks for each member of staff. This, he believes, will ensure that those staff who do not receive additional payments nevertheless will experience the motivation of involvement and results.

With regard to coercive power, he is quick to celebrate success, achievement and effort whilst making clear what is unacceptable practice – at first in private unless there is a whole-school issue to be faced. He is not afraid to be clear in setting demands and in supporting them with sanctions and support.

The new head has considerable charismatic power. He is intensely hard-working, very articulate, very forthright, very clear and very funny! He has a clear vision and communicates this effectively and frequently. He is a mixture of humanity and, where he feels it justified, harshness. He does not operate by personal threat but by the power of argument and evidence, and possesses an enviable grasp of all relevant factors in an issue. He is more liked than disliked; people see that he has the good of the school at heart and leads by example.

With regard to connection power he quickly establishes links with the local community services and industries, local authority networks, regional and national projects, bringing in considerable sums of money to refurbish the school resources.

Indeed the school rapidly builds up a reputation for its IT resources, which it makes available to the local community, running adult training courses. The head communicates extensively with parents and has rapidly become known for spending time with parents in seeing to their children's welfare and progress. The head works efficiently with governors.

With regard to communication power the head communicates rapidly, effectively and widely on all matters of concern. Information is publicly available and staff cannot argue that they have not been consulted about matters. Discussion, consultation and working papers are circulated, indeed the school risks information overload. The head uses communication openly to disseminate and consult, rather than controlling the communication and keeping back matters.

Figure 8.3 Using different types of power

potential for loss (e.g. of face for individuals and/or groups); warning off the opposition (threats that trouble (e.g. from senior management) will ensue if resistance and interference persist).

Judson (1991: 100–37) argues that it is possible for leaders to support change and overcome resistances in a variety of ways that move from the highly coercive to the highly supportive, including, for example: persuasion, argument, bargaining, rewards and incentives, giving guarantees and securities, discussion and negotiation, inviting and giving criticism, building on the best of the past, trialling the changes and adopting a flexible and tentative approach to suggesting changes. Whichever of these strategies is adopted, effective leaders have sufficient foresight to be able to calculate the likely effects of using different types of power and negotiation.

Judson (*ibid.*: 144) offers five prescriptions for the maintenance of a climate of support for change that moves away from a coercive stance. First, it is argued that leaders must be sincere in their invitations to participate and that this must reveal itself in open communication. Secondly, this climate of participation must be widely disseminated and perceived. Thirdly, participation must be given a high profile and priority in the organization. Fourthly, the development of participation should not be *ad hoc* but should be deliberately planned, with concomitant training in such process skills being provided. These include the development of

- an open, inquiring mind;
- a willingness to learn and change;
- interest in the proposals;
- expertise to meet the demands of the proposals;
- an ability to make a positive contribution, voicing opinions and concerns, even in the presence of senior staff;
- an ability to enter into a vigorous discussion and exchange of ideas, leaving aside personalities;
- sensitivity and a willingness to communicate personal concerns and feelings.

Fifthly, Judson argues that it is the managerial style that sets the whole tone of the organization and which is, therefore, the singular most important factor in managing the organization.

Kanter *et al.* (1992) suggest the notion that leaders have to be able to balance the demands of 'bold strokes' (immediate decisive actions) with 'long marches' (the overall development of an organization). In 'bold strokes' time frames are rapid and short, decisions are taken by senior managers with the leader exercising a high degree of control and power, and there is an emphasis on short-term gains as long-term gains are unpredictable. Changing the culture of the organization is not high on the agenda of the management-by-bold-strokes approach. On the other hand 'long marches' are characterized by slow and long time frames, initiatives and changes are spread throughout – and emanate from throughout – the organization, the leadership style is low profile, ceding and spreading power – initiating rather than commanding – and there is an emphasis on achievable and concrete longer-term gains even if the immediate impact is unclear. These more fundamental shifts impact on everyday ways of working; hence in long marches the culture and habits of the organization have to change. The effective leader is able to balance the advantages of bold strokes with the need to address the long marches.

Characteristics of effective leaders

Apart from the ability to 'deliver' on all the issues set out above, the business literature is clear and comprehensive on the range of characteristics of effective leaders. Peters (1987: 248), in a characteristically exuberant style, describes the hallmarks of effective leaders, including, for example: energy, idealism, pragmatism, cunning, 'towering impatience', an unrealistic intolerance of any barrier to success, development or change, and frequent love–hate relationships with subordinates. Clarke (1994: 144–5, 206–7 and Rosener (1990) identify several characteristics of visionary and effective leaders, including: clear focus; decisiveness; effective interpersonal skills; trustworthiness; the demonstration of respect for others; the ability and willingness to take risks; the belief that they actually are able to make changes; the ability to empower others; effective leadership of the organization as a system and effective leadership of the organization as a culture; effective communication skills; personal responsibility and accountability.

Other business writers adopt a less 'inspirational', more sober tone than Peters in identifying key features of effective leaders. For example Galbraith and Lawler (1993) suggest that temperament, values, self-awareness and the ability to be involved in constant learning are characteristics of effective leaders. Charan (1996: 33–4) suggests that top managers should have a strong sense of accountability, an ability to show initiative, astuteness in the selection of staff, intellectual curiosity and an ability to have a global mind-set on matters.

Champy and Nohria (1996b: 263–4) suggest that leaders are ambitious, have a sense of humility, constantly strive for the truth of situations, face up to ambiguity, uncertainty, take responsibility for their actions, are self-disciplined and authentic. Miyashiro (1996b) adds to these the leader's abilities to change people's emotions before making changes in the organization, and to tap into the often hidden knowledge that most people have, as a starting point for subsequent further development. McKaskey (1988) suggests that significant elements of effective leaders of change include the ability to tolerate ambiguity and flexibility, to find problems, to build maps, to look in several directions simultaneously (e.g. to internal and external environments), to balance control and autonomy, to be humorous, and to possess charisma that motivates. In education, Bowring-Carr and West-Burnham (1994: 128–9) identify seven characteristic practices of effective people, viz. their abilities to be proactive, to identify goals, to order tasks and priorities, to think positively (win/win), to understand matters, to make themselves understood and to synergize effectively.

Bennis (1984) identifies four competencies of leadership: the management of: 1) attention (the ability to communicate clear objectives and direction); 2) meaning (the ability to create and communicate meaning clearly so that it is understood and that people's awareness is raised); 3) trust (the ability to be consistent and clear in complex circumstances and dilemmas in which people are placed, so that leaders are seen as dependable); 4) self (self-awareness and the ability to work with one's strengths and weaknesses).

Covey (1992) suggests that effective leaders possess seven key characteristics:

1) being proactive (anticipating the future and making personal and positive, existential choices);
2) beginning with the end in mind (being clear on the main personal motivations for achievement, and articulation of values);
3) putting first things first (self-management: prioritizing, organizing and delegating, identifying key tasks and roles, setting time frames);
4) thinking win/win (seeking solutions that benefit everybody);
5) understanding and being understood (empathic, active listening and communicating/responding effectively);
6) synergizing (catalysing, unifying and unleashing powers in people for a collective enterprise for collective benefit);
7) sharpening the saw (reviewing, renewing and developing oneself, other people and the institution).

Other authors adopt a less generalist approach in defining the characteristics of effective leaders and effective leaders of change. For example, Wickens (1995: 95–9) sets out a range of specific characteristics under the headings of personal attributes, a strategic perspective, communication and achievement thus:

• *personal attributes*: high intelligence; broad knowledge base; empathy; ability to focus on critical success factors; ability to analyse logically and rationally; informed intuition; high integrity; setting high ethical standards for all; knowing when to do nothing; energy; self-motivation; determination; courage; flexibility and adaptability; self-awareness;

- *strategic perspective*: aligning an organization; setting a strategic vision, implementing it and sensing its impact; concern for all stakeholders; challenging existing situations; determination to achieve goals;
- *communication*: inspirational, enthusing other people; effective communication (particularly orally); effective persuasion; communication of vision and strategy; enabling everyone to share and own the vision; being a team member as well as leader; responding to others' feelings; putting people at their ease; respecting and valuing others and listening to them; recognizing everyone's contributions; balancing decisive action with support (see also Harvey-Jones, 1988: 55);
- *achievement*: leading by high-quality example to achieve objectives; showing a commitment to development and constant improvement; taking calculated risks; devolving responsibility, authority and accountability; monitoring intuitively; concern for the processes involved in achievement.

Wickens's work is useful here, for it signals not only that leaders have to look to their own roles as leaders but also to the roles of others as 'followers', echoing previous comments that the management of change is about the management of perception. Effective leaders study hard the likely effects of change on the followers and ensure that everything appropriate is done to ease the effects of the change. Brown and Weiner (1984) suggest that the leader has to avert 'crises of followership' that are caused through: 1) overmanaging and bureaucracy; 2) a belief that only the senior managers know best; 3) a belief that only a selected few factors in the external environment need to be addressed (i.e. missing complexity); 4) isolating mavericks (the need to include the 'plant' was identified by Belbin (1981) in the previous chapter as an essential feature of successful teams).

Effective management of change in education, then, requires appropriate knowledge, skills, personality and characteristics for managing change. Everard and Morris (quoted in Morrison and Ridley, 1988), indicate several aspects of knowledge required for managing change. Knowledge of:

- people and their motivation systems – what makes them tick;
- organizations as social systems – what makes them healthy and effective, able to achieve objectives;
- the environment surrounding the organization – the systems that impinge on and make demands of it;
- managerial styles and their effects on work;
- one's own personal managerial style and proclivities;
- organizational processes such as decision-making, planning, control, communication, conflict management and reward systems;
- the process of change;
- educational and training methods and theory.

They indicate several skills for managing change:

- analysing large complex systems;
- collecting and processing large amounts of information and simplifying it for action;

- goal-setting and planning;
- getting consensus decisions;
- conflict management;
- empathy;
- political behaviour;
- public relations;
- consulting and counselling;
- training and teaching.

They also indicate several personality characteristics for effective managers of change:

- a strong sense of personal ethics which helps to ensure consistent behaviour;
- something of an intellectual by both training and temperament;
- a strong penchant towards optimism;
- enjoyment of the intrinsic rewards of effectiveness, without the need for public approval;
- high willingness to take calculated risks and live with the consequences without experiencing undue stress;
- a capacity to accept conflict and enjoyment in managing it;
- a soft voice and low-key manner;
- a high degree of self-awareness – knowledge of self;
- a high tolerance of ambiguity and complexity;
- a tendency to avoid polarizing issues into black and white, right and wrong;
- high ability to listen.

This latter list of qualities resonates with Adair's (1983: 13) identification of qualities of effective leaders. He includes in his list: perseverance; integrity; ambition; a willingness for and ability to sustain hard work; enthusiasm; enterprise and an ability to identify opportunities; curiosity; single-mindedness; an ability to understand others; a willingness to take risks; a capacity for abstract and analytical thinking; astuteness; decision-making ability; lucidity in writing and communication; efficient administration; imagination and open-mindedness; a willingness to handle difficult or unpleasant situations; responsiveness to change. Harvey-Jones (1988: 87) adds the view that leaders must be prepared to share responsibility when things go wrong. However, Adair also cautions against the simplistic adherence to checklists of skills and qualities, arguing that there is disagreement about exactly which ones they are and whether one should be so prescriptive about the delineation of skills in a democratic society. Buchanan and Boddy (1992: 118–20) suggest a range of characteristics of the expertise of effective change agents that includes:

- excellence in their own fields (e.g. in terms of expertise and experience);
- the ability to see – and work with – wholes, patterns, the overall picture, adopting the 'helicopter' perspective (seeing the overall terrain and the inter-related sections in a detached way and with clarity, avoiding becoming bogged down in details);
- the ability to see to the heart of problems, in terms of principles, theories

and key concepts;
- the ability to simplify complex problems;
- the thirst for information;
- the ability to penetrate and cope with information overload;
- the ability – and practice – of asking demanding questions;
- the ability to become absorbed in a problem and devote time to its analysis rather than plunging into superficial solutions, leading to subsequent rapid, correct and effective solutions;
- high organizational skills and the ability to construct mental maps of problems;
- excellent memories and recall;
- powerful abilities to be self-checking and self-monitoring;
- high self-awareness and self-critique.[9]

Doz and Prahalad (1988) identify a set of competences and skills for change agents that focus on identifying goals, roles, communication, negotiation and 'managing up'. With regard to goals, expert change agents are sensitive to: 1) changes in the leadership and key personnel of an organization; 2) the perceptions of the senior managers; 3) changes in the market; 4) the implications of (1)–(3) for the management of change. Change agents are able to define goals that are achievable and are able to respond to changes that might lie outside the immediate field of the project in question, i.e. taking risks.

With regard to roles, Doz and Prahalad suggest that expert change agents are effective at 1) developing and building teams; 2) identifying and bringing together key people in the organization to work on a change; 3) identifying and delegating key responsibilities in teams; 4) communicating through formal and informal networks both inside the organization and with the world outside; 5) tolerating ambiguity and uncertainty and being able to work effectively in such climates.

With regard to communication, Doz and Prahalad suggest that expert change agents are effective at communicating to everybody: 1) the need for change (echoing Harvey-Jones's (1988: 102) comment that one task of leadership is to make it clear that remaining in the existing situation is more dangerous than stepping into the possibly unknown future); 2) what the changes will imply; 3) how they will impact on individuals. Such expertise is the product of effective interpersonal skills, being good listeners, collating and disseminating information, being able to identify people's concerns, and conveying enthusiasm and commitment that stimulates and motivates others to become committed to the change.

With regard to negotiation, Doz and Prahalad suggest that expert change agents are effective at: 1) 'selling' ideas, plans and visions to those affected; 2) negotiating for required resources and support; 3) resolving conflict; 4) negotiating changes in operations, procedures and activities.

Finally, with regard to managing up, Doz and Prahalad suggest that expert change agents are effective at: 1) identifying and working with the micropolitics of organizations; 2) using influencing skills to secure the commitment of initial resisters; 3) seeing the whole picture and establishing   and communicating – overall priorities.

One can detect in expert leaders, change agents and managers of change the ability to balance the twin concerns of achieving results (task orientation) with promoting positive relationships (people orientation). That this is not a novel suggestion is evidenced by Tannenbaum and Schmidt (1958) in their view that it is possible to locate the managerial styles of 'tell' (autocratic), 'sell' (paternalistic), 'involve' (consultative) and 'co-determine' (democratic) on a continuum of a concern for results to a concern for relationships respectively. One can note here that the concern for results and 'tell' and 'sell' styles resonate with the mechanical and closed systems that, it was argued in previous chapters, are not conducive to positive organizational health and climates and hence are not conducive to change, whereas the concern for relationships and 'involve' and 'co-determine' styles resonate with the organic and open systems that, it was argued, are conducive to positive organizational health and climate and hence are conducive to change. Indeed Harvey-Jones (1988: 87) suggests that leaders should be as much enablers as they are drivers. A balance can be struck between the concern for results and concern for relationships (Blake and Mouton, 1964), by adopting motivational and problem-solving styles of managing change.

Evenden and Anderson (1992: 197) suggest that the concern for relationships is, itself, problematical. Whilst they chart the dangers for the management of change that reside in leaders who are too hostile, aloof or remote (leading to anger, intimidation and sabotage in employees), they also signal danger from too friendly a leadership style (the leader as 'buddy') as this can be intrusive, unfair and maybe two-faced. Rather, they suggest, the effective leader of relationships is approachable and friendly, promoting in colleagues feelings of trust, interest, support, liking, humanity and warmth.

Poor leaders, by contrast, have several distinguishing features (Kotter, 1996):

- an inability to create a sense of urgency;
- an inability to create a sufficiently powerful guiding coalition;
- limited vision;
- inability to remove obstacles to the achievement of the vision;
- undercommunication;
- lack of planning for short-term wins;
- celebrating success to rapidly;
- an inability to institutionalize change.

Summary of implications for education

It has been argued that leaders exist throughout the organization and that senior managers need to foster and nurture the development of leadership potential of everybody in the organization. The question then arises: 'what is being done in the organization to develop and prepare leaders at all levels and in all areas of the organization, not only to fulfil existing leadership roles but also to prepare them for future leadership and senior leadership roles?' In summarizing the preceding discussion in terms of its implication for education there are very many questions that can be generated for leaders of change. These include the need to address issues of how to manage people, culture and structure, and tasks and roles.

People

- Align everybody in the organization whilst still promoting personal autonomy and the tolerance of creative 'mavericks';
- develop and exercise the knowledge, skills, qualities, personalities and change agency abilities of leaders;
- motivate and reward staff – individually and collectively;
- develop commitment;
- ensure that the best leaders for the job are appointed;
- identify and appoint leaders throughout the organization;
- be sensitive to individuals and groups;
- balance pressure and support;
- maximize human resources and human resource management.

Culture and structure

- Promote leadership within a flat management style;
- enable leaders to operate in a collegial, organic and open management structure;
- involve everybody and value everybody in the organization;
- foster appropriate 'followership' and synergy;
- promote openness and trust;
- raise everyone's awareness of each other;
- enable effective communication to occur (e.g. so that the message is not distorted, so that the appropriate channels of communication are utilized and so that the correct message is received);
- ensure that senior managers are effective leaders;
- use power legitimately and avoid the illegitimate use/abuse of power;
- promote the organizational health and positive climate in the organization for change to occur;
- assess the internal and external environment and respond to pressure from it;
- lead change;
- overcome resistance and manage conflict;
- be a transformational and empowering leader.

Tasks and roles

- Lead the development and sharing of the vision, strategy, direction, aims and objectives of the organization;
- achieve the vision, aims and strategy in practice, i.e. linking strategy and operations;
- develop and exercise the required interpersonal, informational, decisional roles of leaders;
- lead for short-term and long-term gains and development;

- set challenging and manageable tasks and goals for everybody;
- adopt flexible and different leadership styles as appropriate;
- prioritize key tasks of leaders;
- balance the push for results with the push for relationships;
- promote problem-solving;
- identify and address challenges to the organization;
- delegate yet share responsibility, i.e. to avoid delegation and the abdication of responsibility;
- balance conflicting leadership roles;
- decide what roles, qualities, tasks an organization wants and requires of its leaders.

The business literature has a wealth of material to offer education in discussing leadership, and this very wealth reveals the complexity and sensitivity of issues of leadership. This argues for a degree of subtlety in leadership that takes it beyond the crude management-by-coercion model (however skilfully and painlessly it appears to be operating), and takes leadership to be a complex and nuanced set of qualities and actions that require both sensitivity and training. Harvey-Jones (1988: 262) closes his account of 'making it happen' in industry (ICI) with the comment that both management and manufacturing are about working effectively with people, leading them, motivating them and harnessing their several and extensive capabilities. That is a salutary message for education.

Notes

1. This builds on McGregor's Theory Y, in which everybody is creative. Whether change agents can exist in Ouchi's Theory Z is another matter (Brandon, 1992: 33) for, by definition, they question, disrupt and even undermine the group and the corporate culture of Japanese companies. In Theory Z change agents are dysfunctional.

2. More recently (1990) Mintzberg has confirmed his original categorization and suggested that the roles and tasks of managers together form a complex *gestalt*; leadership and management are inextricably intertwined.

3. In arguing this Zaleznik is echoing the Weberian principle that the authority of many leaders derives from charisma, presence, expertise and foresight.

4. Clarke (1994: 43) suggests that the new managers for the future will be effective in 'sensing' the environment, acting as catalysts and 'animateurs'.

5. Peters, 1987; Adair, 1983; 1984; 1987; 1988; Harvey-Jones, 1988; Hersey and Blanchard, 1988; Quinn, 1988; Belasco, 1990; Kotter, 1990; Mortiboys and Oakland, 1991; Evenden and Anderson, 1992; Galbraith and Lawler, 1993; Nicholson, 1993; Pettigrew and Whipp, 1993; Bartlett and Ghoshal, 1994; Carnall, 1995; Champy and Nohria, 1996c; Kanter, 1996; Miyashiro, 1996b; Heifetz and Lawrie, 1997.

6. Senior managers, Champy and Nohria aver (1996b: xix), add value to the organization by brokering with – working with, discussing with,

trading with – people rather than by presiding over empires.

7.   The notion of transformational leadership is not without its critics. Riches (1993b: 28) suggests that there is a rhetoric of transformation that neglects essential administrative competencies, overstates its own ability to solve a range of problems, neglects pressing immediate everyday mundane problems, can be too risky, is too reliant on inspirational talk and charisma, and neglects an important debate about values and democracy.

8.   Grace (1994) has made much of the moral component of leadership; rather it is to note its comparative neglect in the business literature. In the business literature one can detect in the increasing advocacy of respect for the humanity of employees and the people-centredness of change through collegiality a clear set of moral principles at work.

9.   Echoing the Japanese model, Brandon (1992: 31) identifies the Senior Managing Director of Toyota as a supreme example of an effective change agent, as he possessed the ability to a) question existing practices and preconceived ideas; b) present problems in a form that was susceptible to solution; c) identify original and creative solutions; d) convince the decision-makers about the correctness of the prescribed solution.

Postscript

The chapters in this book combine to suggest a large range of considerations for educational institutions that derive from an analysis of practices in industry and business. It has been seen that the swing in business towards human resource development as the key to productivity through the fulfilment and self-actualization of employees has been taking place for decades.

The business literature was seen to take with the utmost seriousness the twin notions of organizational development and human resource development in deliberate, planned and supported ways. The achievement of productivity was seen to reside in these rather than simply the development and use of new technologies. The notion of productivity is frequently regarded with suspicion in educational circles, as though it suggests the exploitation of workers in the cause of producing uniform outcomes with as little input as possible. The exploitative view of productivity does not find affirmation in the current business literature because it is based on a win/lose model – the company wins and the workers lose. Rather, this book has suggested that it is to everybody's advantage that a win/win model is adopted. Certainly the business literature is a strong advocate of this. The new form of productivity concerns producing the best for everyone, maximizing everyone's abilities and outputs – a creative rather than exploitative view. That is a message with which many educationists should feel comfortable.

It has been argued that change at a macrosocietal level can be matched by change at the microlevel of organizations, groups and individuals. That this is neither easy nor straightforward is well recognized in the business literature and educational practice. The suggestion has been made here that the business literature offers many valuable insights into the processes of development and change so that everyone can benefit. This is a much more humanistic view of profit than simply economic return.

It would be easy to suggest that the analysis provided in this book is simplistic. The argument could run that our school is already running well so why change it ('if it's not broken, why fix it') but this overlooks the point at issue, which is that the world outside is changing and that it is simply to play the ostrich to ignore this. Further, it is to violate the notion of continuous improvement that, as has been suggested, is a powerful means of self-authentication.

Another potential worry with some of the analysis in this book might suggest that schools do not have the room for manoeuvre that business has because they are starved of resources and there are too many contingencies. To some extent this is unquestionably true. However, it overlooks the points made throughout this book that many of the changes concern human resource development, particularly the need to address issues of motivation.

A third worry with some of the analysis in this book might argue that the portrayal of business is unrealistic, that far from being the delight to work in, many businesses are not the haven they have been portrayed to be here and that many of the suggestions made here are only applicable to those in comparatively exciting jobs. How do we empower a machinist, an assembly-line worker, or somebody whose job, whatever it is in an organization, is largely low-level routine, or a very low-paid worker, or the worker in a small company where there is little room for manoeuvre? This book has provided examples of how motivation and empowerment might be developed through teamwork, the social relations of work and the development of multiskilling. It is also to argue that maybe business needs to look to itself for how to improve employees' work situations.

This book has avoided making specific, detailed prescriptions for educational institutions. This has been deliberate, for the overwhelming message is that these are matters for the people involved in the organization. This is not to avoid responsibility or invite the criticism that academics are long on theory and short on practice. Rather, it is to identify where responsibility for certain decisions about practice both should and do lie (see Dalin *et al.*, 1993). This book has attempted to adopt a responsible attitude by raising agendas, by providing justifications and arguments, by suggesting that practice is – and should be – underpinned by complex, problematical and contestable principles.

Einstein was known to remark that one should make matters as simple as possible, but no simpler. This book has attempted to chart the contours of the complexity of change and to outline proposals for how change might be addressed and managed. The responsibility for specific changes must reside with the participants. People matter.

There is a biblical proverb that states that without vision the people perish; the message of this book has suggested an important inversion of this message: without people the vision perishes.

Bibliography

Adair, J. (1983) *Effective Leadership: A Self-Development Manual*. Aldershot: Gower.

Adair, J. (1984) *The Skills of Leadership*. Aldershot: Gower.

Adair, J. (1987) *Effective Teambuilding: How to Make a Winning Team*. London: Pan.

Adair, J. (1988) *The Action-Centred Leader*. London: The Industrial Society.

Adam Smith Institute (1984) *Education Policy (the Omega Report)*. London: Adam Smith Institute.

Adams, J., Hayes, J. and Hopson, B. (1976) *Transitions – Understanding and Managing Personal Change*. Oxford: Martin Robertson.

Ainscow, M., Hargreaves, D.H., Hopkins, D., Balshaw, M. and Black-Hawkins, K. (1994) *Mapping Change in Schools*. Cambridge: Department of Education, University of Cambridge.

Åm, O. (1994) *Back to Basics. Introduction to Systems Theory and Complexity*. http://www.stud.his.no/~onar/Ess/Back-to-Basics.html.

Amabile, T.M. (1983) *The Social Psychology of Creativity*. New York: Springer Verlag.

Arcaro, J. (1995a) *Quality in Education*. Delray Beach, Florida: St Lucie Press.

Arcaro, J. (1995b) *Teams in Education*. London: Kogan Page.

Argyris, C. (1990) *Overcoming Organizational Defences*. Needham Heights, Mass.: Allyn & Bacon.

Argyris, C. and Schön, D. (1978) *Organizational Learning: A Theory of Action Perspective*. Reading, Mass.: Addison-Wesley.

Arroba, T. and James, K. (1987) *Pressure at Work*. Maidenhead: McGraw-Hill.

Askey, J.M. and Dale, B.G. (1994) From ISO 9000 series registration to total quality management: an examination. *Quality Management Journal*, July, 67–76.

Ball, C. (1985) What the hell is quality? In C. Ball (ed.) *Fitness for Purpose*. Guildford: Society for Research in Higher Education.

Ball, S. (1990) *Politics and Policy Making in Education*. London: Routledge.

Ball, S. (1994) *Education Reform: A Critical and Post-Structuralist Approach*. Buckingham: Open University Press.

Bank, J. (1992) *The Essence of Total Quality Management*. London: Prentice-Hall.

Barker, H. and Bell, M. (1994) The national standard of Investors in People – does it have a place in the management of schools? In H. Green (ed.) *The School Management Handbook*. London: Kogan Page.

Barnard, C.L. (1938) *Functions of the Executive*. Cambridge, Mass.: Harvard University Press.

Bartlett, C.A. and Ghoshal, S. (1994) Changing the role of top management: beyond strategy to purpose. *Harvard Business Review*, 72, Nov/Dec, 79–88.

Bartlett, C.A. and Ghoshal, S. (1995) Changing the role of top management: beyond systems to people. *Harvard Business Review*, 73, May/June, 132–42.

Beale, D. (1994) *Driven by Nissan: A Critical Guide to New Management Techniques*. London: Lawrence & Wishart.

Beckhard, R. (1992) A model for the executive management of transformational change. In G. Salaman (ed.) *Human Resource Strategies*. London: Sage Publications in association with the Open University Press.

Beer, M., Eisenstadt, R.A. and Spector, B. (1990) Why change programs don't produce change. *Harvard Business Review*, 68, Nov/Dec, 158–66.

Belasco, J. (1990) *Teaching the Elephant to Dance: Empowering Change in Your Organisation*. London: Hutchinson Business Books.

Belbin, R.M. (1981) *Management Teams: Why they Succeed or Fail*. Oxford: Butterworth-Heinemann.

Bell, L. (1992) *Managing Teams in the Secondary School*. London: Routledge.

Bendell, T. (1991) *The Quality Gurus*. London: Department of Trade and Industry.

Bennett, J.B. and O'Brien, M.J. (1994) The building blocks of the learning organization. *Training*, June, 41–8.

Bennett, N. (1993) Effectiveness and the culture of the school. Unit 1, E326 Module 2: *Managing for School Effectiveness*. Milton Keynes: Open University Press.

Bennett, N., Crawford, M. and Riches, C. (1992) *Managing Change in Education*. London: Paul Chapman in association with the Open University Press.

Bennis, W. (1969) *Organizational Development: Its Nature, Origins and Projects*. Menlo Park, Calif.: Addison-Wesley.

Bennis, W. (1984) The 4 competencies of leadership. *Training and Development Journal*, 38, 15.

Berman, P. and McLaughlin, M. (1979) *An Exploratory Study of School District Adaptations*. Santa Monica, Calif.: Rand Corporation.

Bessler, T.L. (1995) Rewards and organizational goal achievements: a case study of Toyota Motor Manufacturing in Kentucky. *Journal of Management Studies*, 32 (3), 383–99.

Bettes, D. (1995) Moving from ISO 9000 towards total quality. *Quality World*, Sept, 610–13.

Bierly, P.E. and Spender, J.C. (1995) Culture and high reliability organizations: the case of the nuclear submarine. *Journal of Management*, 21 (4), 639–56.

Blackstone, T., Cornford, J., Hewitt, P., and Miliband, D. (1992) *Next Left: An Agenda for the Nineties*. London: Institute for Public Policy Research.

Blake, R.R. and Mouton, J.S. (1964) *The Managerial Grid*. Houston, Tex.: Gulf Publishing.

Blau, P.M. (1964) *Exchange and Power in Social Life*. New York: Wiley.

Bolman, L. and Deal, T. (1984) *Modern Approaches to Understanding Organizations*. San Francisco, Calif.: Jossey Bass.

Bottery, M. (1994) *Lessons for Schools?* London: Cassell.

Bowe, R., Ball, S. and Gold, A. (1992) *Reforming Education and Changing Schools*. London: Routledge.

Bowman, C. and Asch, D. (1987) *Strategic Management*. Basingstoke: Macmillan Educational.

Bowring-Carr, C. and West-Burnham, J. (1994) *Managing Quality in Schools*. Harlow: Longman.

Brandon, J. (1992) *Managing Change in Manufacturing Systems*. Olney: Productivity Publishing.

Braun, A. and Weiner, E. (1984) *Supermanaging*. New York: McGraw-Hill.

Bridges, D. and Husbands, C. (1996) *Consorting and Collaborating in the Education Market Place*. London: Falmer.

Bridges, D. and McLaughlin, T.H. (eds) (1994) *Education and the Market Place*. London: Falmer.

Brown, A. and Weiner, E. (1984) *Supermanaging*. New York: McGraw-Hill.

Buchanan, D. and Boddy, D. (1992) *The Expertise of the Change Agent*. Hemel Hempstead: Prentice Hall.

Bullock, R.J. and Batten, D. (1985) It's just a phase we're going through: a review and synthesis of OD phase analysis. *Group and Organization Studies*, 10, 383–412.

Burnes, B. (1996) *Managing Change: A Strategic Approach to Organizational Dynamics*. London: Pitman.

Burns, T. and Stalker, G.M. (1961) *The Management of Innovation*. London: Tavistock.

Burridge, E., Ginnis, P., Hammond, L., and Smith, A. (1993) *Quality Development*. Birmingham: Birmingham City Council Education Department.

Bush, T. (1993) Exploring collegiality: theory and practice. Unit 2 of E326 Module 1, *Managing Educational Change*. Milton Keynes: Open University Press.

Bush, T. (1995) *Theories of Educational Management* (second edition). London: Harper & Row.

Buxbaum, P.A. (1993) ISO 9000: paper trail to quality? *Distribution*, 92, 80–4.

Caldwell, B.J. and Spinks, J.M. (1992) *Leading the Self-Managing School*. London: Falmer.

Carnall, C.A. (1982) *The Evaluation of Organisational Change*. Aldershot: Gower.

Carnall, C.A. (1995) *Managing Change in Organizations* (second edition). London: Prentice-Hall.

Carroll, M. (1996) *Workplace Counselling*. London: Sage.

Carroll, M. and Walton, M. (eds) (1997) *Handbook of Counselling in Organizations*. London: Sage.

Cartwright, S. and Cooper, C. (1994) *No Hassle: Taking the Stress out of Work*. London: Century Business Books.

Champy, J. and Nohria, N. (1996a) Into the storm: the cycle of change quickens. In J. Champy and N. Nohria (eds), op. cit.

Champy, J. and Nohria, N. (1996b) The eye of the storm: the force at the center. In J. Champy and N. Nohria (eds), op. cit.

Champy, J. and Nohria, N. (eds) (1996c) *Fast Forward: The Best Ideas on Managing Business Change*. Boston, Mass.: Harvard Business School.

Charan, R. (1996) How networks reshape organizations. In J. Champy and N. Nohria (eds), op. cit.

Chaudhry-Lawton, R., Lawton, R., Murphy, K. and Terry, A. (1992) *Quality: Change through Teamwork*. London: Century Business.

Child, J. (1984) *Organization: A Guide to Problems and Practices* (second edition). London: Paul Chapman Publishing.

Clarke, L. (1994) *The Essence of Change*. London: Prentice-Hall.

Clegg, S.R. (1992) Modernist and postmodernist organization. In G. Salaman (ed), *Human Resource Strategies*. London: Sage Publications in association with the Open University Press.

Coffield, F. (1989) Caught in the act: ERA 1988? In F. Coffield and T. Edwards (eds), op. cit.

Coffield, F. (ed.) (1997) *A National Strategy for Lifelong Learning*. Newcastle upon Tyne: Department of Education, University of Newcastle upon Tyne.

Coffield, F. and Edwards, T. (1989) *Working within the Act*. Durham: Educational Publishing Services.

Cole, R.E. (1979) *Work, Mobility and Participation*. Berkeley, Calif.: University of California Press.

Cole, R.E. and Tominga, K. (1976) Japan's changing occupational structure and its significance. In H. Patrick (ed.) *Japanese Industrialization and its Social Consequences*. Berkeley, Calif.: University of California Press.

Coleman, M. and Bush, T. (1994) Managing with teams. In T. Bush and J. West-Burnham (eds) *The Principles of School Management*. Harlow: Longman.

Coleman, T. (1994) Leadership in educational management. In T. Bush and J. West-Burnham (eds) *The Principles of School Management*. Harlow: Longman.

Collins, P. (1994) Approaches to quality. *The TQM Magazine*, 6 (3), 39–43.

Cool, K.O. and Lengnick-Hall, C.A. (1985) Second thoughts on the transferability of the Japanese management style. *Organizational Studies*, 6 (1), 1–22.

Corrigan, J.P. (1994) Is ISO 9000 the path to TQM? *Quality Progress*, 27 May, 33–6.

Coulson-Thomas, C.J. (1991) Developing tomorrow's professionals today. *Journal of European Industrial Training*, 15 (1), 3–11.

Covey, S. (1992) *The Seven Habits of Highly Effective People*. London: Simon & Schuster.

Cowling, A. and James, P. (1994) *The Essence of Personnel Management and Industrial Relations*. London: Prentice-Hall.

Crosby, P.B. (1980) *Quality is Free*. Harmondsworth: Penguin.

Crosby, P. (1984) *Quality without Tears*. New York: McGraw-Hill.

Cuban, L. (1990) A fundamental problem of school reform. In A. Lieberman (ed.), op. cit.

Dale, R. (1989) *The State and Education Policy*. Milton Keynes: Open University Press.

Dalin, P. (1978) *Limits to Educational Change*. Basingstoke: Macmillan.

Dalin, P., Rolff, H. and Kottkamp, R. (1993) *Changing the School Culture*. London: Cassell.

Dalin, P. and Rust, V. (1983) *Can Schools Learn?* Windsor: NFER-Nelson.

Dalin, P. and Rust, V. (1996) *Schooling for the Twenty-first Century*. London: Cassell.

Davis, L.E. and Kanter, R.R. (1995) Job design. *Journal of Industrial Engineering*, 6 (1), 3.

Dawson, P. (1994) *Organizational Change: A Processual Approach*. London: Paul Chapman Publishing.

Deal, T.E. (1990) Healing our schools: restoring the heart. In A. Lieberman (ed.), op. cit.

Deal, T.E. and Kennedy, A.A. (1983a) *Corporate Cultures: The Rites and Rituals of Corporate*

Life. Reading, Mass.: Addison-Wesley.

Deal, T.E. and Kennedy, A. (1983b) Culture: a new look through old lenses. *Journal of Applied Behavioural Science*, 19 (4), 497–507.

Dean, J. and Evans, J.R. (1994) *Total Quality Management, Organization and Strategy*. St. Paul, Minn.: West Publishing.

Deming, W.E. (1982) *Out of the Crisis: Quality, Productivity and Competitive Position*. Cambridge, Mass.: Cambridge University Press.

Department for Education (1992) *Education Act 1992*. London: HMSO.

Department for Education (1993a) *Education Act 1993*. London: HMSO.

Department for Education (1993b) *Effective Management in Schools*. London: HMSO.

Department for Education and Employment (1997) *Excellence in Schools*. London: HMSO.

Department of Education and Science (1986) *Education Act 1986*. London: HMSO.

Department of Education and Science (1988) *Education Reform Act*. London: HMSO.

Department of Education and Science (1989) *Planning for School Development*. London: HMSO.

Department of Education and Science (1992) *Choice and Diversity: A New Framework for Schools*. London: HMSO.

Department of Trade and Industry (1994a) *BS 5750/ISO 9000/EN 29000: 1987. A Positive Contribution to Better Business*. London: Department of Trade and Industry.

Department of Trade and Industry (1994b) *Quality Circles*. London: Department of Trade and Industry.

Department of Trade and Industry (1995) *Implementing BS EN ISO 9000: A Guide for Small Firms*. London: Department of Trade and Industry.

Doll, W.E. (1993) *A Post-Modern Perspective on Curriculum*. Columbia University, New York: Teachers College Press.

Doz, Y.Z. and Prahalad, C.K. (1988) A process model of strategic redirection in large complex firms: the case of multinational corporations. In A. Pettigrew (ed.), op. cit.

Drucker, P. (1988) The coming of the new organization. *Harvard Business Review*, Jan/Feb, 45–53.

Drucker, P. (1993) *The Ecological Vision: Reflections on the American Condition*. London: Transaction Publishers.

Drucker, P.F. (1995) *Managing in Times of Great Change*. London: Butterworth-Heinemann.

Drucker, P.F. (1996) The coming of the new organisation. In J. Champy and N. Nohria (eds), op. cit.

Duck, J.D. (1993) Managing change: the art of balancing. *Harvard Business Review*, Nov/Dec, 109–18.

Dunphy, D. (1981) *Organizational Change by Choice*. Sydney: McGraw-Hill.

Egan, G. (1993) *Adding Value*. San Francisco, Calif.: Jossey-Bass.

Egan, G. (1994) *Working on the Shadow-Side: A Guide to Positive behind the Scenes Management*. San Francisco, Calif.: Jossey-Bass.

Egan, G. and Cowan, M. (1979) *People in Systems*. Monterey, Calif.: Brooks Cole.

Elliott-Kemp, J. and Elliott-Kemp, N. (1992) *Managing Change and Development in Schools: A Practical Handbook*. Harlow: Longman.

Elliott-Kemp, J. and Williams, G.L. (1979) *The DION Handbook: Diagnosis of Individual and Organisational Needs for Staff Development and In-Service Training in Schools*. Sheffield: Sheffield Polytechnic.

Endrijonas, J. (1994) Is ISO 9000 certification a bane or a boon? *Managing Automation*, May, 38–9.

Entwistle, H. (1981) Work, leisure and life styles. In B. Simon and W. Taylor (eds) *Education in the Eighties*. London: Batsford.

Evenden, R. and Anderson, G. (1992) *Management Skills: Making the Most of People*. Wokingham: Addison-Wesley.

Everard, B. and Morris, G. (1988) Effective school management. Quoted in K.R.B. Morrison and K. Ridley, op. cit.

Everard, B. and Morris, G. (1990) *Effective School Management* (second edition). London: Paul Chapman Publishing.

Feigenbaum, A.V. (1991) *Total Quality Control* (third edition). New York: McGraw-Hill.
Finch, J. (1994) Quality and its measurement: a business perspective. In D. Green (ed), op.cit.
Fink, S., Beak, J. and Taddeo, K. (1971) Organizational crisis and change. *Journal of Applied Behavioural Science*, 13 (1), 15–41.
Fitz-Gibbon, C.T. (1996) *Monitoring Education: Indicators, Quality and Effectiveness*. London: Cassell.
Foucault, M. (1980) *Power/Knowledge; Selected Interviews and Other Writings 1972–77*. Brighton: Harvester.
Frazer, M. (1994) Quality in higher education: an international perspective. In D. Green (ed.), op. cit.
French, J. and Raven, B.H. (1959) The bases of social power. In D. Cartwright (ed.) *Studies in Social Power*. Ann Arbour, Mich.: Michigan University Press.
Fromm, E. (1944) *The Fear of Freedom*. London: Routledge.
Fullan, M. (1991) *The New Meaning of Educational Change*. London: Cassell.
Galbraith, J.R. and Lawler, E.E. (eds) (1993) *Organizing for the Future*. New York: Jossey-Bass.
Gardner, H. (1993) *Multiple Intelligences: The Theory in Practice*. New York: Basic Books.
Garrahan, P. and Stewart, P. (1992) *The Nissan Enigma: Flexibility at Work in a Local Economy*. London: Mansell.
Garvin, D.A. (1993) Building a learning organization. *Harvard Business Review*, July/Aug, 78–91.
Garvin, D.A. (1996) Leveraging processes of strategic advantage: a roundtable with Xerox's Allaire, USAA's Herres, SmithKline Beecham's Leschly, and Pepsi's Weatherup. In J. Champy and N. Nohria (eds), op. cit.
Gibb, J.R. and Gibb, L.M. (1955) *Applied Group Dynamics*. London: National Training Authorities.
Gilmer, B. (1966) *Industrial Psychology* (second edition). New York: McGraw-Hill.
Gleick, J. (1987) *Chaos*. London: Abacus.
Goffin, K. and Szwejczewski, M. (1996) Is management commitment to quality just 'a given'? *The TQM Magazine*, 8 (2), 26–31.
Goldsmith, W. and Clutterbuck, D. (1984) *The Winning Streak*. London: Weidenfeld & Nicolson.
Goodstein, L.D. and Burke, W.W. (1993) Creating successful organizational change. In C. Mabey and B. Mayon-White (eds), op. cit.
Goss, T., Pascale, R. and Athos, A. (1996) The reinvention roller coaster: risking the present for a powerful future. In J. Champy and N. Nohria (eds), op. cit.
Grace, G. (1994) Education is a public good: on the need to resist the domination of economic science. In D. Bridges and T. McLaughlin (eds), op. cit.
Green, D. (ed.) (1994) *What is Quality in Higher Education?* Buckingham: Society for Research in Higher Education and the Open University Press.
Green, G. D. (1992) Document control for BS 5750. *Transition*, July, 28–9.
Greenwood, M.S. and Gaunt, H.J. (1994) *Total Quality Management for Schools*. London: Cassell.
Grundy, T. (1994) *Strategic Learning in Action*. London: McGraw-Hill.
Hall, G., George, A., and Rutherford, W. (1986) *Measuring Stages of Concern about the Innovation: A Manual for Use of the SOC Questionnaire*. Austin, Tex.: Southwest Educational Development Laboratory.
Hall, G. and Hord, S. (1987) *Change in Schools*. New York: State University of New York Press.
Halpin, W. (1966) *Theory and Research in Administration*. New York: Macmillan.
Hammer, M. (1996) Reengineering work: don't automate, obliterate. In J. Champy and N. Nohria (eds), op. cit.
Hampden-Turner, C. (1994) *Corporate Culture*. London: Piatkus.
Handy, C. (1976) *Understanding Organisations*. Harmondsworth: Penguin.
Handy, C. (1989) *The Age of Unreason* (first edition). London: Business Books.
Handy, C. (1991) *The Age of Unreason* (second edition). London: Business Books.
Handy, C. (1994) *The Empty Raincoat: Making Sense of the Future*. London: Hutchinson.

Hargreaves, A. (1994) *Changing Teachers, Changing Times*. London: Cassell.

Hargreaves, D. and Hopkins, D. (1991) *The Empowered School*. London: Cassell.

Harris, R.T. (1987) *Organizational Transitions*. Wokingham: Addison-Wesley.

Harrison, R. (1994) Organisational culture. Cited in A. Cowling and P. James, op. cit.

Hartnett, A. and Naish, M. (1976) *Theory and Practice of Education*. London: Heinemann.

Harvey-Jones, J. (1988) *Making It Happen: Reflections on Leadership*. London: Collins.

Hastings, C., Bixby, P. and Chaudry-Lawton, R. (1986) *The Superteam Solution*. Aldershot: Gower.

Hayek, F. (1960) *The Constitution of Society*. London: Routledge & Kegan Paul.

Hayek, F. (1973) *Law, Legislation and Liberty, Volume One: Rules and Order*. London: Routledge & Kegan Paul.

Hayek, F. (1979) *Law, Legislation and Liberty, Volume Three: The Political Order of a Free People*. London: Routledge & Kegan Paul.

Hayek, F. (1986) *The Road to Serfdom*. London: Routledge & Kegan Paul.

Healy, M. (1994) BS 5750 and beyond in a secondary school. In C. Parsons (ed.) *Quality Improvement in Education*. London: David Fulton.

Heifetz, R.A. and Lawrie, D.L. (1997) The work of leadership. *Harvard Business Review*, Jan/Feb, 124–34.

Herbig, P.A. and Palumbo, F.A. (1996) Innovation – Japanese style. *Entrepreneurship, Innovation and Change*, 5 (3), 227–44.

Hersey, P. and Blanchard, K. (1988) *Organizational Behavior*. New York: Prentice-Hall.

Herzberg, F. (1968) One more time: how do you motivate employees? *Harvard Business Review*, Jan/Feb, 53–62.

Ho, S.K. and Gemil, S. (1996) Japanese 5-S practice. *The TQM Magazine*, 8 (1), 45–53.

Homans, G.C. (1971) *Institutions and Social Exchange*. Indianapolis, Ind.: Bobbs-Merrill.

Hopkins, D. (1985) *A Teacher's Guide to Classroom Research*. Milton Keynes: Open University Press.

Hopkins, D. (1994) School improvement in an ERA of change. In P. Ribbins and E. Burridge (eds), *Improving Education: Promoting Quality in Schools*. London: Cassell.

Hopkins, D., Ainscow, M. and West, M. (1994) *School Improvement in an Era of Change*. London: Cassell.

Hoy, W.K., Tarter, C.J. and Kottkamp, R.B. (1991) *Open Schools: Healthy Schools*. Newbury Park, California: Sage Publications.

Hoyle, E. (1969) How does the curriculum change? *Journal of Curriculum Studies*, 1 (2) pp. 132–41.

Hoyle, E. (1975) The creativity of the school in Britain. In A. Harris, M. Lawn and M. Prescott (eds) *Curriculum Innovation*. London: Croom Helm and the Open University Press.

Hoyle, E. (1976) Strategies of curriculum change. Unit 23, E203: *Curriculum Design and Development*. Milton Keynes: Open University Press.

Hoyle, E. (1986) *The Politics of School Management*. Sevenoaks: Hodder & Stoughton.

Hunt, T.M. and Carter, J.C. (1995) Getting it done: new roles for senior executives. *Harvard Business Review*, Nov/Dec, 133–45.

Iles, P. and Auluck, R. (1993) Team building, inter-agency team development and social work practice. In C. Mabey and B. Mayon-White (eds), op. cit.

International Job Survey Research Ltd (1992) *Employee Satisfaction – Achieving Competitive Advantage in the 90s*. London: International Survey Research.

Ishikawa, K. (1976) *Guide to Quality Control*. Tokyo: Asian Productivity Organization.

Ishikawa, K. (1985) *What is Total Quality Control? The Japanese Way* (trans. D.J. Lu). Englewood-Cliffs, NJ: Prentice-Hall.

Jacobs, R.L. (1995) Impressions about the learning organisation. *Human Resource Development Quarterly*, 6 (2), 119–22.

Jameson, F. (1991) *Postmodernism, Or, The Cultural Logic of Late Capitalism*. London: Verso.

Japan Auto Workers Union (1992) *Japanese Automobile Industry in the Future*. Tokyo: Japan Auto Workers Union.

Jaques, E. (1990) In praise of hierarchy. *Harvard Business Review*, Jan/Feb, 127–33.

Johnson, G. (1993) Processes of managing strategic change. In C. Mabey and B. Mayon-White (eds), op. cit.

Johnson, G. and Scholes, K. (1993) *Exploring Corporate Strategy.* London: Prentice-Hall.

Jonathan, R. (1989) Choice and control in education: parental rights, individual liberties and social justice. *British Journal of Educational Studies,* 37 (4), 321–38.

Joseph, K. (1976) *Stranded on the Middle Ground.* London: Centre for Policy Studies.

Judd, D.K. and Winder, R.E. (1995) The psychology of quality. *Total Quality Management,* 6 (3), 287–91.

Judson, A.S. (1991) *Changing Behaviour in Organizations: Minimizing Resistance to Change.* Oxford: Blackwell.

Juran, J.M. (1988) *Juran on Planning for Quality.* London: Collier-Macmillan.

Juran, J.M. (1993) *Quality Planning and Analysis* (third edition). London: McGraw-Hill.

Kamata, S. (1983) *Japan in the Passing Lane.* London: Allen & Unwin.

Kanji, G.P. (1996) Can total quality management help innovation? *Total Quality Management,* 7 (1), 3–9.

Kanji, G.P. and Asher, M. (1993) *Total Quality Management Process: A Systematic Approach.* Abingdon: Carfax Publishing.

Kanter, R.M. (1983) *The Change Masters: Corporate Entrepreneurs at Work.* London: Allen & Unwin.

Kanter, R.M. (1989) *When Giants Learn to Dance: Mastering the Challenges of Strategy, Management and Careers in the 1990s.* London: Unwin.

Kanter, R.M. (1994) Collaborative advantage: the art of alliances. *Harvard Business Review,* July/Aug, 96–108.

Kanter, R.B. (1996) The new managerial work. In J. Champy and N. Nohria (eds), op. cit.

Kanter, R.M., Stein, B.A. and Jick, T.D. (1992) *The Challenge of Organizational Change.* New York: Maxwell Macmillan International.

Katzenbach, J.R. and Smith, D.K. (1993a) The discipline of teams. *Harvard Business Review,* Mar/April, 111–20.

Katzenbach, J.R. and Smith, D.K. (1993b) *The Wisdom of Teams: Creating the High-Performance Organization.* Boston, Mass.: Harvard Business School Press.

Kauffman, S. (1995) *At Home in the Universe.* Harmondsworth: Penguin.

Kelly, G.A. (1955) *The Psychology of Personal Constructs.* New York: Norton.

Kemmis, S. and McTaggart, R. (1981) *The Action Research Planner.* Victoria, Australia: Deakin University Press.

Kenney, M. and Florida, R. (1988) Beyond mass production: production and the labour process in Japan. *Politics and Society,* 16 (1), 121–58.

Kerka, S. (1995) *Myths and Realities: The Learning Organization* (Document RR 93002001). Office of Educational Research and Improvement, United States Department of Education, Washington, D.C.

Keys, J.B. and Miller, T.R. (1994) The Japanese management theory jungle revisited. *Journal of Management,* 20 (2), 373–402.

Kline, P. and Saunders, B. (1993) *Ten Steps to a Learning Organization.* Arlington, Va.: Great Ocean Publishers.

Kosko, B. (1994) *Fuzzy Thinking.* London: Flamingo.

Kotter, J.P. (1978) *Organizational Dynamics.* Reading, Mass.: Addison-Wesley.

Kotter, J.P. (1990) What leaders really do. *Harvard Business Review,* May/June, 103–11.

Kotter, J.P. (1995) Why transformation efforts fail. *Harvard Business Review,* 73, March/April, 59–67.

Kotter, J.P. (1996) Leading change: why transformations fail. In J. Champy and N. Nohria (eds), op. cit.

Kubler-Ross, E. (1990) On death and dying. Cited in T. Deal, op. cit.

Kuchinke, K.P. (1995) Managing learning for performance. *Human Resource Development Quarterly,* 6 (3), 307–17.

Lash, S. and Urry, J. (1987) *The End of Organized Capitalism.* Cambridge: Polity Press.

Lawler, E.E. (1991) *Pay and Organizational Development.* Reading, Mass.: Addison-Wesley.

Lawton, D. (1983) *Curriculum Studies and Educational Planning.* Sevenoaks: Hodder & Stoughton.

Lawton, D. (1989) *Education, Culture and the National Curriculum.* Sevenoaks: Hodder & Stoughton.

Layder, D. (1994) *Understanding Social Theory.* London: Sage.

Leavitt, H.J. and Lipman-Blumen, J. (1995) Hot groups. *Harvard Business Review*, July/Aug, 109–16.

Legge, K. (1995) *Human Resource Management: Rhetorics and Realities*. Basingstoke: Macmillan.

Le Grand, J. (1990) *Quasi-Markets and Social Policy*. Bristol: School for Advanced Urban Studies.

Leigh, A. (1988) *Effective Change*. London: Institute of Personnel Management.

Levitas, R. (1986) Competition and compliance: the utopias of the New Right. In R. Levitas (ed) *The Ideology of the New Right*. Cambridge: Polity Press.

Lewin, K. (1958) Group decisions and social change. In G.E. Swanson, T.M. Newcomb and L. Hartley (eds) *Readings in Social Psychology*. New York: Holt, Rinehart & Winston.

Lewin, R. (1993) *Complexity: Life on the Edge of Chaos*. London: Phoenix.

Lieberman, A. (ed) (1990) *Schools as Collaborative Cultures*. London: Falmer.

Lincoln, J.R. and McBride, K. (1987) Japanese industrial organizations in comparative perspective. *Annual Review of Sociology*, 13, 289–312.

Linton, R. (ed) (1940) *Acculturation*. New York: Appleton-Century-Crofts.

Litwin, G.H. and Stringer, R.A. (1968) *Motivational and Organizational Climate*. Boston, Mass.: Harvard University Graduate School of Business Administration.

Lung, C.L. (1998) School improvement: effectiveness management of personal and social education in an era of change. Paper submitted towards the award of Doctorate of Education, School of Education, University of Durham.

Mabey, C. and Mayon-White, B. (eds) (1993) *Managing Change* (second edition). London: Paul Chapman Publishing in association with the Open University.

Macmillan, I.C. (1978) *Strategy Formation: Political Concepts*. New York: West.

Margerison, C. and McCann, D. (1990) *Team Management*. London: Mercury.

Markus, M.L. (1983) Power, politics and MIS implementation. *Communications of the ACM*, 26 (6), 430–4.

Marris, P. (1993) The management of change. In C. Mabey and B. Mayon-White (eds), op. cit.

Martin, J. (1985) Can organizational culture be managed? Quoted in P.J. Frost, L.F. Moore, M.R. Louis, C.C. Lundberg and J. Martin (eds) *Organizational Culture*. Beverly Hills, Calif.: Sage.

Mayo, E. (1945) *The Social Problems of Industrial Civilization*. Boston, Mass.: Harvard University Graduate School of Business Administration.

McDaniel, R.R. (1997) Strategic leadership: a view from quantum and chaos theories. *Health Care Management Review*, 22 (1), 321–37.

McGregor, D. (1960) *The Human Side of Enterprise*. New York: McGraw-Hill.

McKaskey, M. (1988) The challenge of managing ambiguity and change. In L. Pondy, R.J. Boland and H. Thomas (eds) *Managing Ambiguity and Change*. Chichester: Wiley.

McLachlan, V.N. (1996) In praise of ISO 9000. *The TQM Magazine*, 8 (3), 21–3.

McPherson, E.D. (1995) Chaos in the curriculum. *Journal of Curriculum Studies*, 27 (3), 263–79.

Merli, G. (1996) The third generation total quality approach. *The TQM Magazine*, 8 (6), 30–6.

Miles, M. (1965) Planned change and organizational health. In R. Carlson (ed) *Change Processes in the Public Schools*. Corvallis, Oreg.: University of Oregon Press.

Miller, D. (1996) A preliminary typology of organizational learning: synthesizing the literature. *Journal of Management*, 22 (3), 485–505.

Mintzberg, H. (1973) *The Nature of Managerial Work*. New York: Harper & Row.

Mintzberg, H. (1987) Crafting strategy. *Harvard Business Review* Mar/April, 66 (2), 66–75.

Mintzberg, H. (1990) The manager's job: folklore and fact. *Harvard Business Review*, Mar/April, 162–76.

Mintzberg, H. (1994) The fall and rise of strategic planning. *Harvard Business Review*, Jan/Feb, 107–14.

Mintzberg, H. (1996) Musings on management. *Harvard Business Review*, July/Aug, 61–7.

Mintzberg, H., Quinn, J.B. and James, R.M. (1988) *The Strategy Process: Concepts, Contexts and Cases*. London: Prentice-Hall.

Miyashiro, M. (1996a) Communicating change. *The TQM Magazine*, 8 (4), 45–8.
Miyashiro, M. (1996b) Exploring the many faces of leadership. *The TQM Magazine*, 8 (2), 17–19.
Mizuno, S. (ed) (1988) *Management for Quality Improvement: the Seven New Tools*. Cambridge, Mass.: Productivity Press.
Møller, C. (1988) *Personal Quality*. Denmark: Time Manager International.
Morrison, K.R.B. (1986) Primary school subject specialists as agents of school-based curriculum change. *School Organisation*, 6 (2), 175–83.
Morrison, K.R.B. (1993) *Planning and Accomplishing School-Centred Evaluation*. Dereham, Norfolk: Peter Francis Publishers.
Morrison, K.R.B. (1994) Centralism and the education market: why emulate the United Kingdom? *European Journal of Education*, 29 (4), 415–24.
Morrison, K.R.B. (1996) Structuralism, postmodernity and the discourses of control. *Curriculum*, 17 (2), 164–77.
Morrison, K.R.B. (1997a) Quality development for effective schools. Paper presented at the Regional Centre for Education in Science and Mathematics, Penang, Malaysia.
Morrison, K.R.B. (1997b) *Establishing School–Industry Links for Low-Achieving Form 4 Students in Malaysia: A Consultation Document*. Durham: School of Education, University of Durham.
Morrison, K.R.B. and Carroll, J. (1986) Preparing for school based curriculum change in primary schools. Unpublished mimeo, School of Education, University of Durham.
Morrison, K.R.B. and Ridley, K. (1988) *Curriculum Planning and the Primary School*. London: Paul Chapman Publishing.
Mortiboys, J. and Oakland, J. (1991) *Total Quality Management and Effective Leadership*. London: Department of Trade and Industry.
Mottram, R. (1982) Team skills management. *Journal of Management Development*. 1 (1), 22–3.
Murgatroyd, S. and Morgan, C. (1993) *Total Quality Management and the School*. Buckingham: Open University Press.
Nadler, D.A. (1993) Concepts for the management of organizational change. In C. Mabey and B. Mayon-White (eds), op. cit.
Nash, R. (1973) *Classrooms Observed*. London: Routledge & Kegan Paul.
National Economic Development Council (1991) *The Experience of Nissan Suppliers*. London: National Economic Development Council.
National Economic Development Office (1991) *The Roles, Competences and Training of Supervisors*. London: National Economic Development Office.
Nicholson, N. (1993) Organisational change. In C. Mabey and B. Mayon-White (eds), op. cit.
Nomura, M. (1992) *The End of Toyotaism*. Frankfurt: IG Metall Conference.
Nonaka, I. (1991) The knowledge creating company. *Harvard Business Review*, Nov/Dec, 96–104.
Normann, R. and Ramirez, R. (1996) From value chain to value constellation: designing interactive strategy. In J. Champy and N. Nohria (eds), op. cit.
Obeng, E. (1990) Avoiding the fast-track pitfalls. *The Sunday Times*, 11 Nov, F1.
O'Brien, L. and Jones, C. (1995) Do rewards really create loyalty? *Harvard Business Review*, May/June, 75–82.
Office for Standards in Education (1993) *Handbook for the Inspection of Schools*. London: Office for Standards in Education.
Ohno, T. (1988) *Workplace Management*. Cambridge, Mass.: Productivity Press.
O'Leary, L. (1993) Mental health at work. Cited in M. Carroll (1996) *Workplace Counselling*. London: Sage.
O'Neill, J. (1994) Organizational structure and culture. In T. Bush and J. West-Burnham (eds) *The Management of Educational Institutions*. Harlow: Longman.
O'Neill, J. (1995) *The Poverty of Postmodernism*. London: Routledge.
Ostell, A. (1996) Managing dysfunctional emotions in organizations. *Journal of Management Studies*, 33 (4), 526–57.
Otala, M. (1995) The learning organisation: theory into practice. *Industry and Higher Education*, 9 (3), 157–64.

Ouchi, W. (1981) *Theory Z*. Reading, Mass.: Addison-Wesley.

Owen, A.A. (1993) How to implement strategy. In C. Mabey and B. Mayon-White (eds), op. cit.

Paine, L.C. (1994) Managing for organizational integrity. *Harvard Business Review*, March/ April, 106–17.

Parker, M. and Slaughter, J. (1988) Managing by stress: the dark side of the team concept. *Industrial and Labour Relations Report*, cited in P. Wickens, op. cit.

Peak, D. and Frame, M. (1994) *Chaos Under Control: The Art and Science of Complexity*. New York: W.H. Freeman.

Peters, T. (1987) *Thriving on Chaos*. New York: Knopf.

Peters, T. (1989) *Thriving on Chaos*. London: Pan.

Peters, T. (1992) *Liberation Management: Necessary Disorganization for the Nanosecond Nineties*. New York: Knopf.

Peters, T. and Austin, N. (1985) *A Passion for Excellence*. London: Fontana.

Peters, T. and Waterman, R.H. (1982) *In Search of Excellence: Lessons from America's Best-Run Companies*. London: Harper & Row.

Pettigrew, A.M. (1985) *The Awakening Giant: Continuity and Change in ICI*. Oxford: Blackwell.

Pettigrew, A.M. (1988) *The Management of Strategic Change*. Oxford: Blackwell.

Pettigrew, A. and Whipp, R. (1993) Understanding the environment. In C. Mabey and B. Mayon-White (eds), op. cit.

Pfeffer, J. (1981) *Power in Organizations*. Cambridge, Mass.: Pitman.

Pfeffer, J. (1993) Understanding power in organizations. In C. Mabey and B. Mayon-White (eds), op. cit.

Pinchott, G. (1985) *Intrapreneuring*. New York: Harper & Row.

Plant, R. (1987) *Managing Change and Making it Stick*. London: Fontana.

Pollard, A. (1982) A model of coping strategies. *British Journal of Sociology of Education*, 3 (1), 19–37.

Pollard, A., Broadfoot, P., Croll, P., Osborn, M. and Abbott, D. (1994) *Changing English Primary Schools?* London: Cassell.

Porter, M.E. (1996) What is strategy? *Harvard Business Review*, Nov/Dec, 61–78.

Preedy, M. and Wallace, M. (1993) Managing sustained change. Unit 3 of E326, Module 1: *Managing Educational Change*. Milton Keynes: Open University Press.

Price, C. and Murphy, E. (1993) Organization development in British Telecom. In C. Mabey and B. Mayon-White (eds), op. cit.

Prigogine, I. and Stengers, I. (1985) *Order out of Chaos*. London: Flamingo.

Pucick, V. and Hatvany, N. (1991) Management practices in Japan and their impact on business strategy. In H. Mintzberg and B. Quinn, *The Strategy Process: Concepts, Contexts, Cases*. Englewood Cliffs, NJ: Prentice-Hall.

Pugh, D. (1993) Understanding and managing organizational change. In C. Mabey and B. Mayon-White (eds), op. cit.

Quinn, J.B. (1980) *Strategies for Change: Logical Incrementalism*. Homewood, Ill.: Irwin.

Quinn, J.B. (1993) Managing strategic change. In C. Mabey and B. Mayon-White (eds), op. cit.

Quinn, R.E. (1988) *Beyond Rational Management*. San Francisco, Calif.: Jossey-Bass.

Raisbeck, I. (1994) Royal Mail: developing a total quality organization. In D. Green (ed), op. cit.

Ranson, S. (1990) From 1944 to 1988: education, citizenship and democracy. In M. Flude and M. Hammer (eds) *The Education Reform Act 1988: Its Origins and Implications*. Lewes: Falmer.

Reynolds, D. (1991) School effectiveness in secondary schools: research and its policy implications. In S. Riddell and S. Brown (eds) *School Effectiveness Research: Its Messages for School Improvement*. Edinburgh: HMSO.

Reynolds, D. (1994) School effectiveness and quality in education. In P. Ribbins and E. Burridge (eds) *Improving Education: Promoting Quality in Schools*. London: Cassell.

Reynolds, D. (1995) The effective school: an inaugural lecture. *Evaluation and Research in Education*, 9 (2), 57–73.

Reynolds, D. and Farrell, S. (1996) *Worlds Apart: A Review of International Surveys of*

Educational Achievement Involving England. London: HMSO.

Riches, C. (1993a) Building teams for change and stability. Unit 4 of E326, Module 1: *Managing Educational Change.* Milton Keynes: Open University Press.

Riches, C. (1993b) Leadership in the effective school. Unit 4 of E326, Module 2: *Managing for School Effectiveness.* Milton Keynes: Open University Press.

Robertson, I.T., Smith, M. and Cooper, D. (1992) *Motivation: Strategies, Theory and Practice.* London: Institute of Personnel Management.

Rodger, I. and Richardson, J.A.S. (1985) *Self-Evaluation for Primary Schools.* Sevenoaks: Hodder & Stoughton.

Rogers, E. and Shoemaker, F. (1971) *Communication of Innovations: A Cross-Cultural Approach.* New York: Free Press.

Rosener, J.B. (1990) Ways women lead. *Harvard Business Review,* Nov/Dec, 68 (6), 119–25.

Roth, S. (1993) *Lean Production in German Motor Manufacturing.* P + *European Participation Monitor* No. 5, cited in P. Wickens, op. cit.

Schaffer, R.H. and Thompson, H.A. (1996) Successful change programs begin with results. In J. Champy and N. Nohria (eds), op. cit.

Schein, E.H. (1985) *Organizational Culture and Leadership.* San Francisco, Calif.: Jossey-Bass.

Schön, D. (1971) *Beyond the Stable State.* Harmondsworth: Penguin.

Schwartz, H.M. and Davis, S.M. (1981) Matching corporate culture and business strategy. *Organizational Dynamics,* 59 (1), 30–48.

Selznick, P. (1957) *Leadership in Administration.* New York: Harper & Row.

Senge, P. (1990) *The Fifth Discipline: The Art and Practice of the Learning Organization.* New York: Doubleday.

Senge, P. (1993) Transforming the practice of management. *Human Resource Development Quarterly,* 4 (1), pp. 5–37.

Sergiovanni, T.J. (1990) *Value-added Leadership: How to Get Extraordinary Performance in Schools.* San Diego, Calif.: Harcourt Brace Jovanovich.

Sergiovanni, T.J. (1992) *Moral Leadership: Getting to the Heart of School Improvement.* San Francisco, Calif.: Jossey-Bass.

Shingo, S. (1986) *Zero Quality Control: Source Inspection and the Poka-yoke System.* Cambridge, Mass.: Productivity Press.

Shingo, S. (1988) *Non-Stock Production.* Cambridge, Mass.: Productivity Press.

Shoji, M. (1988) Without muda, muri, mura. *Mechanical Engineering,* Jan, 41.

Simons, R. (1995) Control in an age of empowerment. *Harvard Business Review,* March/April, 80–8.

Smith, G.F. (1996) Identifying quality problems: prospects for improvement. *Total Quality Management,* 7 (5), 535–52.

Smith, R. (1990) Kaizen. *British Medical Journal,* 301, Oct., 679–80.

Stake, R. (1976) The countenance of educational evaluation, cited in D. Jenkins, Six alternative models of curriculum evaluation. Unit 20, E203: *Curriculum Design and Development.* Milton Keynes: Open University Press.

Stevens, M.J. and Campion, M.A. (1994) The knowledge, skills and ability for teamwork: implications for human resource management. *Journal of Management,* 20 (2), 503–30.

Stewart, I. (1990) *Does God Play Dice?* Harmondsworth: Penguin.

Stewart, V. (1990) *The David Solution: How to Reclaim Power and Liberate your Organization.* London: Gower.

Strebel, P. (1996) Why do employers resist change? *Harvard Business Review,* May/June, 86–92.

Street, P.A. and Fernie, J.M. (1993) Costs, drawbacks and benefits – the customer's view of BS 5750. *Training for Quality,* 1 (1), 21–3.

Stringfield, S. (1997) Underlying the chaos: factors explaining exemplary US elementary schools and the case for high-reliability organisations. In T. Townsend (ed) *Restructuring and Quality: Issues for Tomorrow's Schools.* London: Routledge.

Tagiuri, R. (1968) The concept of organizational climate. In R. Tagiuri and G.W. Litwin (eds) *Organizational Climate: Explorations of a Concept.* Boston, Mass.: Harvard University Graduate School of Business Administration.

Taguchi, G. (1986) *Introduction to Quality Engineering.* Tokyo: Asian Productivity

Organization.
Tannenbaum, R. and Schmidt, W. H. (1958) How to choose a leadership pattern. *Harvard Business Review*, May/June 36, 95–101.
Thomas, D.A. and Ely, R.J. (1996) Making differences matter: a new paradigm for managing diversity. *Harvard Business Review*, Sept/Oct, 79–90.
Thomas, W.I. (1928) *The Child in America*. New York: Knopf.
Thompson, J.L. (1993) *Strategic Management: Awareness and Change* (second edition). London: Chapman & Hall.
Toffler, A. (1985) Science and change. Foreword to I. Prigogine and I. Stengers, op. cit.
Toffler, A. (1990) *Powershift*. New York: Bantam Books.
Tomlinson, J. (1993) *The Control of Education*. London: Cassell.
Tooley, J. (1996) *Education without the State*. London: Institute of Economic Affairs.
Tuckman, B.W. (1965) Development sequence in small groups. *Psychological Bulletin*, 63, 384–99.
Turner, A.N. and Lawrence, P.R. (1965) *Industrial Jobs and the Worker: An Investigation of Response to Task Attributes*. Boston, Mass.: Harvard University Graduate School of Business Administration.
Tyler, R. (1949) *Basic Principles of Curriculum and Instruction*. Chicago, Ill.: University of Chicago Press.
Tylor, E.B. (1871) *Primitive Culture*. London: Murray.
UNESCO (1996) *Learning: The Treasure Within*. Paris: UNESCO.
Usher, R. and Edwards, R. (1994) *Postmodernism and Education*. London: Routledge.
Vroejenstijn, A. (1995) *Improvement and Accountability: Navigating between Scylla and Charybdis*. London: Jessica Kingsley.
Vroom, V.H. (1964) *Work and Motivation*. New York: Wiley.
Waldrop, M.M. (1992) *Complexity: The Emerging Science at the Edge of Order and Chaos*. Harmondsworth: Penguin.
Wallace, M. (1991) Flexible planning: a key to the management of multiple innovations. *Educational Management and Administration*, 19 (3), 180–92.
Walsh, K. (1991) *Going for Quality*. Luton: Local Government Training Board.
Walton, M. (1997) Counselling as a form of organisational change. In M. Carroll and M. Walton (eds) *Handbook of Counselling in Organizations*. London: Sage.
Watson, G. (1966) *Resistance to Change*. Washington, DC: National Training Laboratories.
Weller, L.D. (1995) Quality teams: problems, causes, solutions. *The TQM Magazine*, 7 (3), 45–9.
Weller, L.D. (1996) Benchmarking: a paradigm for change to quality education. *The TQM Magazine*, 8 (6), 24–9.
Weller, L.D. and Hartley, S.A. (1996) Why are educators stonewalling TQM? *The TQM Magazine*. 6 (3), 23–8.
West, N. (1995) *Middle Management in the Primary School*. London: David Fulton.
West, P. (1994) The concept of the learning organisation. *Journal of European Industrial Training*, 18 (1), 15–21.
West-Burnham, J. (1991) *Quality Management for Schools*. Harlow: Longman.
West-Burnham, J. (1992) *Managing Quality in Schools*. Harlow: Longman.
West-Burnham, J. (1994) Management in educational organizations. In T. Bush and J. West-Burnham (eds) *The Principles of Educational Management*. Harlow: Longman.
West-Burnham, J. (1997) *Managing Quality in Schools* (second edition). London: Pitman.
Whitehead, M. (1997) All new heads must pass test. *The Times Educational Supplement*, 14 Nov, 9.
Wickens, P. (1987) *The Road to Nissan: Flexibility, Quality, Teamwork*. Basingstoke: Macmillan.
Wickens, P. (1995) *The Ascendant Organisation*. Basingstoke: Macmillan.
Wilby, P. (1997) Business doesn't mean best when it comes to schools. *The Times Educational Supplement*, 12 Dec, 18.
Woodcock, M. (1989) *Team Development Manual* (second edition). Aldershot: Gower.
Young, M.F.D. (ed) (1971) *Knowledge and Control*. Basingstoke: Collier-Macmillan.
Zaleznik, A. (1992) Managers and leaders: are they different? *Harvard Business Review*, Mar/April, 126–35.

Index

Acceptable Quality Levels (AQLs), 81-4
accountability, 5-8, 37, 72, 186
action planning, see targets *and* school development plans
action research, 20, 24, 55
aligned organization, 42, 45-6, 90, 208
autocatalysis, 3-5, 154

bureaucracy, see organizations *and* hierarchy
Belbin, 190-3, 204
benchmarking, 98-9
brainstorming, 22-3, 29, 110
BS 5750, 81, 102-5, 117-8
bureaucracy, see hierarchy
business, 5-11

career, 46-8, 52, 132, 146
cause-and-effect diagrams, 90, 95-8
change:
    as fermentation, 35
    as loss, 136-9
    bottom up, 16
    definitions of, 13-16
    elements of, 16-17
    evaluation of, 80-1
    evolutionary, see incremental change
    formulae for, 17-18
    incremental, 30-6, 67
    levers of, 14, 29
    linear, 15
    models of, 13-18
    nature of, 13-18, 49
    planning of, 13-42, 51
    processual approaches to, see processual change
    problem-solving in, see problem-solving
    psychological factors in, 10-11, 56, 121-47
    radical, 30-5
    rational views of, 3, 26, 35
    resistance to, see resistance
    stages of, 18-42, 110-7, 137, 143, 175
    strategic, 35-8
    top down, 16
chaos theory, 3-5, 14
charter marks of quality, see quality marks
choice, 5-8
classical organization theory, 150
collegiality, 45, 48, 155-64, 169, 179, 196-7
commitment, 29, 44, 79, 106-8
commodification, 8
communication, 5-8, 42, 59, 64, 126-8, 144, 159-61, 166, 196
competition, 5
complexity theory, 3-5, 14, 26, 154, 160
conflict, 44, 46, 53, 96, 139-41, 155
consensus, 50-7, 67-8
consonance, 16
consultation, 48, 50-7, 67-8, 154
consumerism, 5-8, 59, 74-6, 79, 81, 95, 111
contingency theory, 26-8, 34, 42, 150-4
continuous improvement, 44, 47, 51, 53-7, 69, 71, 85, 92-4, 108
continuous professional development (CPD), 47, 108
co-operation, 43-4
counselling, 10-11, 137-8
creativity, 15, 44, 67, 78-9, 90, 96, 140-2
Crosby, see quality gurus

Deming, see quality gurus
dissemination, 20, see communication
diversity, 5-8
dynamical systems, 3-5

efficiency, 5-8, 57-60, 69
emergence, 3-5, 13, 26, 154
empowerment, 2, 11, 37, 56, 79, 90, 121, 131-2, 138, 144, 173, 183, 212-7
entrepreneurship, 6, 141-2
equality, 6-7, 66